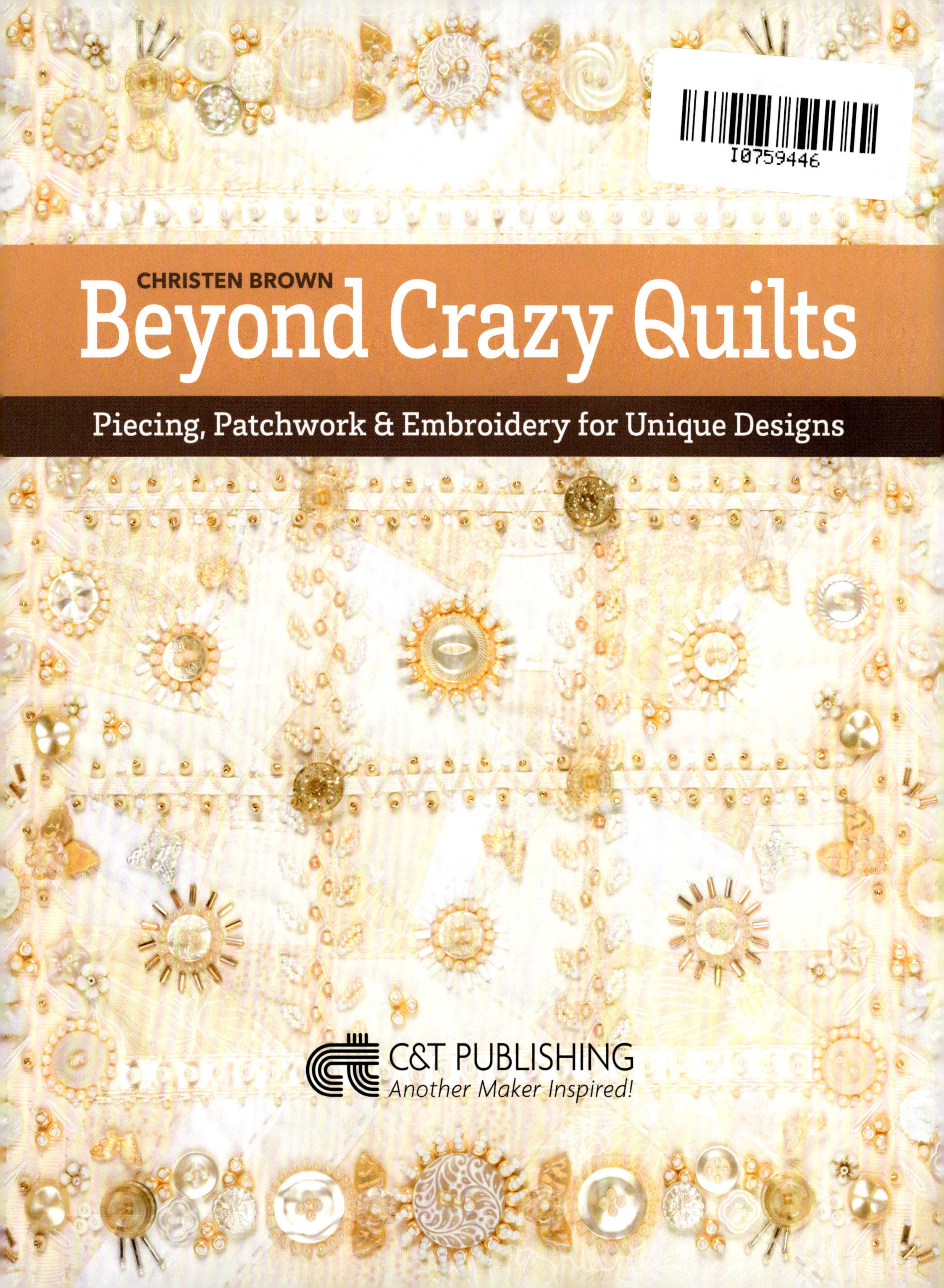

CHRISTEN BROWN

Beyond Crazy Quilts

Piecing, Patchwork & Embroidery for Unique Designs

C&T PUBLISHING
Another Maker Inspired!

Text copyright © 2025 by Christen Brown

Photography and artwork copyright © 2025 by C&T Publishing, Inc.

Publisher: Amy Barrett-Daffin

Creative Director: Gailen Runge

Senior Editor: Roxane Cerda

Technical Editor: Debbie Rodgers

Proofreader: Second Glance Editorial

Cover/Book Designer: April Mostek

Production Coordinator: Tim Manibusan

Illustrators: Christen Brown and Linda Johnson

Photography Coordinator: Rachel Ackley

Front cover photography by C&T Publishing

Photography by C&T Publishing, unless otherwise noted

Published by C&T Publishing, Inc., P.O. Box 1456, Lafayette, CA 94549

All rights reserved. No part of this work covered by the copyright hereon may be used in any form or reproduced by any means—graphic, electronic, or mechanical, including photocopying, recording, taping, or information storage and retrieval systems—without written permission from the publisher. The copyrights on individual artworks are retained by the artists as noted in *Beyond Crazy Quilts*. These designs may be used to make items for personal use only and may not be used for the purpose of personal profit. Items created to benefit nonprofit groups, or that will be publicly displayed, must be conspicuously labeled with the following credit: "Designs copyright © 2025 by Christen Brown from the book *Beyond Crazy Quilts* from C&T Publishing, Inc." Permission for all other purposes must be requested in writing from C&T Publishing, Inc.

Attention Copy Shops: Please note the following exception—publisher and author give permission to photocopy pages 168—173 for personal use only.

Attention Teachers: C&T Publishing, Inc., encourages the use of our books as texts for teaching. You can find lesson plans for many of our titles at ctpub.com or contact us at ctinfo@ctpub.com.

We take great care to ensure that the information included in our products is accurate and presented in good faith, but no warranty is provided, nor are results guaranteed. Having no control over the choices of materials or procedures used, neither the author nor C&T Publishing, Inc., shall have any liability to any person or entity with respect to any loss or damage caused directly or indirectly by the information contained in this book. For your convenience, we post an up-to-date listing of corrections on our website (ctpub.com). If a correction is not already noted, please contact our customer service department at ctinfo@ctpub.com or P.O. Box 1456, Lafayette, CA 94549.

Trademark (™) and registered trademark (®) names are used throughout this book. Rather than use the symbols with every occurrence of a trademark or registered trademark name, we are using the names only in the editorial fashion and to the benefit of the owner, with no intention of infringement.

Library of Congress Control Number: 2025936816

Printed in China

10 9 8 7 6 5 4 3 2 1

Strip-pieced heart

Wedge-pieced heart

Crazy-pieced heart

DEDICATION

Happy Creating

I dedicate this book to all my students and readers. Thank you for giving me this opportunity to share my knowledge with you. May you always find the time to enjoy the creative adventure.

~Christen

SPECIAL ACKNOWLEDGMENTS

Special thank you to my team, Roxane, Gailen, and April, you know how special you are, and I do appreciate you.

My Biggest Fans

To my husband, Kevin and daughter, Gwen – thank you for your unconditional love and support and for allowing me to play in my room. Love you both to the moon and back!

Wine and Roses Needle Keep

A NOTE TO THE READER

Yes, *Beyond Crazy Quilts* is indeed a bold statement. For this book, I have created examples that share my own unique ideas that combine a variety of techniques and embroidery and embellishment stitches. I hope that the projects and gallery examples help you to create your own designs. Please note that I have done my best to provide accurate measurements and guidelines!

Happy Stitching to you!—CB

Contents

PROJECTS

Visual Guide

The Visual Guide is meant to be an index and reference for you, the reader. The more than 155 stitches are worked in a variety of threads, silk embroidery ribbons, beads, and ephemera.

BORDER ROW STITCHES FOR SHORT SEAMS OR NARROW SPACES (page 51)

Stitch along a seam line, in the open spaces between seams, or over a length of ribbon or lace.

Backstitch (page 51)

Bead strand stitch single or double (page 52)

Cable stitch (beaded) (page 54)

Chain stitch (page 52)

Chain stitch (beaded) (page 54)

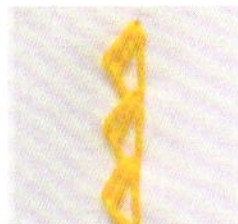

Chain stitch double (page 52)

Chain stitch feathered (page 52)

Chain stitch long-short (beaded) (page 54)

Chain stitch spiny (page 52)

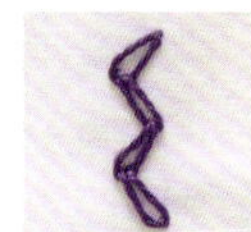

Chain stitch zigzag (page 52)

Continuous bead stitch (page 53)

Continuous bead stitch fancy (page 53)

Continuous bead stitch knobbed (page 53)

Couched stitch (page 51)

Double bubble stitch (beaded) (page 54)

Outline stitch (page 51)

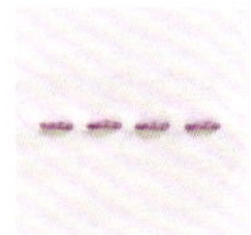

Running stitch (page 51)

Spine vine stitch (beaded) (page 53)

Stem stitch (page 51)

Stem/outline fern stitch (page 51)

BORDER ROW STITCHES FOR MEDIUM SEAMS OR MEDIUM SPACES (page 55)

Stitch along a seam line, in the open spaces between seams, or over a length of ribbon or lace.

Beaded vine stitch (page 58)

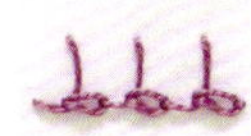

Blanket and chain stitches (page 56)

Blanket stitch (page 55)

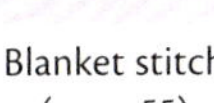

Blanket stitch angled (page 55)

Blanket stitch closed (page 55)

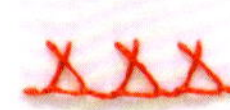

Blanket stitch crossed (page 56)

Blanket stitch even (beaded) (page 58)

Blanket stitch fancy (beaded) (page 58)

Blanket stitch frilled (beaded) (page 58)

Blanket stitch looped (page 56)

Blanket stitch up and down (page 55)

Blanket stitch with loose knot (page 56)

Chain and cross stitches (page 56)

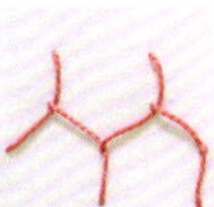

Cretan stitch (page 57)

Cretan stitch looped (page 57)

Cretan stitch with knot tip (page 57)

Cross stitch row (page 57)

Cross stitch row (beaded) (page 69)

Cross stitch long arm row (beaded) (page 59)

Fishhook stitch (page 57)

Fly stitch chain link (page 57)

Herringbone stitch (beaded) (page 59)

Serpentine stitch fancy (beaded) (page 59)

Serpentine stitch V-shape (beaded) (page 59)

Snail trail stitch (page 56)

BORDER ROW STITCHES FOR LONG SEAMS OR WIDE SPACES (page 60)

Stitch along a seam line, in the open spaces between seams, or over a length of ribbon or lace.

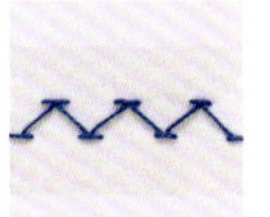
Chevron stitch (page 61)

Cretan stitch fancy (beaded) (page 62)

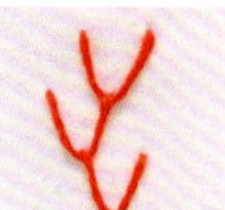
Feather stitch (page 60)

Feather stitch (beaded) (page 62)

Feather stitch double (page 60)

Feather stitch fancy (beaded) (page 62)

Feather stitch looped (page 60)

Feather stitch single (beaded) (page 62)

Feather stitch straight side (page 60)

Feather stitch variations (page 60)

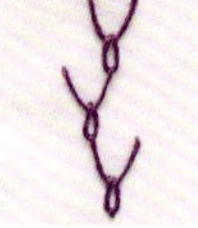
Feather stitch with chain stitch center (page 60)

Fishnet stitch (page 61)

Herringbone stitch (page 61)

Herringbone long arm stitch (page 61)

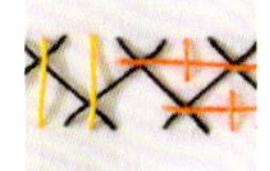
Herringbone stitch with details (page 61)

Sawtooth stitch (page 61)

VINES AND STALKS (page 63)

Stitch along a seam line or in the open spaces between seams.

Blanket stitch stalk or row (page 63)

Fern stitch modern (page 64)

Leaves and stem stalk or row (page 64)

Looped petal row (page 64)

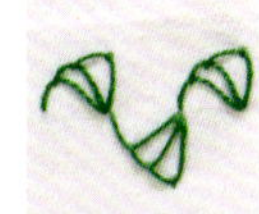
Shell stitch row (page 64)

Stalks (page 63)

Thorn stitch (page 64)

Vines (page 63)

DECORATIVE STITCHES (page 65)

Can be worked off the border rows, vines, stalks, or over a length of ribbon or lace.

Barb stitch (page 66)

Crossed lazy daisy stitch (page 66)

Cross stitch (page 66)

Cross stitch (beaded) (page 69)

Cross stitch doubled (page 66)

Cross stitch with details (page 66)

Fleet stitch (page 66)

Fly stitch (page 67)

Fly stitch (beaded) (page 69)

Fly stitch fancy (beaded) (page 69)

Fly stitch offset (page 67)

Fly stitch with French knot stitch (page 67)

Fly stitch with lazy daisy stitch (page 67)

Fly stitch with loop (page 67)

Fly stitch with straight edge (page 67)

French knot bud stitch (page 68)

Lazy daisy piggyback stitch (page 65)

Lazy daisy stitch (page 65)

Lazy daisy stitch (beaded) (page 69)

Lazy daisy stitch fancy (beaded) (page 69)

Lazy daisy square tip stitch (page 65)

Lazy daisy tulip stitch (page 65)

Lazy daisy with bullion tip stitch (page 65)

Lazy daisy with French knot stitch (page 65)

Padded straight stitch (page 68)

Pointed petal stitch (page 68)

Ribbon loop stitch (page 68)

Ribbon stitch (page 68)

Ruched rose stitch (page 68)

DETAIL STITCHES (page 70)

Can be worked off or around border row stitches, vines, stalks, decorative stitches, flowers, and filler shapes.

Bead cascade stitch (page 71)

Bead combination stitch (page 71)

Beaded pistil stitch (page 72)

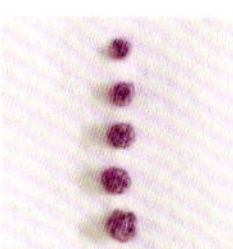

French knot stitch (page 70)

Front-to-back hole charm stitch (beaded) (page 72)

Grouped bead stitch (page 71)

Knotted seed stitch (page 70)

Picot tip stitch (beaded) (page 71)

Pistil stitch (page 70)

Seed stitch (page 70)

Sequin decoration stitches (beaded) (page 72)

Single bead stitch (page 71)

Snap and hook decorative stitches (page 72)

Stacked bead stitch (page 71)

Stamen stitch (page 70)

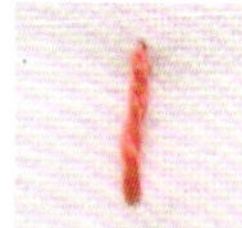

Straight stitch (page 70)

Stem and flower stitch (beaded) (page 72)

Top-to-bottom hole charm dangle stitch (beaded) (page 72)

FLOWERS (page 73)

Can be used alone or combined with decorative and detail stitches and used in the open spaces between seams, the center, corner sections, or in the triangle shapes.

Bell flower stitch (page 76)

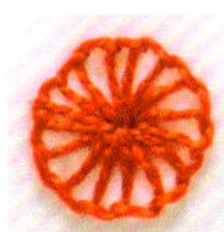

Buttonhole circle stitch (page 76)

Button bezel stitch (beaded) (page 74)

Button flower with petals stitch (beaded) (page 75)

Fly stitch flowers (page 73)

Floret stitch (beaded) (page 75)

Flower with petite petals (beaded) (page 74)

Flower with straight petals (beaded) (page 73)

French knot stitch flower (page 74)

Lazy daisy stitch flower (page 73)

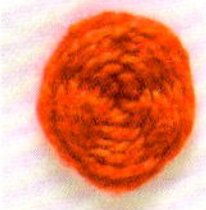

Spiderweb rose stitch and variation (page 76)

Straight stitch flowers (page 73)

Silk ribbon flower stitch (page 74)

Silk ribbon petal stitch (page 73)

Woven rose stitch and variation (page 76)

FILLER SHAPES (page 77)

Can be used alone or combined with decorative and detail stitches and used in the open spaces between seams, the center, corner sections, or in the triangle shapes.

Bead spider stitch (page 80)

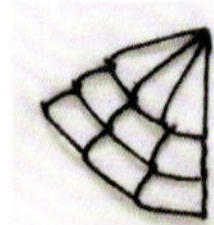

Blanket stitch cobweb (page 80)

Button bug stitch (page 80)

Button spider stitch (page 80)

Butterfly stitch (page 78)

BzzyBee stitch (page 78)

Crossed triangle stitch (page 77)

Crosshatch stitch (page 77)

Curved wing butterfly stitch (page 78)

Dragonfly stitch (page 78)

Fly stitch stacked (page 77)

Herringbone and cross stitch single (page 77)

Looped tendril stitch (page 77)

Sideview butterfly stitch (page 78)

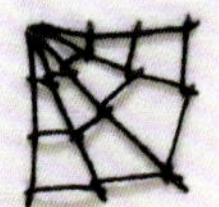

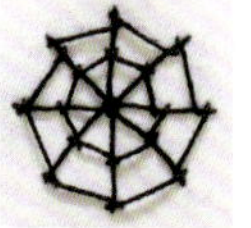

Spiderwebs: corner and round (page 79)

Spiderweb stitch (beaded) (page 80)

Steampunk bugs (page 79)

Whip-stitch star (page 77)

BUTTON EMBELLISHMENT STITCHES (page 81)

Can be used alone or combined with decorative and detail stitches and used in the open spaces between seams, the center, corner sections, or in triangle shapes.

Button cascade (page 81)

Button flower (page 81)

Buttonhole decoration stitches (beaded) (page 81)

Clustered buttons (page 81)

Embroidered buttons (page 83)

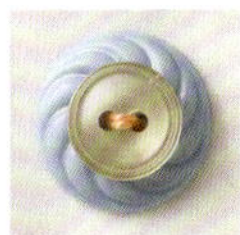

Stacked buttons (page 81)

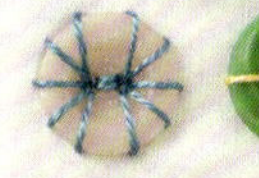
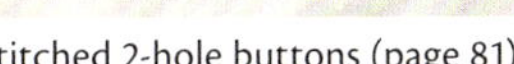

Stitched 2-hole buttons (page 81)

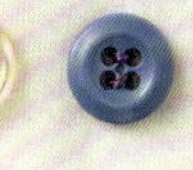

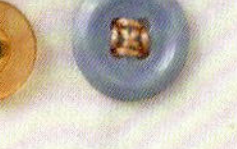

Stitched 4-hole buttons (page 81)

A SPECIAL NOTE

Allow yourself the time to learn and experiment when you are working a new stitch or refreshing your skills. You are worth the time it takes to get it right.

Let's get to stitching! -CB

Still Stitchin' After All These Years

THE SEWING CUPBOARD

I have always been drawn to creating with fiber, whether it be clothing, quilts, or home decor. I learned how to sew on a Singer sewing machine, the same one that my mom used to create matching outfits for herself, her girls, and our Barbie dolls.

I made the Scrap Apron below for a home economics class. We didn't have a lot of extra money, so I asked to rummage through Mom's sewing cupboard. Some of the more exotic fabrics came from my Aunt Murt, who gave us the scraps from her tailor-made wardrobe.

To no one's surprise, my first real job was working at a fabric store. The answer to the inevitable question is YES, I do still have some of these fabrics hanging around, waiting for the right project! See *Woof and Warp Scrap Strip* (page 18).

Table Scraps was my first attempt at a quilt. I didn't really know anything about color theory, fabric combinations, cutting properly, trueing up edges, or really **anything**. I was dismayed by the unevenness of my finished blocks and set this aside for over 30 years. I finally decided to make a tablecloth instead of a quilt. I stitched ribbon down the long seams to camouflage the more obvious discrepancies.

Silver Linings I find that every day is a learning process. Give yourself time to grow, and think of mistakes as a new design opportunity.

Scrap Apron

Table Scraps, 42″ x 42″ (1.07 × 1.07m)

PROGRESSION OF AN IDEA

In the 1990s I was a board member for Visions, Quilt San Diego, an organization which promoted art quilts, quilting, and artists. My fellow board member Julia Zgliniec and I created an exhibit for Visions: QuiltArt explaining how a craft and a technique can evolve from its traditional roots to a contemporary art form. We chose a Log Cabin quilt design—see block example in *Summer Picnic* (page 16)—for the samples below, and Julia wrote the text that accompanied the display.

When a craft is first taught or learned, the traditional fundamentals and mechanics are covered. Once these are mastered, an artist's choices are vast and exciting. Some artists choose to stay with the tradition of the craft, honing and honoring those skills and legacies passed on and passed down through the generations. Other artists choose to create contemporary works using these traditionally learned skills. With reverence to their roots these artists bend the rules, which in turn expand the horizons for those to come.

This quilt honors the traditional pattern using a red center with light and dark scraps of fabrics.

The contemporary color scheme and fabrics in this quilt bend the tradition slightly.

In this quilt, the rules are changed by the size of the strips and the use of hand-dyed fabrics in non-traditional colors, which offer an interesting change.

The bold color palette, the choice of silk fabrics, and the non-traditional pieced design take the design further.

Summer Picnic

Size: 10½″ x 13″ (26.7 × 33cm)

The piecing of the base diagram below is loosely related to the traditional Log Cabin block that you can see below. In this example, wedge shapes were used instead of rectangular shapes. Pattern piece 1 is slightly askew, and pieces 2 and 3, then 4 and 5, are stitched to opposite sides of piece 1. Pieces 6, 7, 8, 9, and 10 follow the Log Cabin pattern, then pieces 11 and 12 are added to the bottom edge to extend the pattern. See the Wedge-Pieced Block pattern (page 95) for a similar but smaller block to work with.

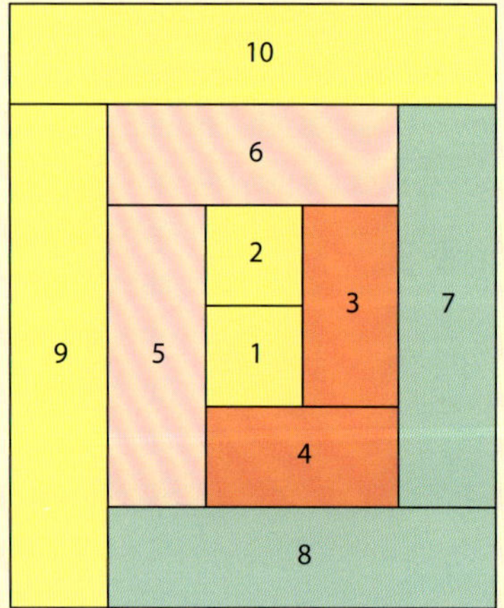

Log Cabin quilt pattern example

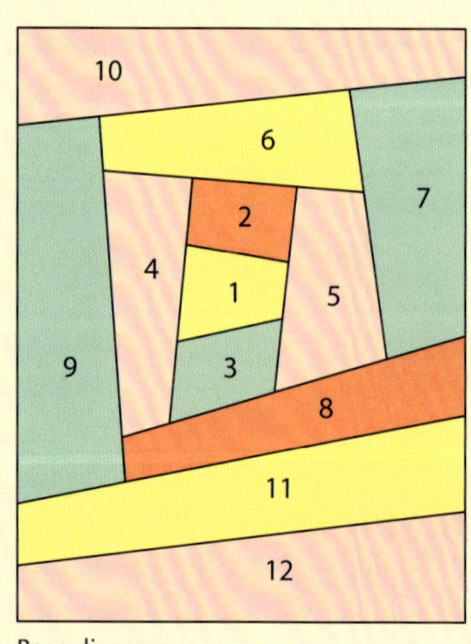

Base diagram

Crazy Quilt Seam Designs

This piece showcases the variety of stencil designs that are offered in my set of Embroidery Stencils, Crazy Quilt Seam Design Collection by C&T Publishing.

Getting It Together

In this chapter you will find suggestions for the types of materials you should gather for a project, including fabrics, trims, embroidery materials, and embellishments. You will also find the types of tools you will need as well as some helpful tips along the way. First, though, let's look at some ideas to help spark your imagination and to try something new.

PROJECT BEGINNINGS

Each project has a moment when an idea is born, a thought is reached, or inspiration is discovered. My favorite projects are those that combine a variety of materials and textures, and I bet that they are yours too!

Jean's Kitchen Curtains, and the Garden Beyond the Window

Size: 13″ x 13″ (33 × 33cm)

This project started with the colorful printed fabric with the white background, leftover scraps from a friend's curtain project. I incorporated a variety of other fabrics, ribbons, and trims to make the blocks. I worked the embroidery in perle cotton, cotton floss, and silk embroidery ribbon, with buttons, charms, and sewing notions for embellishments. For similar block patterns, see Strip-Pieced Block (page 168), and Crazy-Pieced Block (page 170).

Woof and Warp Scrap Strip

Size: 10″ x 18½″ (25.4 × 47cm), a free scrap table runner project on ctpub.com

I like to build a piece around something special, such as a thrift store find or a gift from a family member or friend. This piece started with the tatted components that my mom made, and yes, fabric that I acquired at my first job. I used a piece of muslin for the foundation, cut random widths of fabric, and sewed the sections down the length. I worked the embroidery in perle cotton and cotton floss, with beads and charms for embellishments.

Garden Party

Size: 4½″ x 14¾″ (11.4 × 37.5cm), a project included in my class Ugly Bug Ball on creativespark.ctpub.com

This is another example of a simple strip-pieced base created from scraps leftover from other projects. I treated each strip as an individual vignette, using leftover buttons and embellishments from other projects. This produced an eclectic group of creepy crawlers, spiders, webs, and bugs. See Embroidery and Embellishment Stitches (page 46) for inspiration.

FABRICS

Gather a variety of fabrics in solid colors, and prints with small, medium, or large designs.

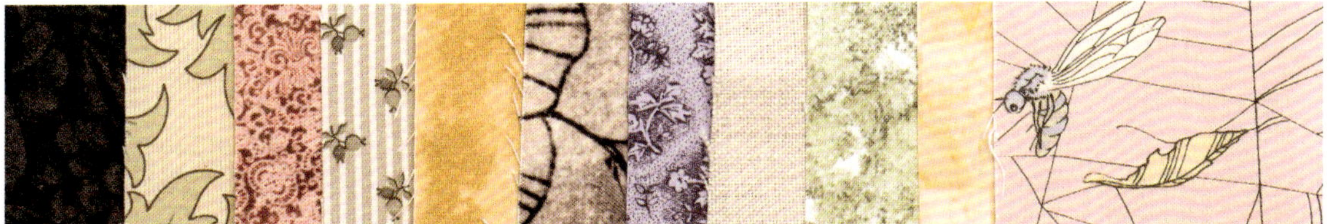

Cotton print and batik fabrics

Specialty fabrics: upholstery, tapestry, sari border, silk ties, silk, and velvets

TRIMMINGS

Collect a variety of trims for added interest and design.

Appliqués, lace, rattail cord, ribbons, rickrack, and trims

STABILIZERS

I use a variety of stabilizers.

- **100% cotton muslin:** *use for foundation piecing*
- **Décor-Bond:** *a lightweight stabilizer, use for mod hexies (page 29).*
- **fast2fuse Interfacing, Heavy:** *a heavy-duty stabilizer, use for fabric circles (page 31) and firm back assembly*
- **Poly-fil:** *polyester fiberfill stuffing*
- **Shape-Flex:** *an iron-on stabilizer, use to add support and to minimize distortion of fabric bases*
- **Warm & Natural batting:** *use for quilting and to add stability to the fabric base*

EMBROIDERY MATERIALS

Threads, Ribbons, and Beads

I use a variety of materials for the embroidery stitches, including perle cotton in a variety of sizes, cotton floss, silk embroidery ribbon (2mm, 4mm, and 7mm), and seed beads (6°, 8°, 11°, and 15°).

Embellishments

Include items such as larger glass beads, buttons, charms, sequins, sewing notions, and found objects.

Note: *Stitch buttons, charms, and found objects in place with sewing thread, floss, perle cotton, or seed beads.*

Stitching Tips

Using a skein of embroidery floss: Pull and cut a length of thread from the skein, then split the threads into a group of two or three. Separate each thread individually from the group, then reassemble these back together to eliminate tangling. For the projects in this book I use cotton floss.

Using a skein of perle cotton: Cut through the knot and entire skein to create separate lengths. Loop the threads over a ring and tie into a loose knot. Remove one length of thread and cut in half so that you have a shorter length.

Working with silk embroidery ribbon: In most stitches, the ribbon should lie flat against the fabric while stitching. If the ribbon is concave (the edges roll down toward the fabric), hold the ribbon next to the fabric, then stitch. If the ribbon is convex (the edges roll up away from the fabric), rub the ribbon until it is flat or concave.

Smooth stitching: Run floss over Thread Magic thread conditioner to prevent the tail from knotting or wrapping around the working portion of the thread.

Tangle-free stitching: Threads and ribbons naturally twist. To untwist hold the fabric base upside down and briefly let go of the needle and thread; they will dangle and unwind.

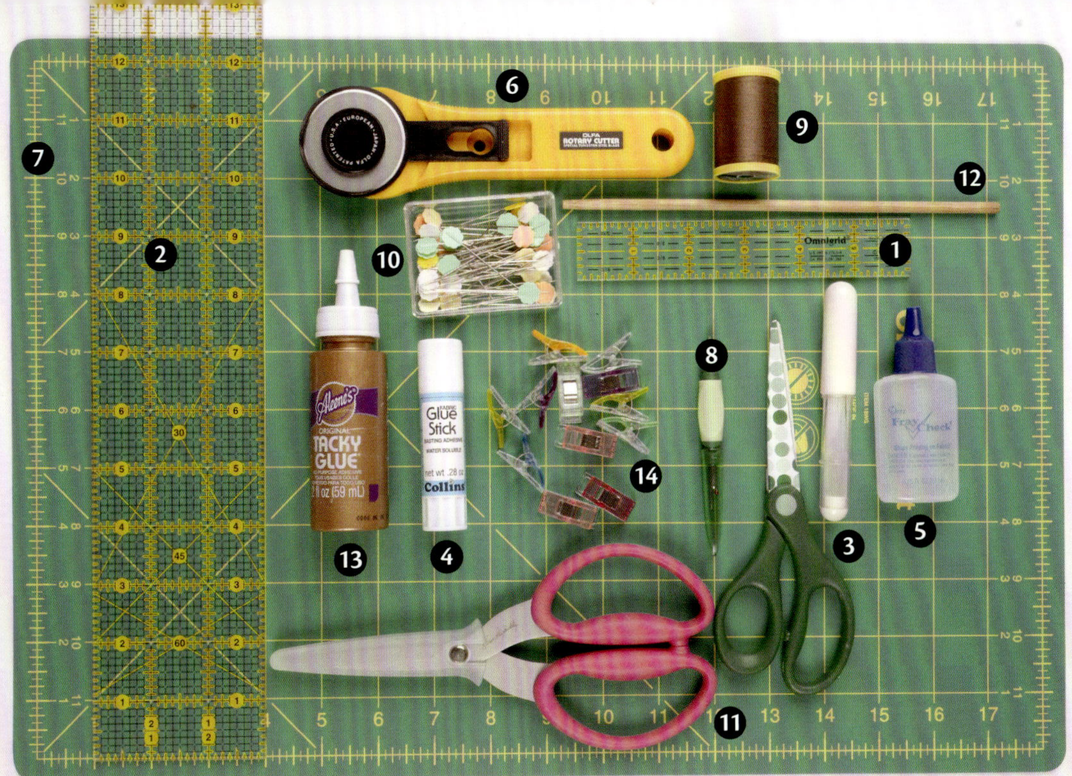

SEWING TOOLS

These are the basic tools and supplies that you should have on hand, in addition to your sewing machine, iron, and ironing board.

1. 6″ clear quilter's ruler with ⅛″ and ¼″ markings
2. 18″ quilter's ruler
3. Chalk pencil
4. Fabric glue stick
5. Fray Check, used on fabric, lace, and ribbon to keep the edges from fraying
6. Rotary cutter
7. Rotary mat
8. Seam ripper
9. Sewing thread
10. Straight pins
11. Scissors: fabric and craft
12. Stuffing tool
13. Tacky Glue, to attach small fiber items
14. Wonder Clips by Clover to hold binding in place

Sewing Tips

- *Prewash cotton fabrics to eliminate chemicals and to prevent shrinkage or bleeding.*
- *When using a fusible stabilizer, follow the manufacturer's instructions.*
- *Apply a thin layer of the fabric glue stick to temporarily hold a piece of ribbon or lace in place.*
- *When machine stitching, do not backstitch at the beginning or end of the seam; this adds bulk to the sections that you will embroider.*
- *To prevent the finished fabric base from fraying, serge or zigzag around the edges. For ribbons, trims, and lace, apply a thin line of Fray Check to the raw edges.*
- *Always wash your hands before working with the fabric base, embroidery threads, and ribbons.*

EMBROIDERY TOOLS

These are the basic tools that you will need for hand sewing and embroidery.

1. ¼″ quilter's tape, for marking seam designs

2. Air-erasable or water-soluble pen

3. Appliqué pins, for trims or appliqués

4. Bead scoop, for picking up loose beads

5. Beading thread: Nymo or other thread

6. Needle grabber, to pull the needle through layers of fabric

7. Needles: beading, chenille, cotton darner, crewel, embroidery, milliner, and small sharps

8. Needle puller

9. Permanent fabric marking pen

10. Pincushion

11. Porcupine quill, for use in silk ribbon embroidery

12. Scissors: embroidery, craft

13. StitchBow floss holders, to keep floss from tangling

14. Synthetic beeswax, to condition beading thread

15. Thread burner, to use on synthetic-fiber ribbon to melt the edges and prevent fraying

16. Thread Magic thread conditioner, to minimize knotting of embroidery and sewing threads

17. Thimble

Note: *Special thanks to Colonial Needle company for providing the needles shown above and the perle cotton used throughout the samples.*

Embroidery Stencils

Even the most experienced embroiderer knows that stitching a row or shape evenly can be made easier with a few drawn lines. I have developed three sets of embroidery templates for that basic purpose.

Embroidery Stencils, Essential Collection

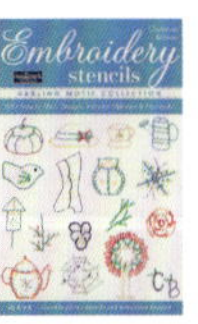
Embroidery Stencils, Darling Motif Collection

Embroidery Stencils, Crazy Quilt Seam Designs

STASH INSPIRATION

Tudor on the Moors

Size: 18¾" x 18¾" (47.6 × 47.6cm)

This piece showcases a collection of linen and cotton fabrics that were combined with vintage laces, ribbons, trims, buttons, and ephemera. The large square center section was cut into four triangles; these sections and the stripped borders (page 38) were then pieced with sections of fabric. See Fabric or Ribbon Sashing (page 37), Embroidery and Embellishment Stitches (page 46), and Embroidery by Design (page 85) for inspiration.

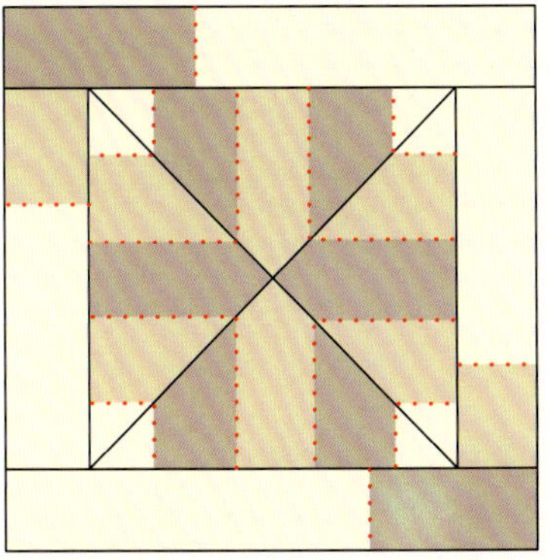

Base diagram

Sizzle and Pop

Size: 15¾" x 15⅞" (40 × 40.3cm)

This colorful collection of batik fabrics is another example of how you can take a larger square and cut it into sections. The beaded embroidery stitches are worked with an exuberant collection of seed and bugle beads, buttons, and sequins in a variety of shapes.

PLAY DAY

Once you begin to collect all your materials, your imagination will be ignited and the ideas will begin to flow. I suggest that you make time for a "play day" at least once a week, so that you can explore the possibilities!

Strip, Patch, or Get Crazy

Wabi Sabi Tic Tac Toe (page 157), using the Crazed Crumbles Block pattern (page 173)

Well, that is the question, and the answer lies in how much fabric you have, and the shapes and sizes of these bits, pieces, and scraps. There are six different block patterns to choose from that can be used in a variety of ways. The base can be comprised of a single block or grouped together with the same or different blocks.

Each of the Strip-Pieced, Wedge-Pieced, and Crazy-Pieced Blocks (page 25) are designed to use four to seven different fabrics. The Stripped Crumbles, Wedged Crumbles, and Crazed Crumbles Blocks (page 26) can use three to five fabrics depending on the sections of the design, or a random mix, combining as many fabrics as you want to "crumble" into these sections.

Crumble, Crumbles, Crumbled A technique where you stitch two or more pieces of fabric together and then cut a pattern piece from this new fabric.

STRIP-PIECED, WEDGE-PIECED, AND CRAZY-PIECED BLOCKS

The following block designs are foundation pieced to a base.

Strip-Pieced Block

The strip- and rectangular-shaped pattern pieces of the Strip-Pieced Block (page 168) offer simple seam lines for embroidery and embellishment. Choose pattern piece 1 or 2 for the center of the block.

4-fabric combination

7-fabric combination

Wedge-Pieced Block

The wedge-shaped pattern pieces of the Wedge-Pieced Block (page 169) offer a variety of angled seam lines and open spaces for embroidery and embellishment.

4-fabric combination

7-fabric combination

Crazy-Pieced Block

The 5-sided center, wedge, and triangle-shaped pattern pieces of the Crazy-Pieced Block (page 170) offer a variety of seam lines and open spaces for embroidery and embellishment.

4-fabric combination

7-fabric combination

STRIPPED CRUMBLES, WEDGED CRUMBLES, AND CRAZED CRUMBLES BLOCKS

The pattern pieces of these blocks can be "crumbled" with scrap pieces of fabric, or they can be cut from whole cloth. A seam allowance can be added to the pattern pieces, or the raw edge seams can be covered with ribbon or a folded fabric strip.

Stripped Crumbles Block

The pattern pieces of the Stripped Crumbles Block (page 171) offer simple seam lines for embroidery and embellishment.

5-fabric combination

Random-mix combination

Wedged Crumbles Block

The pattern pieces of the Wedged Crumbles Block (page 172) offer a variety of angled seam lines and open spaces for embroidery and embellishment.

3-fabric combination

Random-mix combination

Crazed Crumbles Block

The pattern pieces of the Crazed Crumbles Block (page 173) offer a variety of seam lines with a larger center for embroidery and embellishment.

5-fabric combination

Random-mix combination

BLOCK GENERAL DIRECTIONS

1. Choose a block. Use it as is, or enlarge or reduce the size.

Note: *Enlarge or reduce the size of a block pattern by placing the pattern on the scanner plate and programming the printer to the desired percentage.*

2. Print 2 copies of the block pattern.

3. Cut out the pattern pieces of one copy, and use the other copy as a piecing guide.

Option: *Cut a swatch of each fabric, and tape to the chosen pattern piece/s.*

4. Follow the directions for Pieced Blocks (below) or Crumbles Blocks (page 28).

PIECED BLOCKS

Use a ¼″ (6mm) seam allowance.

Strip-Pieced Block (page 168), Wedge-Pieced Block (page 169), or Crazy-Pieced Block (page 170)

1. Follow Block General Directions (above).

2. Add seam allowance to each pattern piece (below).

3. Place each pattern piece face up onto the fabric, and cut around the pattern.

4. Follow the directions for Foundation Piecing (below), and stitch the pieces onto a muslin base.

Foundation Piecing

Use a ¼″ (6mm) seam allowance.

Note: *For a piecing guide, trace the lines of the block onto the muslin base using a lightbox, ruler, and chalk pencil.*

1. Place the first piece of fabric right-side up on the muslin base.

2. Place the second piece of fabric on top of the first, right sides together. Pin, then machine stitch.

3. Flip the current piece of fabric over and press.

4. Follow Steps 2–3 for each remaining piece of fabric.

ADDING SEAM ALLOWANCE

1. Paste each pattern piece face up onto a larger piece of paper.

2. Using a ruler, draw a ¼″ (6mm) seam allowance around each pattern piece.

3. Cut the pattern pieces along these lines.

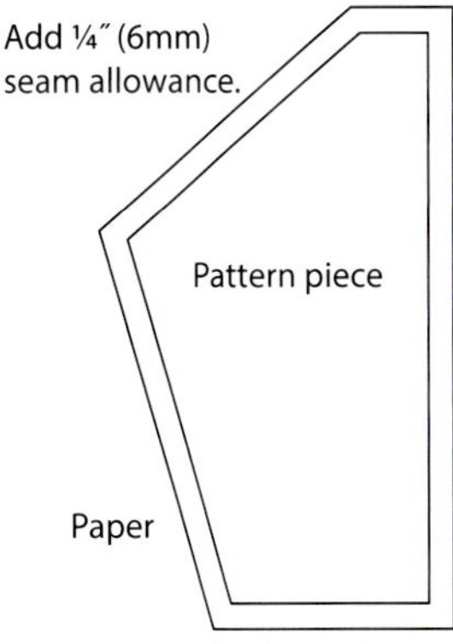

Pattern piece glued to a piece of paper, with seam allowance added

CRUMBLES BLOCKS

Stripped Crumbles Block (page 171), Wedged Crumbles Block (page 172), or Crazed Crumbles Block (page 173)

1. Follow Block General Directions (page 27).

2. Follow the directions for Crumbled Fabric Piecing (at right), using the suggested dotted red lines on the block pattern as a guide, or use your own design.

3. Place each pattern piece face up onto the crumbled fabric section, then cut around the pattern.

4. Assemble the sections together onto the muslin base, kissing the raw edges together.

5. Machine or hand stitch the inner raw edge seams and the outer edges in place.

6. Place a length of ribbon over the shortest raw edge seam, then machine or hand stitch in place. Continue this process, covering all the open raw edge seams and raw edges of ribbon.

Option: *These block patterns can also be cut and assembled following the directions for the Pieced Blocks (page 27).*

Foundationless Piecing

Use a ¼" (6mm) seam allowance.

1. Place the first piece of fabric right-side up on the work surface.

2. Place the second piece of fabric on top of the first, right sides together. Pin and machine stitch together using a ¼" (6mm) seam allowance.

3. Flip the current piece of fabric over and press.

4. Follow Steps 2–3 for each remaining piece of fabric.

Disappearing Seam

Use a ¼" (6mm) seam allowance.

Add a seam allowance (page 27) to each pattern piece. Stitch the pattern pieces in order.

1. Place pattern piece 1 (center) right-side up on the work surface.

2. Pin pattern piece 2 right sides together onto piece 1, leaving a ¼"(6mm) seam allowance open at the beginning of the seam.

3. Machine stitch in place. Flip over and press the seam to one side.

4. Working clockwise, follow Steps 2–3, for pattern pieces 3 and 4, except sew the full seam.

5. Open piece 2, to expose the raw edge of the seam, pin pattern piece 5, and follow Step 3.

CRUMBLED FABRIC PIECING

Use a ¼" (6mm) seam allowance.

1. Select your scrap pieces, cutting straight edges for the seams.

2. Place the first piece of fabric right-side up on the work surface.

3. Place the second piece of fabric on top of the first, right sides together. Pin and machine stitch together.

4. Flip the current piece of fabric over and press.

5. Follow Steps 3–4 for each remaining piece of fabric.

BITS AND PIECES

Glossary of Hand-Sewn Stitches

Note: *For hand sewing, use a small sharps needle and sewing thread.*

Anchor knot: Bring the needle through the selvage edge of the ribbon. Repeat, inserting the needle through the loop that is created; tighten the knot.

Assembly stitch: A series of short, even stitches used to stitch two pieces together to form a seam.

Gather stitch: A series of long, even stitches used to gather and form a center or the edge of a component.

Loop-over: The thread is looped over an edge any time the direction of the gather stitches is changed.

Tack stitch: A small, straight stitch used to attach the components together.

Whipstitch: A series of short, angled straight stitches used to attach the components together.

MOD HEXIES

1. Cut 1 piece of Décor-Bond from the pattern piece.

2. Glue the Décor-Bond to the wrong side of a piece of fabric with a glue stick.

3. Draw a ¼″ (6mm) seam allowance on the fabric around the Décor-Bond.

4. Cut the fabric on the lines.

5. Fold over one edge, finger press, and glue to the Décor-Bond.

6. Repeat Step 5 for each remaining edge, folding the last edge under the first.

7. Tackstitch the raw edges of the fabric in place.

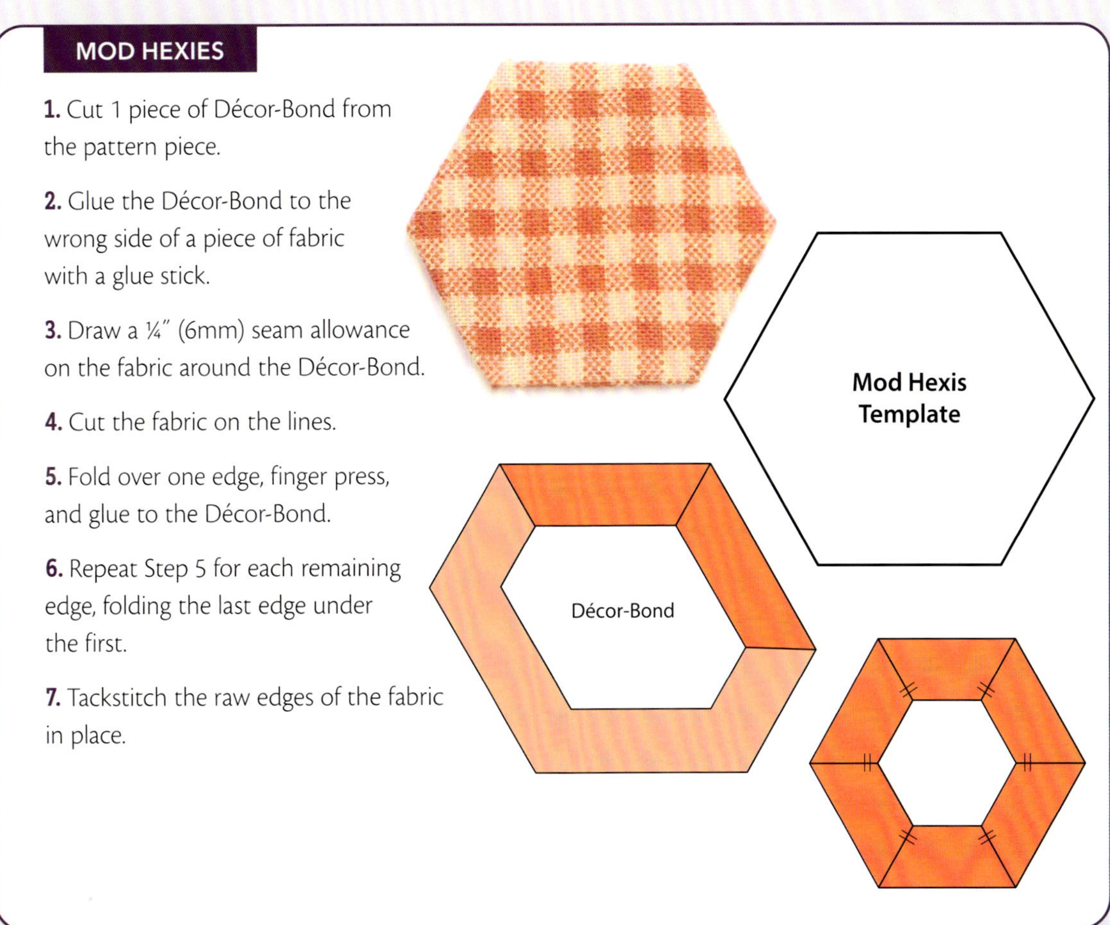

PRAIRIE POINTS

1. Cut a strip 2″–3″ (5.1–7.6cm) by the length of fabric.

2. Fold and press the width (short) edges in half, wrong sides together.

3. Fold the left end down 45° and press.

4. Fold the right edge down, kissing the folds of fabric together, and press.

5. Cut off the excess fabric flush with the raw edge.

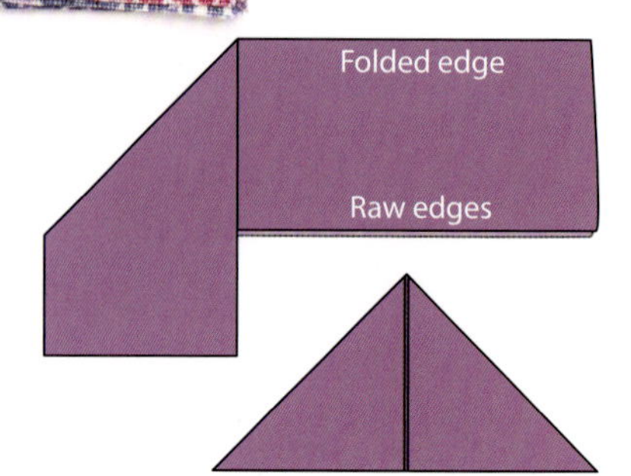

LINED PRAIRIE POINTS

1. Cut 1 strip 1″ (2.5cm) and a second strip 1¼″ (3.2cm) by the length of fabric.

2. Pin, and machine stitch the 2 rectangles right sides together.

3. Flip open and press.

4. Follow Steps 2–5 for prairie points (above).

MOCK PRAIRIE POINTS

1. Cut 1 strip 2″–2¾″ (5.1–7cm) strip by the length of the fabric.

2. Fold one end down 45° to meet the raw edges and press.

3. Fold the remaining edge down 45°, folding the point down ¼″ (6mm) along the first fold, and press.

4. Cut off the excess fabric flush with the raw edge of the first section folded.

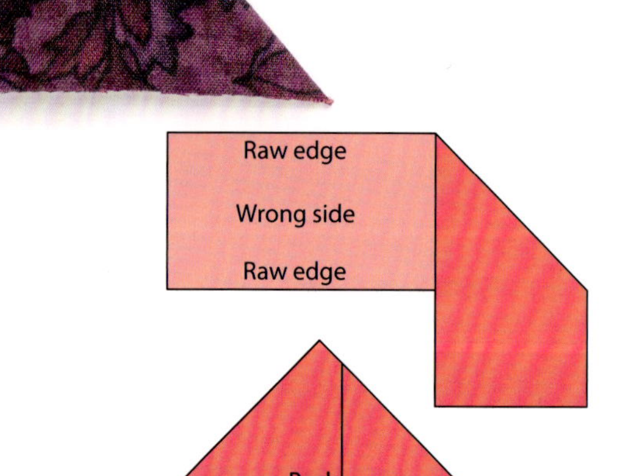

FABRIC YO-YOS

1. Cut a 2⅛″ (5.4cm) or larger circle from fabric or a crazy-pieced base (below).

2. Working with the wrong side of the fabric facing up, fold over a ⅛″ (3mm) seam, and insert the needle under the seam and into the fold.

3. Gather stitch close to the folded edge through both layers of fabric. End the stitching on the right side of the fabric.

4. Pull the thread to gather the stitches and anchor knot the thread into a fold of the fabric. Bury the needle through a fold of the fabric; knot and cut the thread.

Solid fabric and crazy-pieced base

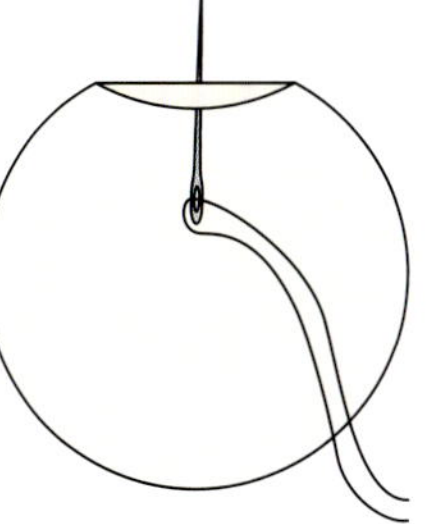
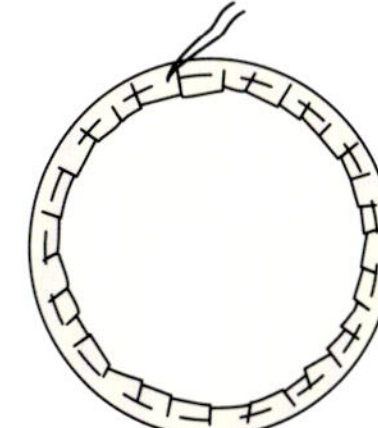
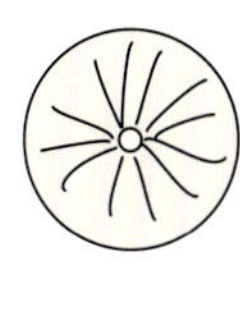

FABRIC CIRCLES

1. Cut a 1¼″ (3.2cm) circle from fast2fuse and a 1⅛″ (2.9cm) circle from batting. Glue the batting to the fast2fuse with a glue stick.

2. Cut a 2″ (5.1cm) circle from fabric or a crazy pieced base (below).

3. Stitch a basting stitch ⅛″ (3mm) from the raw edge of the fabric, ending the needle on the right side.

4. Place the batting side of the fast2fuse circle in the center of the wrong side of the fabric. Pull the thread to gather the stitches; knot and cut the thread.

Solid fabric and crazy-pieced base

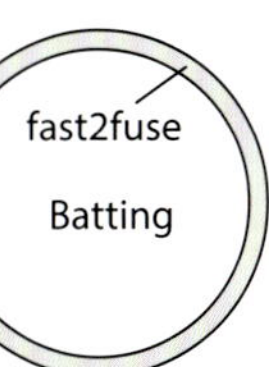

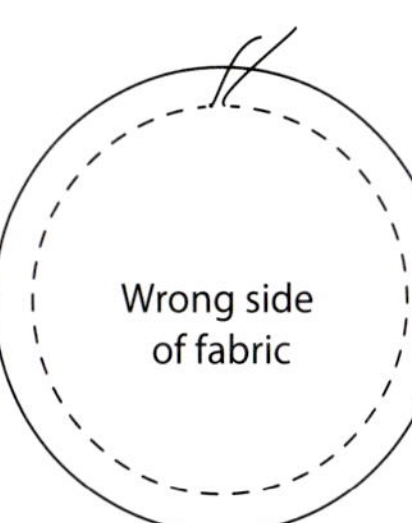

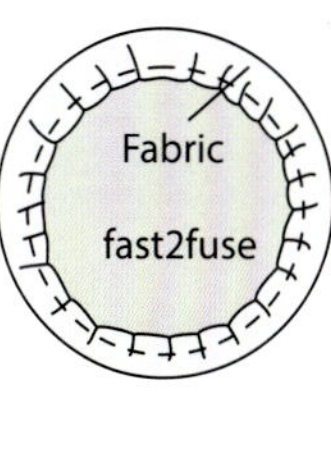

CRAZY-PIECED BASE

1. Hand stitch 2 or more pieces of fabric together, slightly larger than the pattern piece.

2. Press the seams to one side.

RIBBON BUTTON

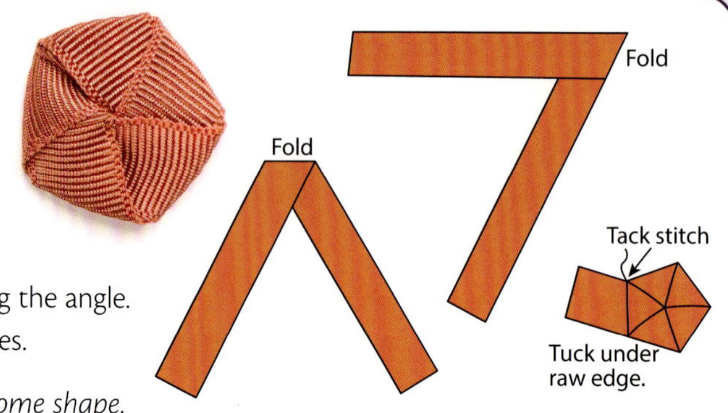

1. Cut 1 length of ribbon ⅜″ × 4⅞″ (1 × 12.4cm).

2. Fold the left edge of the ribbon down at an angle, dividing the length in half.

3. Fold the right side over the left, matching the angle. Continue to fold right over left 3 more times.

Note: *The folds will create a slight curved dome shape.*

4. Tackstitch the point of the first fold to the shorter edge of ribbon. Tuck the remaining edge under to the back. Tackstitch, anchor knot, and cut the thread.

ROSETTE

1. Cut 1 length of ⅜″ (1cm) ribbon by 3″ (7.6cm) or 6″ (15.2cm).

2. Fold the ribbon length in half, right side in, matching the raw edges. Stitch the raw edges together with a ⅛″ (3mm) seam allowance using the assembly stitch.

3″ and 6″ ribbon rosettes

3. Starting at the inner selvage edge next to the seam, gather stitch through 1 layer of ribbon along the continuous selvage edge back to the seam.

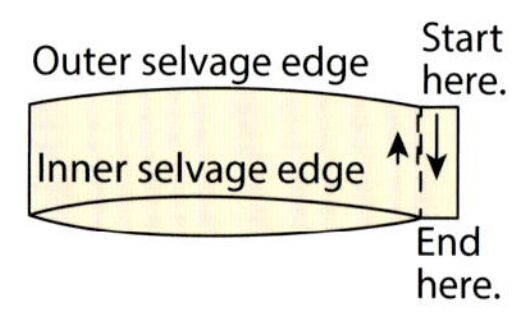

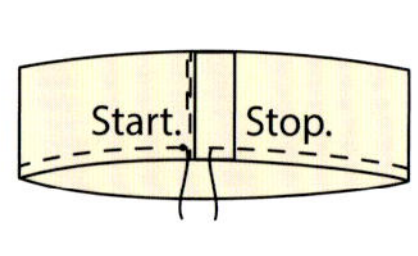

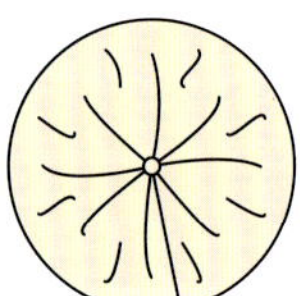

4. Gently pull the thread to gather the stitches and form the middle of the flower. Anchor knot, and cut the thread.

EXPANDING UPON AN IDEA

This is an example of how I took the Wedge-Pieced Block pattern (page 169) further. I cut a larger foundation and continued to add rectangles and wedge-shaped fabric to the edges of the foundation.

Sparkling Midnight Lights

Size: 14″ x 14½″ (35.6 × 36.8cm)

The base is pieced with both cotton prints and solids, vintage and new cotton and polyester ribbons, vintage lace appliqués, and vintage metallic lace. I added fabric circles (page 31) made from sari borders, fabric yo-yos (page 31) cut from cotton fabric from India, and satin ribbons from a wedding invitation for rosettes (page 32). The embroidery stitches were worked in perle cotton, with vintage and new glass beads; embellishments include vintage sequins, glass, and fabric buttons. See the Embroidery and Embellishment Stitches (page 46) and Embroidery by Design (page 85) for inspiration.

Block Party: Making a Base, from Start to Finish

Close-up of *Kaleidoscope* (page 121)

3-Patch Block Ideas

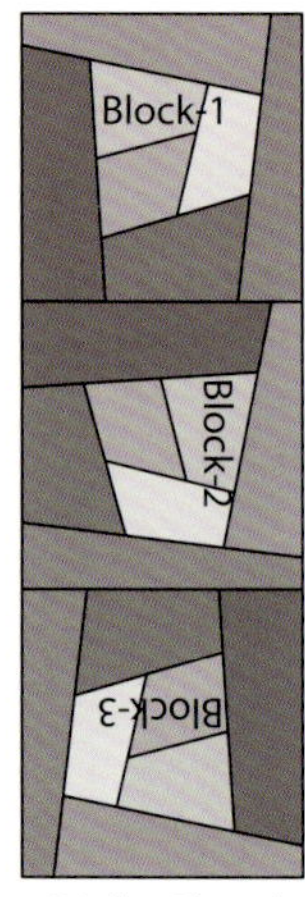

Wedge-Pieced Block pattern (page 169): **Block-1** original position, **Block-2** rotated 90° to the right, **Block-3** rotated 180°

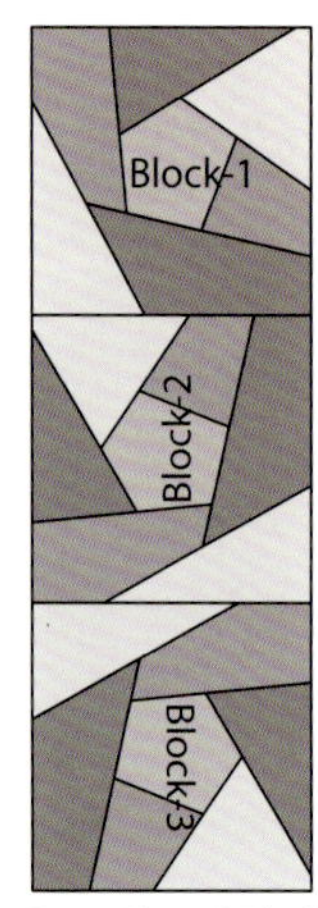

Crazy-Pieced Block pattern (page 170): **Block-1** original position, **Block-2** rotated 90° to the left, **Block-3** rotated 90° to the right

ARRANGEMENT IDEAS

The projects in the chapter Custom Design Ideas (page 101) offer a variety of ways to assemble the blocks to create a design. This chapter includes additional ideas, as well as basic instructions.

4-Patch Block Ideas

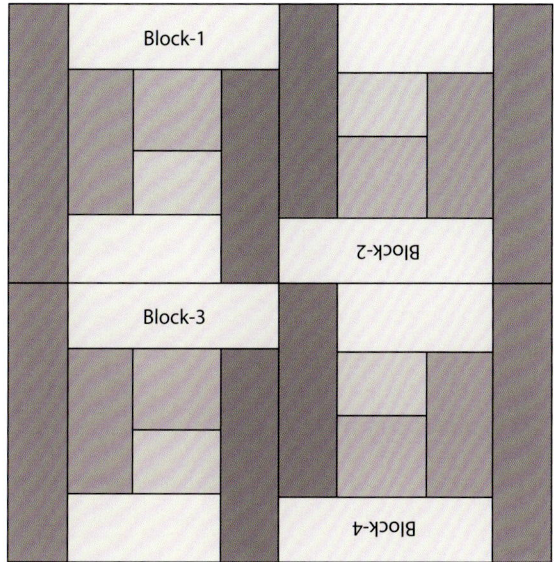

Strip-Pieced Block pattern (page 168): **Block-1** and **Block-3** original position, **Block-2** and **Block-4** rotated 180°

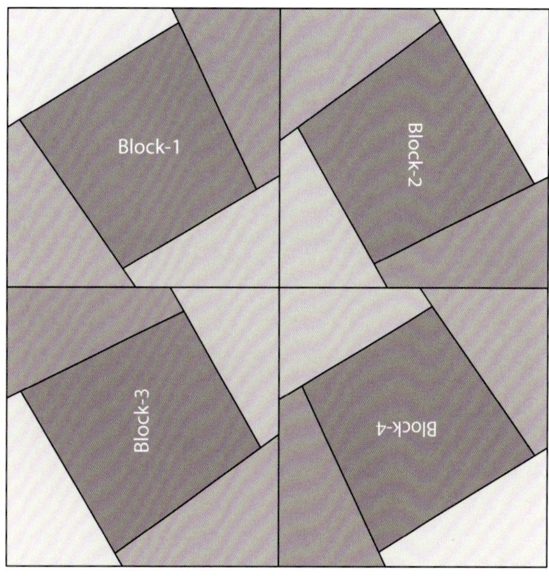

Crazed Crumbles Block pattern (page 173): **Block-1** original position, **Block-2** rotated 90° to the right, **Block-3** rotated 90° to the left, **Block-4** rotated 180°

9-Patch Block Base

Note: *Use a ¼" (6mm) seam allowance.*

1. Choose 1 or more block designs, and make 9 blocks.

2. Pin 3 blocks together, in 3 rows.

3. Machine stitch. Press the seams open.

4. Pin the first and second row together, aligning the seams; follow Step 3.

5. Repeat Step 4 for the remaining row.

Note: *Fabric or ribbon sashing (page 37) can be used to enlarge the size of the base.*

9-Patch Diagram using the Wedged Crumbles Block pattern (page 172)

BASIC BASE INSTRUCTIONS

Note: *Use a ¼" (6mm) seam allowance, unless otherwise instructed.*

Follow the directions included for each project or create your own design.

1. Stitch a block or group blocks following the Block General Directions (page 27).

2. See Arrangement Ideas (page 34) or choose your own.

3. Choose an option from the Base Design Options (at right).

4. Add trims or lace; see Trimmings (page 19).

Note: *Extend the trim to the raw edges of the block or cover the raw edges of a short length with the next trim, or with embellishments.*

5. Add additional details; see Two-Layer Quilting (page 40) and Bits and Pieces (page 29).

Base Design Options

Use the measurements for each project, or if you are making your own design, cut a piece of batting 1" (2.5cm) larger on all sides than the block/s and or sashing and borders.

Option A: Cut a piece of batting. Pin the block/s in the center the batting, and staystitch around the raw edges.

Option B: Stitch a group of individual blocks, following Steps 3–5 of Basic Base Instructions (at left). Choose a sashing (page 37); follow option **A**, spacing the blocks to accommodate the width of the sashing.

Option C: Choose a Border (page 38); follow option **A**, adding the width of the border/s to the batting measurement.

Option D: Choose a sashing and a border; follow option **A**, adding the width of the sashing and border/s to the batting measurement.

Example of option B, using the Wedged Crumbles Block pattern (page 172)

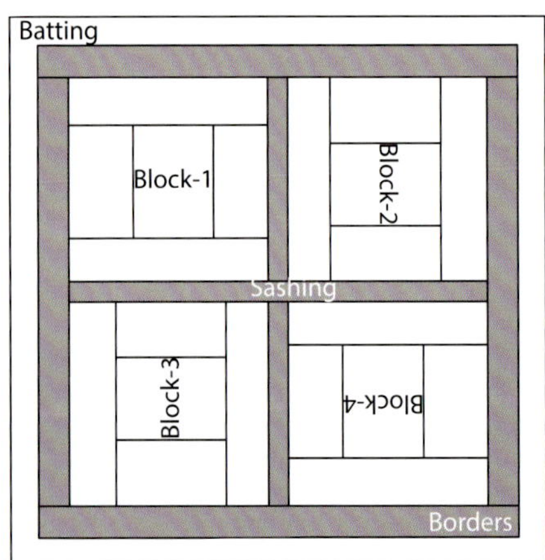

Example of option D, using the Stripped Crumbles Block pattern (page 171)

BORDERS AND SASHING

This is a detailed example showing your options for adding a border and/or sashing, Use the measurements for each project, or if you are making your own design, see the suggestions under the Base Design Options (page 36).

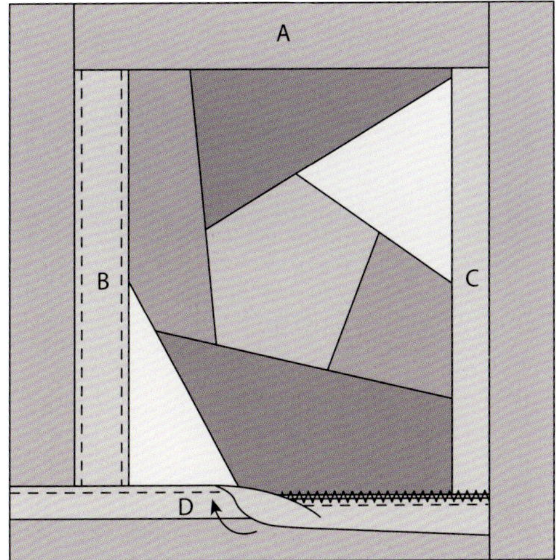

Block Diagram: **A.** Finished Seam Option **B.** Fabric Sashing **C.** Ribbon Sashing **D.** Folded Edge Fabric Sashing

ADDING A BORDER

1. Cut a piece of batting large enough for the block/ base, including the size of the border/s.

2. Place the block/base in the center of the batting. Staystitch in place, zigzag over raw edges.

3. Choose from the Border Designs (page 38), then one of the following options.

Finished Seam Option

Note: *Use a ¼" (6mm) seam allowance.*

1. Cut a rectangle the desired width of the border by the length of the block/base.

2. Pin to the block/base right sides together and machine stitch. Fold over and press open.

3. Repeat Steps 1–2 for any additional borders.

Raw Edge Option

1. Pin the raw edges of the border next to the raw edges of the block/base. Zigzag in place over the raw edges of the seam.

2. Cover the raw edges of the seam with a sashing.

SASHING

A sashing can be added between blocks or between the block and border.

Fabric or Ribbon Sashing

1. Cut a length of fabric the desired width plus 1" (2.5cm) by the length needed.

2. Press the raw edges under ½" (1.2cm) to the wrong side of the vertical (long) edges.

Option: *Substitute a ⅜" (1cm) or wider length of woven edge ribbon.*

3. Pin the length over the raw edges of the seam; machine stitch along the folded edges (or woven edges if using ribbon).

Folded Edge Fabric Sashing

1. Cut a 1½" (3.8cm) rectangle of fabric by the desired length.

2. Fold and press the width (short) edges in half, wrong sides together.

3. Pin the raw edges of the rectangle over the raw edges of the seam. Machine stitch with a ⅛" (3mm) seam allowance.

4. Fold over, and press flat, covering the remaining raw edges of the seam. Machine or hand stitch in place.

BORDER DESIGNS

Stripped Borders

1. See options below and select fabrics to create the width and length of the border.

2. Follow the directions for Foundationless Piecing (page 28).

3. Cut the stripped border the length needed.

4. Follow the directions for Adding a Border (page 37), choosing one of the following finishing options.

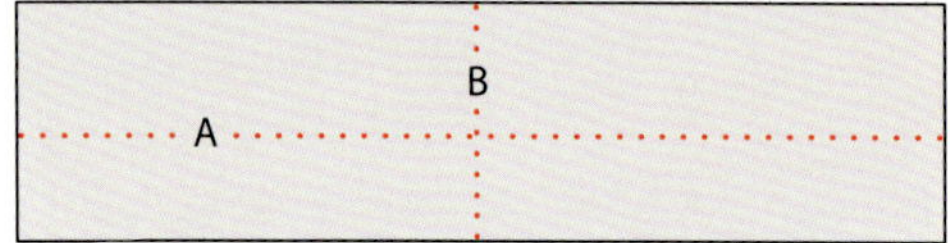

Double Strip Border: Select 2 fabrics **A.** Same or different widths **B.** Same or different lengths

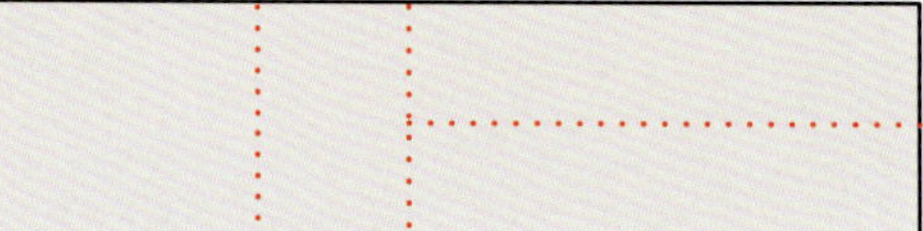

Crumbled Strip Border: 2 or more fabrics, the same width, or crumble strips to create a width

Disappearing Seam Border

Note: *Use a ¼″ (6mm) seam allowance.*

1. Follow Steps 1–2 for Adding a Border (page 37).

2. Cut 4 fabric rectangles the desired width by the same length of the block/base plus the width of one border.

3. Pin the first rectangle to the block/base right sides together, with one edge flush with the base, and the other overlapping the base. Leave a ¼″ (6mm) seam allowance open at the overlapping end.

4. Machine stitch. Open and press in place.

5. Working clockwise, pin the second rectangle flush with the previous strip and base; repeat Step 4.

6. Repeat Step 5 for the third rectangle.

7. Open the first rectangle to expose the raw edge of the seam. Repeat Step 5 for the last rectangle.

Option: *The raw edges of the borders can be assembled next to the raw edges of a block/base and covered with a sashing (page 37).*

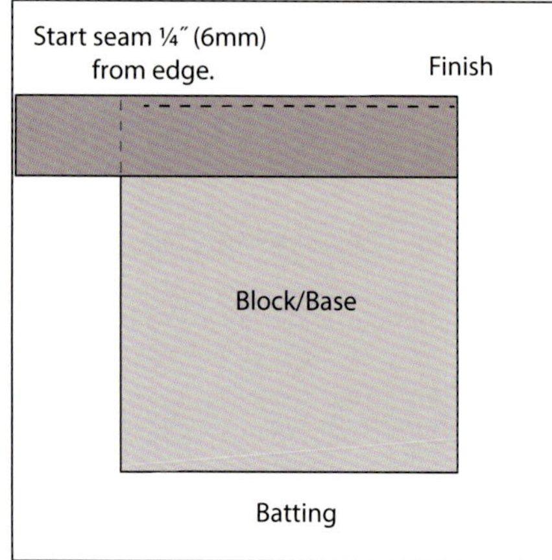

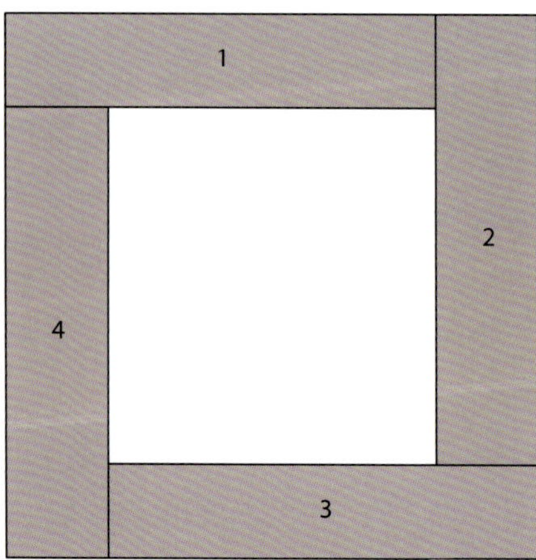

Prairie Point or Mock Prairie Point Border

1. Cut a rectangle the desired width and length for the border.

2. Follow the directions for prairie points (page 30) or mock prairie points (page 30).

3. Follow the directions for Adding a Border (page 37) and Option **A, B,** or **C** below.

4. Hand stitch the pieces from Step 2 in the desired position.

A. Follow the directions for Finished Seam Option (page 37) for the border. Place the pieces from Step 2, with the raw edges on the outer edge of the border.

B. Follow the directions for the Raw Edge Option (page 37), placing the pieces from Step 2 on the seam with the raw edges next to the block/base.

C. Combine options **A** and **B**.

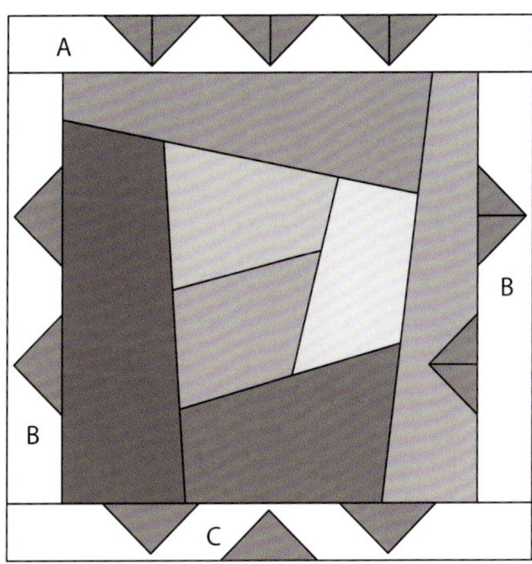

Foundation-Pieced Borders

1. Select a group of fabrics and 1 of the border design options below:

A. Strip-Pieced Border: Cut strips in a variety of widths.

B. Wedge-Pieced Border: Cut strips and wedge shapes in a variety of widths.

2. Cut a rectangle of muslin the desired width and length of the border.

3. Follow the directions for Foundation Piecing (page 27), using the suggested dotted red lines or your own design.

4. Follow the directions for Adding a Border (page 37) and the Raw Edge Option (page 37).

Multiple Pieced Borders Option: *Cut the rectangle of muslin twice the desired width; cut the width in half after Step 3.*

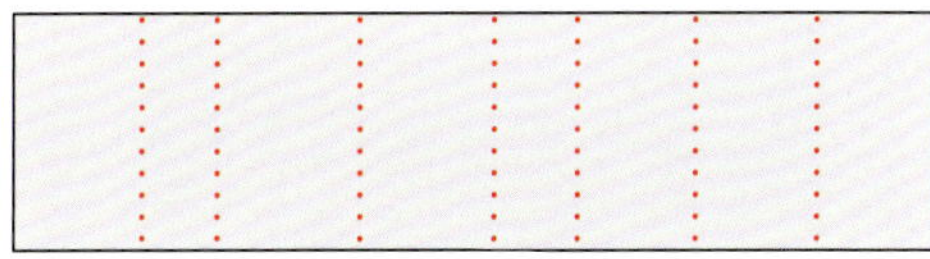

A. Strip-pieced border

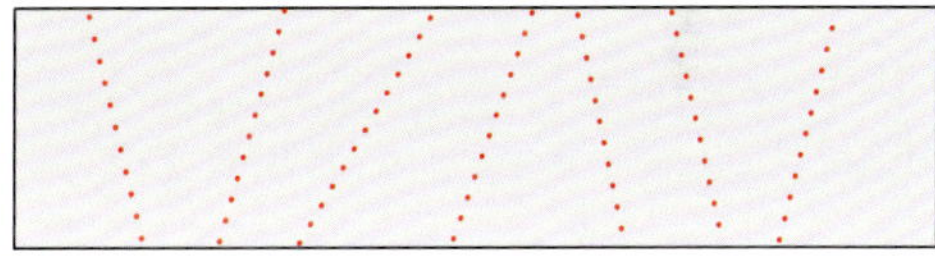

B. Wedge-pieced border

TWO-LAYER QUILTING

Machine- or hand-stitched quilt lines add an additional design element and will prevent the batting from traveling or distorting.

Free-Form Machine Quilting

1. Thread the machine with decorative or top-stitching thread.

2. Begin in the center of the base, in either a straight line or curved design, working to the outer edge.

3. Continue to stitch lines emanating from the center of the base.

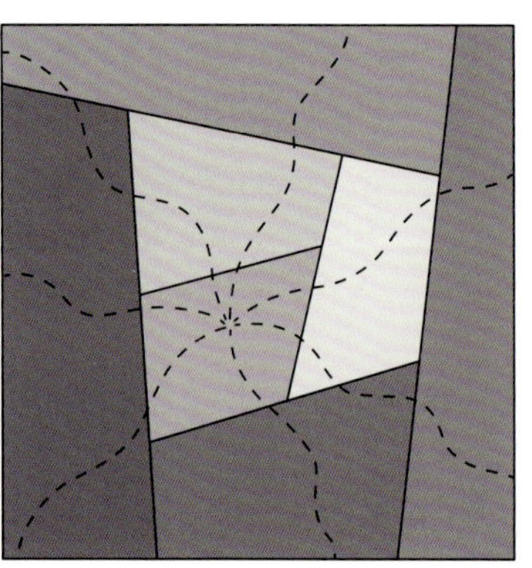

Hand Quilting

1. Draw a line with an erasable pen.

2. Thread a small sharps or quilting needle with decorative or top-stitching thread or pearl cotton #12.

3. Follow the directions for the running stitch (page 51).

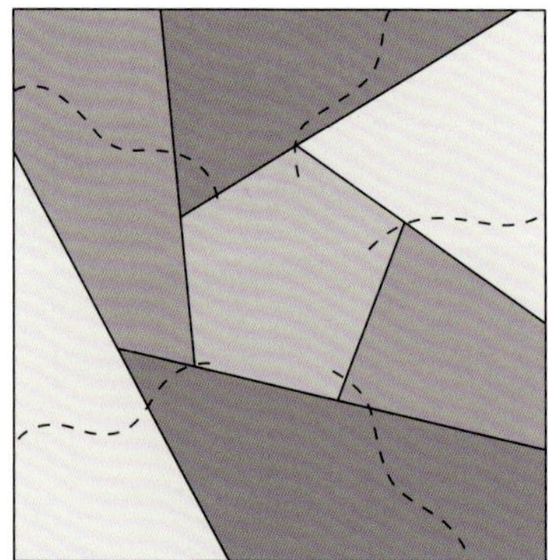

Sashiko Quilting

1. Choose a Sashiko pattern like the one shown (from *Sashiko Stencils, Traditional Collection*, by Sylvia Pippen, from C&T Publishing).

2. Follow Steps 1–3, Hand Quilting (above).

Note: *Another great resource for information is the* Sashiko Handy Pocket Guide *by Sylvia Pippen, from C&T Publishing.*

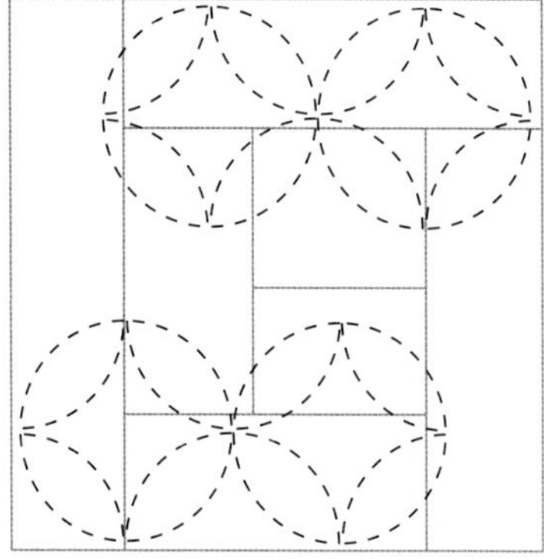

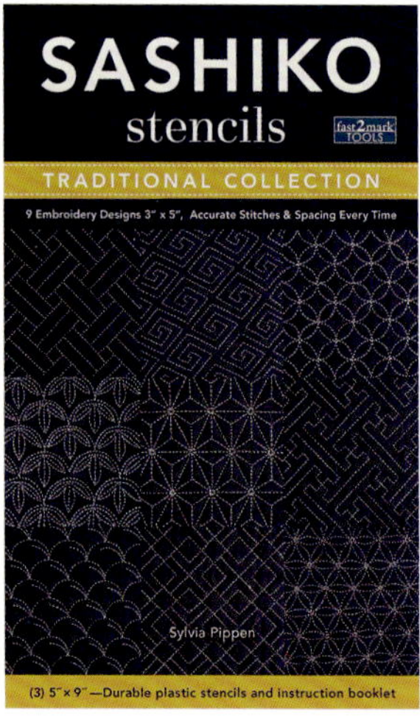

Sashiko Stencils, Traditional Collection

FINISHING TECHNIQUES

Hanging Sleeve

1. Fold and press the hanging-sleeve rectangle in half lengthwise. Unfold and press under ¼″ (6mm) on the short ends; machine stitch along the folds. Refold the piece.

2. Center and pin in place with the raw edges 2″ (5.1cm) below the top edge of the backing and the folded edge extending up and beyond the backing.

3. Machine stitch the raw edges of the sleeve to the backing using a ¼″ (6mm) seam.

4. Fold the sleeve down, enclosing the seam, and press flat. Hand stitch in place.

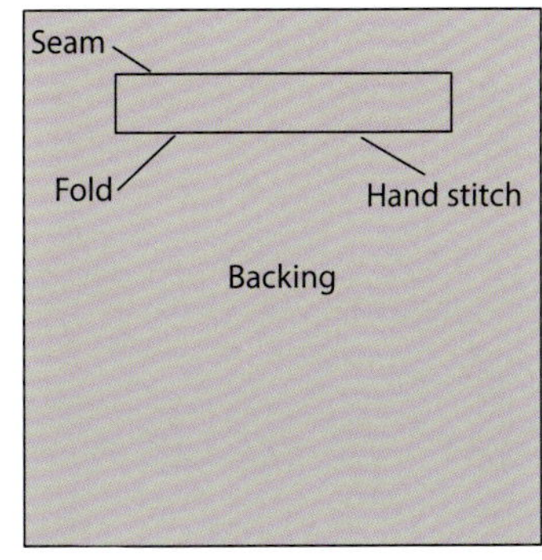

Hanging sleeve

Bound Edge Assembly

Note: *Use a ⅜″ (1cm) seam allowance.*

1. Sandwich the block/base and the backing with wrong sides together.

2. Fold and press the width (short) edges of the binding rectangles in half, wrong sides together.

3. Pin the shorter rectangles to the vertical edges of the block/base, right sides together and raw edges even.

4. Machine stitch.

5. Open and press the seam flat. Press and pin the folded edge to the backing. Hand stitch in place.

6. Follow Steps 3–4, using the longer rectangles on the horizontal edges of the block/base. Follow Step 5, pressing and tucking in the raw edges at the ends first.

Bind the vertical edges.

Bind the horizontal edges.

Firm-Back Assembly

1. Press the wrong side of the backing to a piece of fast2fuse.

2. Center and press the batting to the other side of the fast2fuse.

3. Follow Steps 2–6 of Bound Edge Assembly (above).

Border-Edge Assembly

1. Sandwich the block/base and the backing with wrong sides together.

2. Pin and stitch the shorter borders to the vertical edges of the block/base, following the Finished Seam Option (page 37) or the Raw Edge Option (page 37).

3. Repeat Step 2, using the longer borders on the horizontal edges.

4. Fold the raw edges of the border under ¼" (6mm); machine top-stitch along the fold.

5. Fold the vertical edges over the backing; press. Pin, and hand stitch in place.

6. Follow Step 5 for the horizontal edges: pressing and tucking in the raw edges at the ends first.

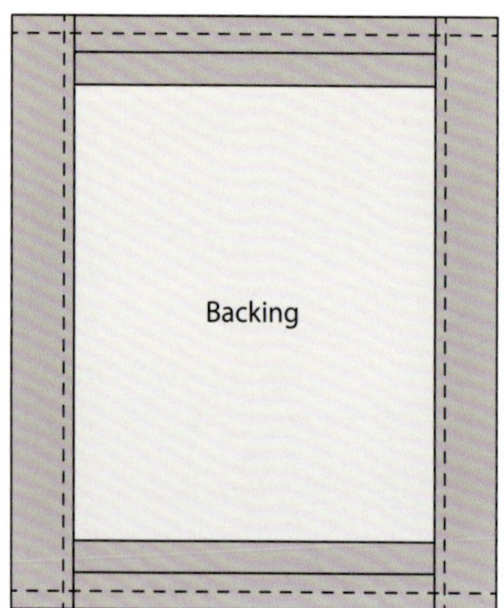

Bind the vertical edges.

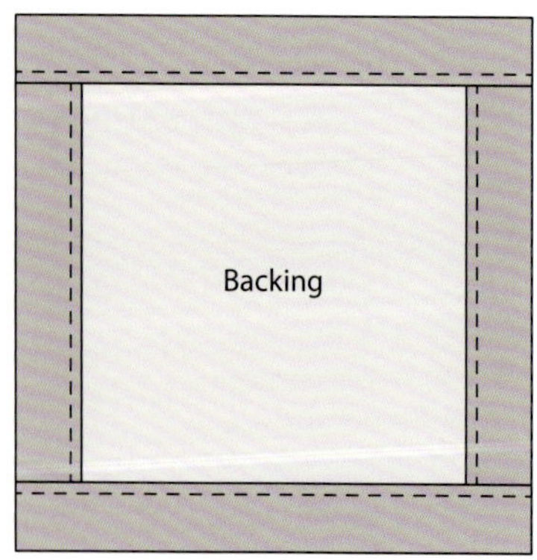

Bind the horizontal edges.

Ribbon-Edge Binding

1. Machine stitch the shorter lengths of grosgrain ribbon to the right side of each vertical raw edge of the block/base ¼" (6mm) from the raw edge.

2. Repeat Step 2, stitching the longer lengths of grosgrain ribbon to each horizontal raw edge.

3. Sandwich the block/base and the backing with wrong sides together. Fold the edges of the base over the backing; press.

4. Pin the ribbon to the backing on the vertical edges. Hand stitch in place.

5. Repeat Step 4 for the ribbon on the horizontal edges, folding and tucking in the ends first.

Option: *The ribbon can be stitched to the backing, then folded over to cover the front of the base.*

Bind the vertical edges.

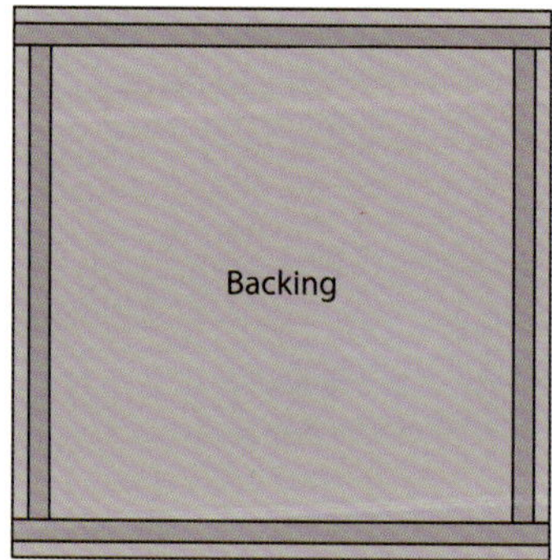

Bind the horizontal edges.

Soft-Edge Assembly

Note: *Use a ⅜″ (1cm) seam allowance.*

1. Sandwich the batting in between the block/base and the backing.

2. Fold and press each square into a triangle.

3. Fold and press under ⅜″ (1cm) on one long side of each binding rectangle; machine stitch along the folds.

4. Pin the raw edges of each triangle into the corners of the right side of the block/base.

5. With right sides together, pin the raw edges of the rectangles even with the edges of the block/base, leaving a 1″ (2.25cm) space from each corner.

6. Machine stitch around the perimeter. Trim the excess at the corners.

7. Turn the triangles out, gently poking out the corners.

8. Press, pin, and hand stitch the finished edges of the binding to the backing.

9. Press, pin, and hand stitch the folded diagonal edge of the triangles to the backing.

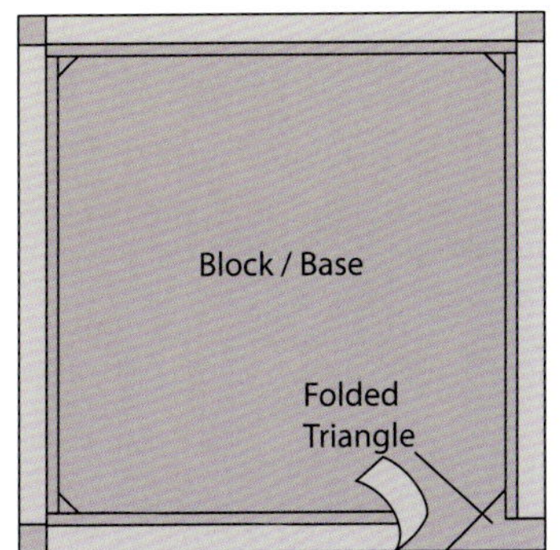

Pin the triangles, vertical strips, and horizontal strips.

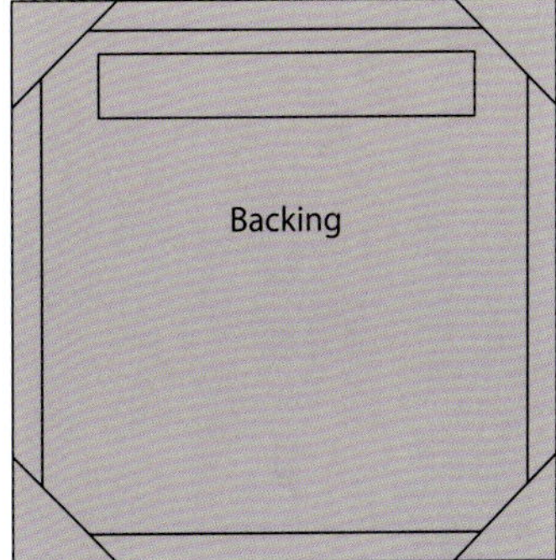

Hand stitch the strips and triangles in place.

Custom Hanger

1. Cut 2 pieces of ⅜″ (1cm) ribbon twice the length needed, plus ½″ (1.2cm).

2. Fold the length in half, right side in. Hand stitch the raw edges together with a ¼″ (6mm) seam allowance.

3. Turn the ribbon right side out. Pin the seamed end of the ribbon to the backing 1½″ (3.8cm) down from the top edge and 3″ (7.6cm) in from the side edges.

4. Hand stitch to the backing.

5. Insert a wooden knitting needle, ruler, or other object for the hanger.

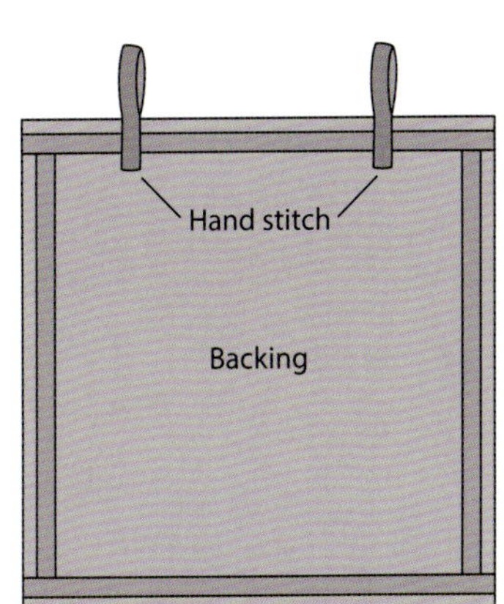

EVERY SCRAP USED

Still have fabric left, or little bits you want to incorporate onto the project? Here are a few additional ideas.

Yo-Yo Edging

1. Tackstitch the side edges of 2 finished fabric yo-yos (page 31) together with 2 or 3 stitches; bury the thread through the second yo-yo, and through to the following edge.

2. Repeat Step 1 for each additional yo-yo until you have the desired length.

3. Tackstitch each yo-yo in the row to the finished edge of the base.

Signature Label

1. Cut 1 piece of fabric for the center of the label; piece around this with leftover sections of fabric. Iron this section onto a piece of Shape-Flex.

2. With a fabric marking pen, write your name or the title of your artwork.

Option: *Embroider the information with the stem stitch, chain stitch, or backstitch.*

3. Embroider or embellish sections with leftover bits and pieces.

A

4. Stitch lace, ribbon, or strips of fabric onto the raw edges.

5. Hand stitch this to the backing with a tack stitch, running stitch, or embroidery stitch.

B

C

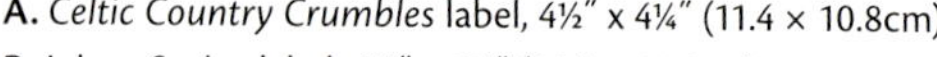

A. *Celtic Country Crumbles* label, 4½″ x 4¼″ (11.4 × 10.8cm)
B. *Jaipur Spring* label, 4½″ x 4½″ (11.4 × 11.4cm)
C. *Saltwater Taffy Trimmings* label, 5″ x 3½″ (12.7 × 8.9cm)
D. *Lumber Jack Picnic* label, 5″ x 4″ (12.7 × 10.2cm)

Tutorial: Signature Labels and Keepsake Pockets, Creative Spark Online Learning

Project: Hand Embroidery Basics and Beyond, Creative Spark Online Learning.

D

LARGER CRUMBLED SECTIONS

If you have a good number of small scraps and want to make a larger project, cut a larger rectangle of muslin, then cut that into smaller sections.

Celtic Country Crumbles

In this example, each section of cotton fabrics was foundation pieced (page 27), then embroidered. I used ribbon for the fabric or ribbon sashing (page 37) to assemble the base, with mock prairie point borders (page 39). I created fabric yo-yos from a crazy-pieced base (page 31) for the Yo-Yo Edging (page 44).

Base diagram

Size: 16¾" x 14¾" (42.5 × 37.5cm)

Embroidery and Embellishment Stitches

STITCH TO YOUR HEART'S CONTENT!

In this chapter you will find a robust selection of stitches that includes traditional stitches, silk ribbon embroidery stitches, beaded embroidery stitches, and embellishment stitches which incorporate buttons, sequins, and other ephemera.

To access the pattern through the tiny url, type the web address provided into your browser window. **tinyurl.com/11539-download**

Crazy Colorful

Size: 27½" x 24½" (69.9 x 62.2cm)

Piecing together a larger base gives you more embroidery and embellishment opportunities. This piece started with a block like the Stripped Crumbles Block (page 171). I added additional sections of foundation piecing (page 27) along with longer strips and wedges of fabric. I used rickrack trim to break up sections and add interest.

I used my *Embroidery Stencils, Crazy Quilt Seam Designs* (page 22) for the embroidery stitches, which were worked in perle cotton, cotton floss, and seed and larger beads. See Embroidery by Design (page 85) for ideas.

Primarily Crazy for Kevin

Size: 15½″ x 20″ (39.4 × 50.8cm)

I made this base with the same fabrics as *Crazy Colorful* (page 46). However, the embroidery stitches are all worked in seed beads, larger beads, sequins, charms, and buttons. This base was created like the base diagram (page 84), with rickrack trim used to break up areas and to add interest. For more beaded embroidery stitches, check out my book *Beaded Embroidery Stitches*, by C&T Publishing.

If these two examples have sparked your imagination, then get out your needles, threads, ribbons, and beads, and let's get stitching!

THREAD AND BEAD EMBROIDERY COMPARISONS

A variety of thread embroidered stitches can be translated into beaded embroidery stitches. Here is an example of the cross stitch, worked in perle cotton and size 11° seed beads.

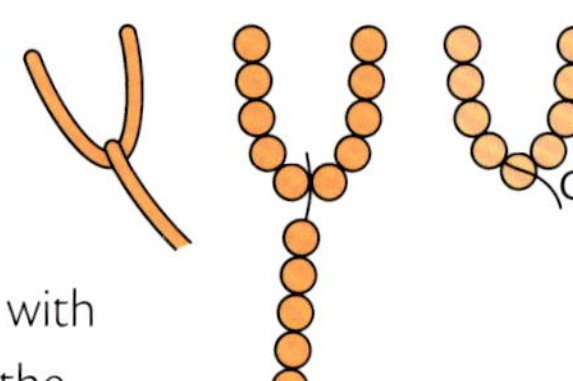

In thread embroidery, when forming a curved stitch, such as the feather stitch, the thread comes out of the cup of the stitch, to catch the stitch and begin the next stitch.

In bead embroidery, the needle can be stitched inside the cup to catch the stitch, with beads added to form the next stitch, or the needle is passed through the bead in the middle of the cup, then beads are added to form the next stitch.

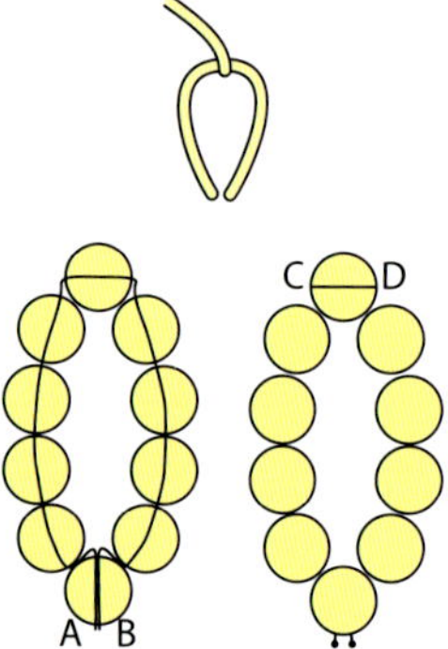

Another comparison is the lazy daisy stitch; in thread embroidery the working thread is wrapped under the needle, the thread is pulled through the fabric, then pulled taut to form the loop. The stitch is finished by catching the loop with a short stitch.

In bead embroidery, the beads are added onto the needle, and the needle is passed in the opposite direction back through the first bead, to form the loop. The stitch is finished by passing the needle through the middle bead in the loop.

Note: *For more information, please read Embroidery Materials (page 20), Stitching Tips (page 20), and Embroidery Tools (page 22).*

EMBROIDERY SPECIFICS

Needle and Thread Lengths

Perle cotton: Cut 16"–18" (40.6–45.7cm) of thread. Use a cotton darner or crewel needle.

Stranded floss: Cut a 16"–18" (40.6–45.7cm) length from the skein, then split the length into sections of 2–3 strands. Use an embroidery needle.

Silk embroidery ribbon: Cut 16" (40.6cm) of ribbon. Use a chenille needle size 18–24, depending on the width of the ribbon.

Note: *The higher the number listed on the package, the finer the needle.*

Nymo B or Silamide beading thread: Cut 2 yards (1.9m) of thread. Match the tails, use the thread doubled, and wax with synthetic bee's wax. Use a beading needle (size 10).

The Form of a Stitch

The shape of a stitch can be altered by changing the positioning and distance between the points the needle will take.

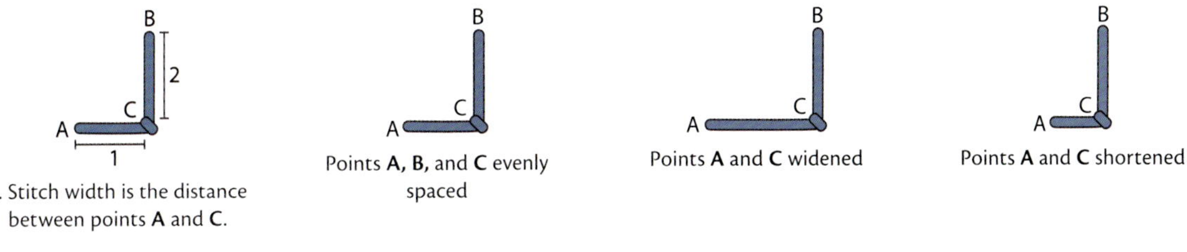

1. Stitch width is the distance between points **A** and **C**.

Points **A**, **B**, and **C** evenly spaced

Points **A** and **C** widened

Points **A** and **C** shortened

2. Stitch height is the distance between points **B** and **C**.

VARIATIONS IN STITCH TECHNIQUE

In some cases, it is easier to form a caught stitch like the chain stitch in 3 strokes—up, down, up—rather than in 2 strokes as the directions indicate.

1. Come up at **A**.
2. Go down at **B**, pulling the thread slightly to form the stitch.
3. Come up at **C**, pulling the thread all the way through.

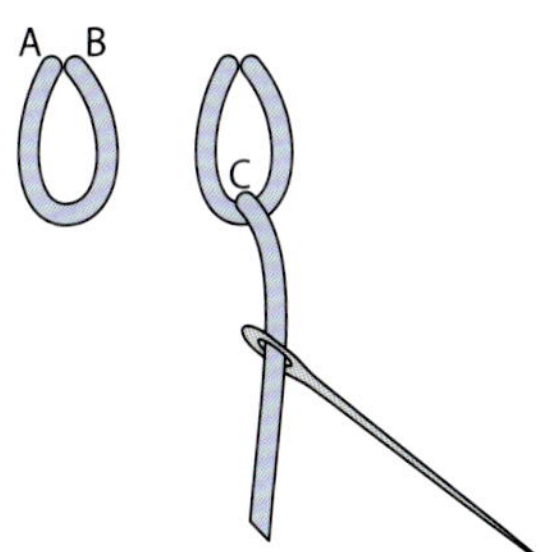

Adding Thread

CAUGHT STITCHES: FEATHER, BLANKET, CRETAN, OR CHAIN STITCHES

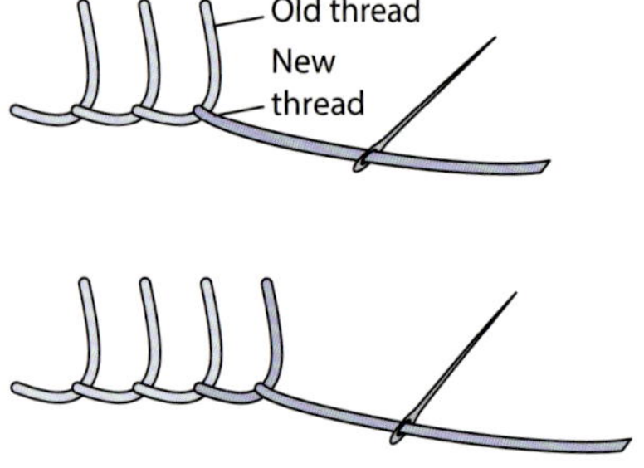

1. Stitch **B** of a looped stitch down through the fabric, but do not pull the thread taut. Stitch the new thread through the loop at **C**. Pull the old thread to form the loop.

2. Stitch 1 or 2 stitches with the new thread; then knot and cut the old thread. Continue to stitch with the new thread.

STRAIGHT STITCHES: OUTLINE, STEM, HERRINGBONE, OR CHEVRON

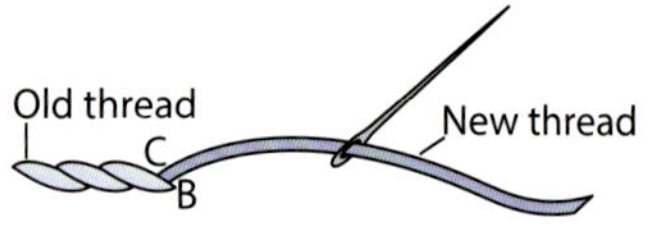

Knot and cut the old thread after **B**; start the new thread at **C**.

BEADED STITCHES

When the thread is too short to continue a stitch, cut the thread after the directions have instructed you to knot the thread. Bring the new thread up through the fabric and continue to follow the directions.

Evenly Spaced Stitches

For a single row of stitches, like the chain stitch, draw a straight line using a ruler and an erasable marking pen, then mark off the line at even increments.

Muslin with line marked off in ¼″ (6mm) intervals, chain stitch

For a stitch that has two points that are spaced, like the blanket stitch, use quilters tape as a temporary spacing guide. Place a row of tape on two lines, then mark the tape at even increments with a permanent marking pen.

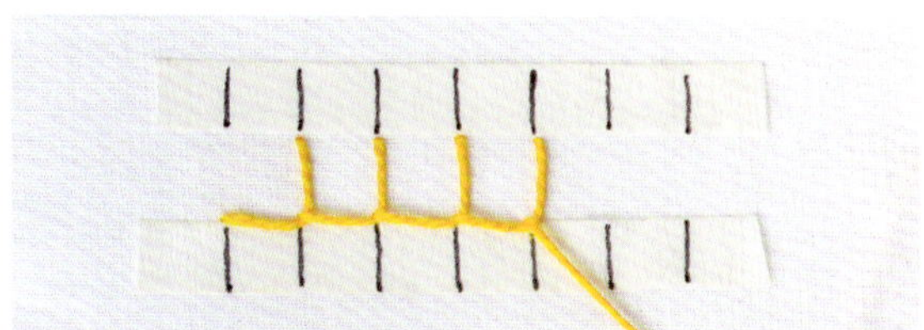

Quilters tape marked off in ¼″ (6mm) intervals, blanket stitch

Stencils can offer even the most experienced stitcher's work a more evenly spaced design. Place the template on the fabric, then mark the design with an erasable pen.

Embroidery Stencils, Darling Motif Collection, spool

Serendipity Beaded stitches create evenly spaced stitches, simply due to the nature of the shape of the beads.

BORDER ROW STITCHES FOR SHORT SEAMS OR NARROW SPACES

Outline Stitch

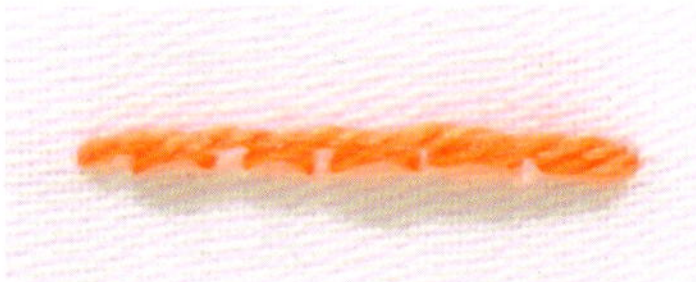

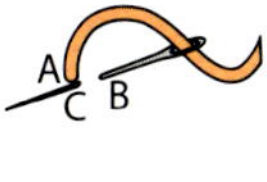

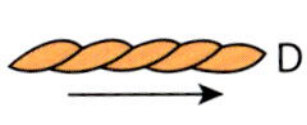

1. Come up at **A**, with the thread above the line. *Backstitch the needle in one motion down at **B** and up at **C**. Pull the needle through the fabric.

2. Repeat from * to finish the row, with **C** of the next stitch next to **B** of the previous stitch. To end the stitch, go down at **D**.

Stem Stitch

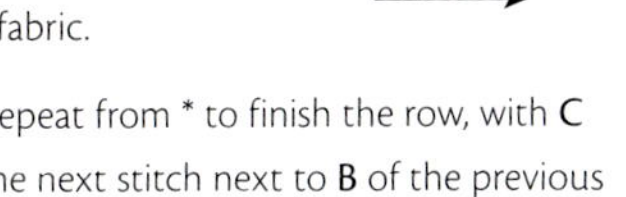

1. Come up at **A**, with the thread below the line. *Backstitch the needle in one motion down at **B** and up at **C**. Pull the needle through the fabric.

2. Repeat from * to finish the row, with **C** of the next stitch next to **B** of the previous stitch. To end the stitch, go down at **B**.

Stem/Outline Fern Stitch

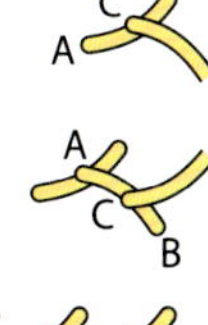

Work 1 stem stitch (at left) and then 1 outline stitch (at far left), working points **B** and **C** in both stitches at an angle. Alternate the stitches along the row.

Running Stitch

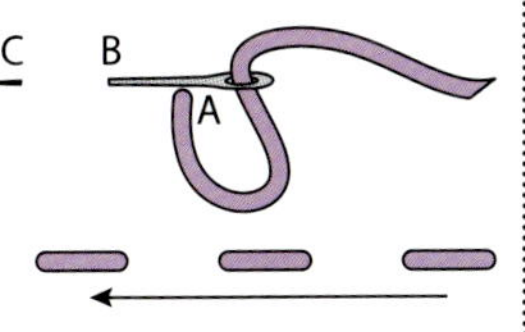

1. Come up at **A**. *In one motion, go down at **B** and up at **C**. Pull the needle through the fabric. **C** now becomes **A**.

2. Repeat from * to finish the row. To end the stitch, go down at **B** of the last stitch.

Note: *This stitch can be used for Sashiko and hand-quilted stitches.*

Couched Stitch

1. Stitch a length of thread onto the fabric; knot and cut the end.

2. With a different color or type of thread, come up next to one end of the thread. Work straight stitches (page 70) across the row.

Variation: *A heavier weight thread or a ribbon can be used in Step 1.*

Backstitch

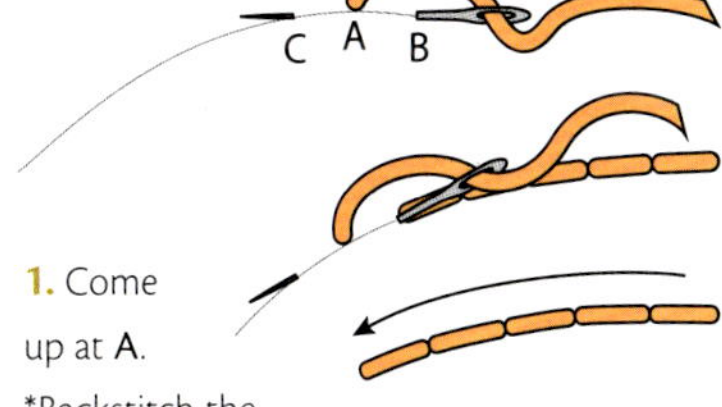

1. Come up at **A**. *Backstitch the needle in one motion, down at **B** and up at **C**. Pull the needle through the fabric. **C** now becomes **A**.

2. Repeat from * to finish the row. To end the stitch, go down at **B**.

Bead Strand Stitch Single or Double

Single

Double

1. Come up at A, with the thread below the line. *In one motion, go down at B and up at C. Wrap the working thread under the eye and the tip of the needle.
2. Place your thumb over the loop and pull the needle through the fabric. Go down at D. Come up at E.
3. Repeat from * to finish the row. To end the stitch, go down at F.

Chain Stitch Spiny

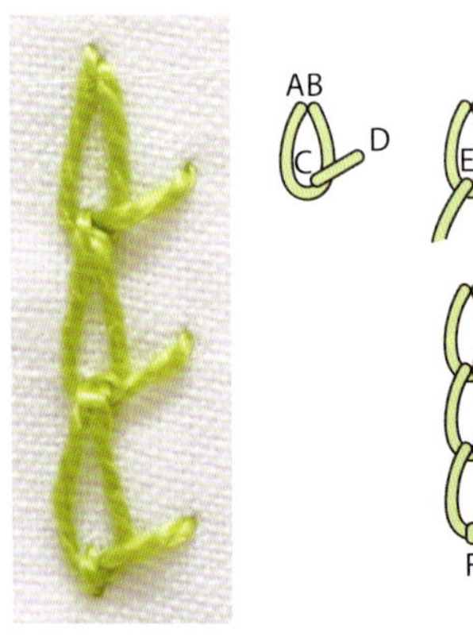

1. Come up at A. Follow Step 1 of the chain stitch (above) from *. Go down at D, angling up. Come up at E, which now becomes A of the chain stitch.
2. Repeat from * to finish the row, working a spine outside each chain. To end the stitch, do down at F.

Chain Stitch

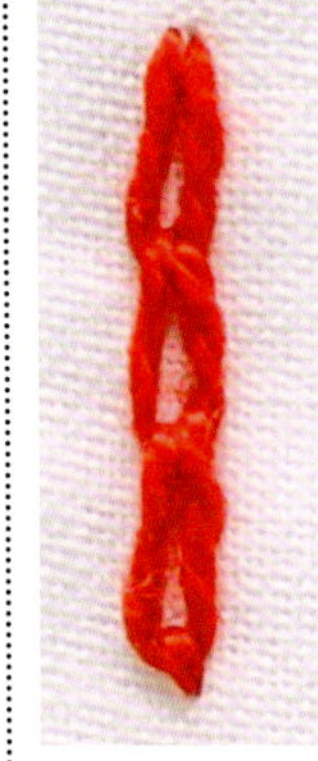

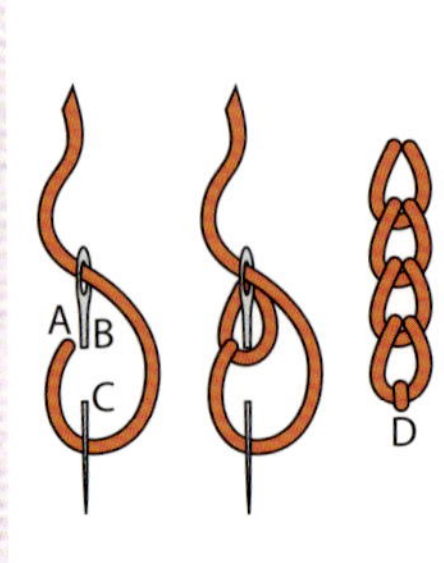

1. Come up at A. *In one motion, go down at B and up at C. Wrap the working thread under the tip of the needle. Pull the needle through the fabric.
2. Repeat from * to finish the row, starting inside the previous loop. To end the stitch, go down at D.

Chain Stitch Double

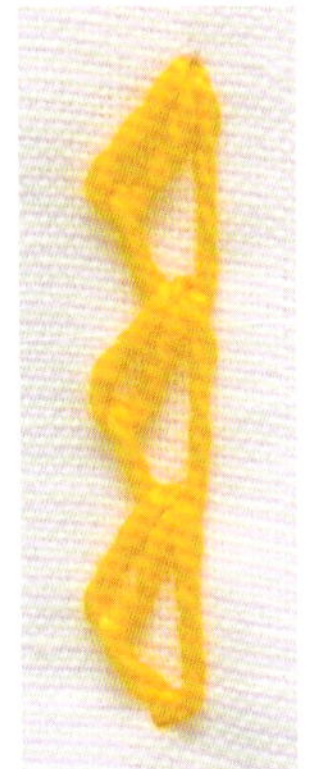

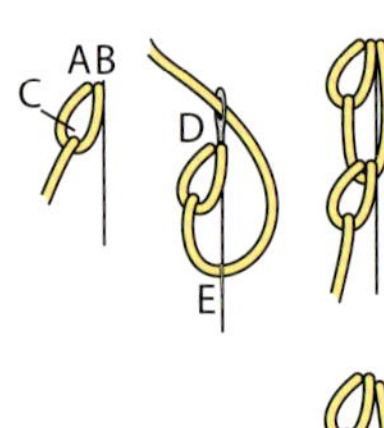

1. *Follow Step 1 of the chain stitch (above), working the stitch slightly angled and next to the seam.
2. In one motion, go down at D next to B and up at E on the seam.
3. Repeat from * to finish the row, beginning in the loop of the previous stitch. To end the stitch, go down at F.

Chain Stitch Zigzag

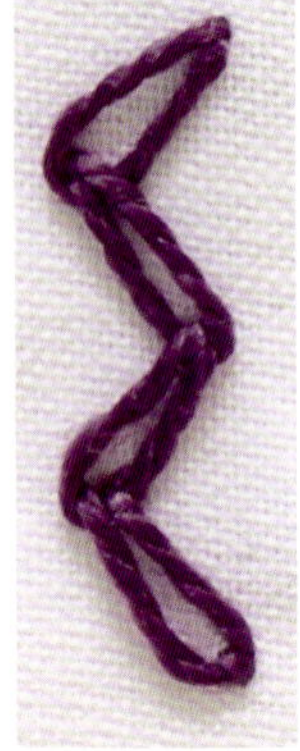

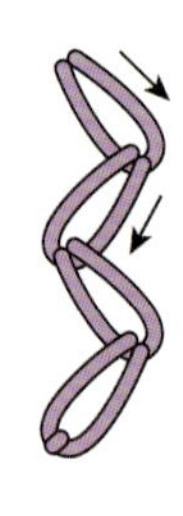

Follow the directions for the chain stitch (at left), angling the first stitch away from the seam and the next stitch toward the seam. Repeat the pattern across the row.

Chain Stitch Feathered

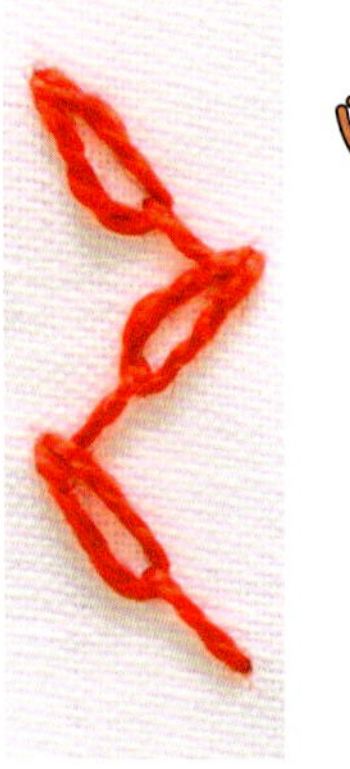

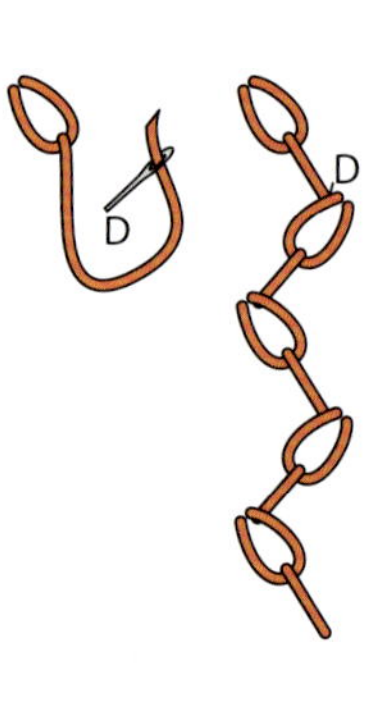

1. *Follow Step 1 of the chain stitch (above), angling the stitch away from the seam. Go down at D a short distance away.
2. Beginning at D, repeat from *, angling the stitch toward the seam.
3. Repeat Steps 1 and 2 to finish the row, angling the stitches from side to side.

Note: *The stitches on this page are worked with seed beads in a variety of sizes.*

Continuous Bead Stitch

1. Come up and *thread 6 beads onto the needle; lay the beads flat against the fabric. Go down just beyond the edge of the last bead.

2. Come up at A, between the third and fourth beads in the row. Thread the needle through the remaining 3 beads in the row. To finish the row, continue from *.

3. To end the stitch, come up at A, go through the last 3 beads in the row, and go down at B. Knot the thread.

Note: *If the line of beads is not straight, pass the needle through the entire row of beads.*

Continuous Bead Stitch Fancy

1. Come up and *thread 3 size 11° and 1 size 8° seed beads onto the needle; lay the beads flat against the fabric. Go down just beyond the edge of the last bead.

2. Come up at A, between the second and third size 11° seed beads in the row. Thread the needle through the size 11° and the size 8° seed beads. To finish the row, continue from *.

3. To end the stitch, come up at A, go through the last 2 beads in the row, and go down at B. Knot the thread.

Spine Vine Stitch (Beaded)

1. Come up at A and *thread 6 size 11°, 1 size 8°, and 1 size 11° seed beads onto the needle. Lay the beads flat against the fabric. Pass the needle through the size 8° and the remaining beads in the row. Go down at B. Knot the thread.

2. Come up at C, between the size 8° and 11° beads; go down at D to couch the bead thread. Knot the thread.

3. Come up at the beginning of the previous row; pass the needle through the first 3 beads. Repeat from *, to continue the row.

Continuous Bead Stitch Knobbed

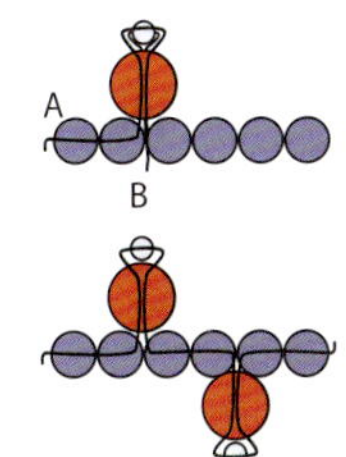

1. Work a row of continuous bead stitches (above) using size 11° seed beads.

2. Come up at A and go through the first 2 beads in the row. *Thread 1 size 8° and 1 size 15° seed beads onto the needle. Thread the needle back through the size 8° seed bead and down through the fabric at B. Knot the thread.

3. Come up close to B of the previous stitch. Thread the needle through the next 2 beads in the row. To finish the row, continue from *, working the stitches on either side of the row.

Note: *The stitches on this page are worked with seed beads in a variety of sizes.*

Chain Stitch (Beaded)

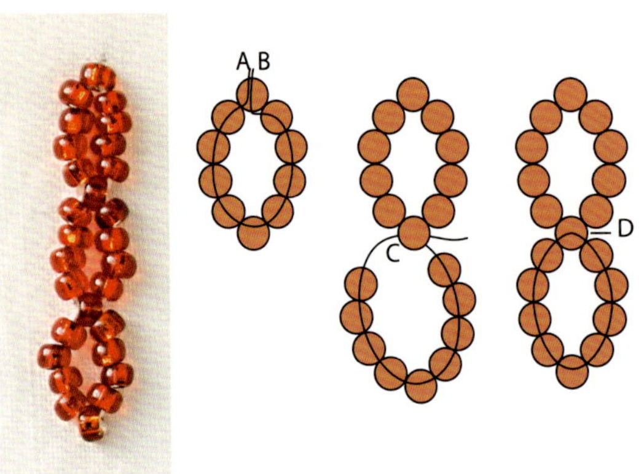

1. Come up at A. Thread 10 size 11° seed beads onto the needle; lay the beads flat against the fabric. Take the needle back through the first bead. Go down at B. Knot the thread.

2. *Come up at C and stitch through the middle bead of the previous loop. Thread 9 size 11° seed beads onto the needle; lay the beads flat against the fabric. Stitch through the middle bead again and down through the fabric at D. Knot the thread.

3. To finish the row, continue from * through the middle bead of the previous loop. To end the stitch, come up at C and go down at D.

Variation: *To make a longer stitch, increase the number of beads by 4 in Steps 1 and 2.*

Chain Stitch Long-Short (Beaded)

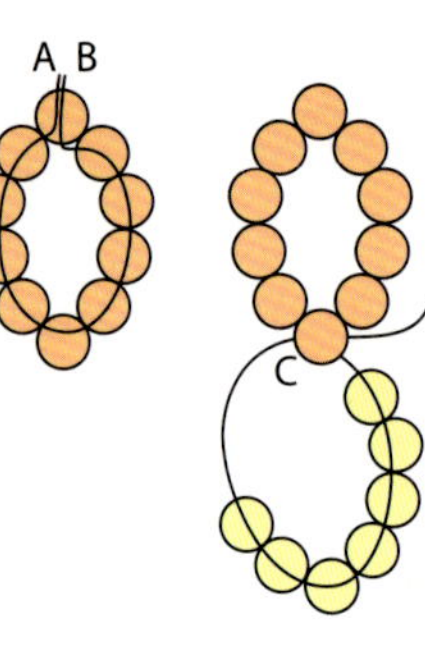

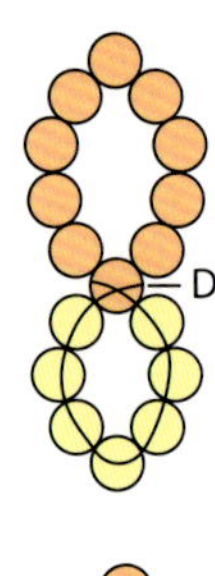

1. Follow Step 1 of the chain stitch (beaded) (at left) using 10 size 11° seed beads.

2. *Come up at C; stitch through the middle bead of the previous loop. Thread 7 (short) or 9 (long) size 11° seed beads onto the needle and lay the beads flat against the fabric.

Stitch through the middle bead again and down through the fabric at D. Knot the thread.

3. To finish the row, continue from *, through the middle bead of the previous loop, alternating the number of beads. To end the stitch, come up at C and go down at D.

Double Bubble Stitch (Beaded)

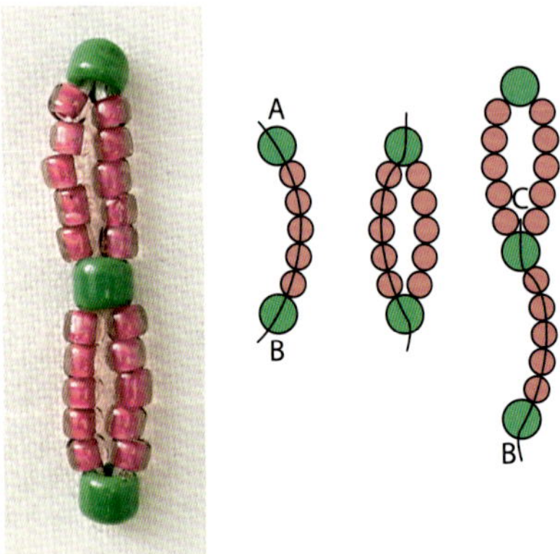

1. Come up at A. Thread 1 size 8°, 5 size 11°, and 1 size 8° seed beads onto the needle. *Lay the beads flat against the fabric. Go down at B.

2. Come back through the first size 8° bead in the row. Thread 5 size 11° seed beads and pass the needle through the next size 8° bead in this row. Go down through the fabric. Knot the thread.

3. To continue the row, come up at C and pass the needle through the last size 8° bead in the previous row. Thread 5 size 11° and 1 size 8° seed beads onto the needle. Follow Step 1 from *.

Cable Stitch (Beaded)

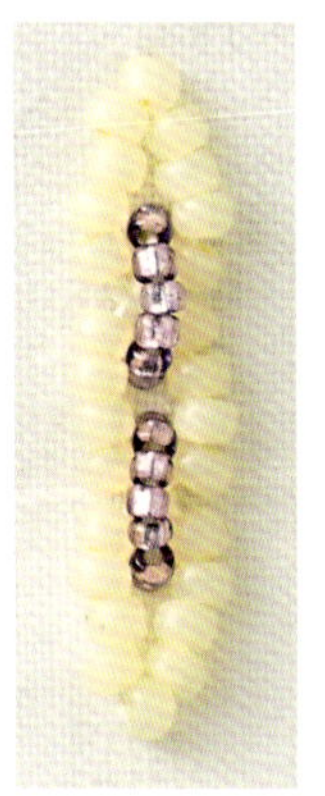

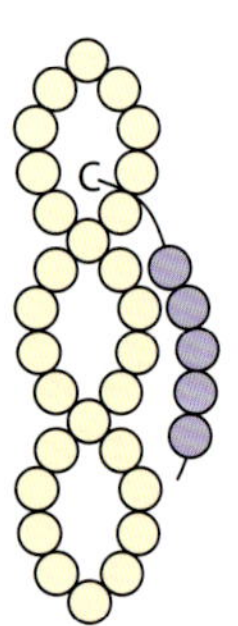

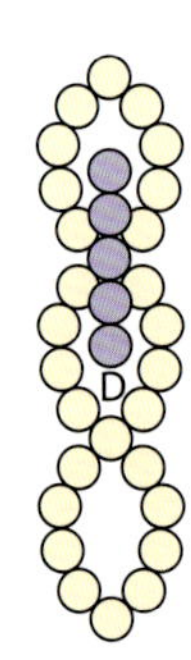

1. Work a row of chain stitches (beaded) (above) using size 11° seed beads.

2. *Come up through the loop at C; thread 5 size 11° seed beads onto the needle and pass them down through the next loop at D. Knot the thread.

3. To finish the row, repeat from * for each remaining loop.

Variation: *Substitute 7 size 15° seed beads in Step 2.*

BORDER ROW STITCHES FOR MEDIUM SEAMS OR MEDIUM SPACES

Blanket Stitch

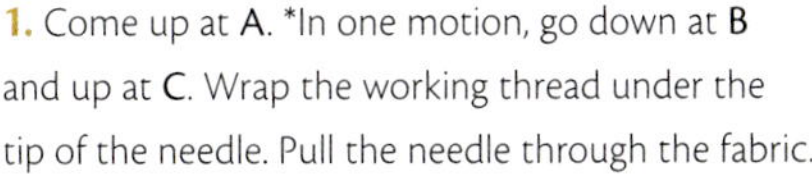

1. Come up at **A**. *In one motion, go down at **B** and up at **C**. Wrap the working thread under the tip of the needle. Pull the needle through the fabric.

2. Repeat from * to finish the row. To end the stitch, go down at **D**, or a short distance away.

Variations: *Change the spacing or the pattern of the stitches.*

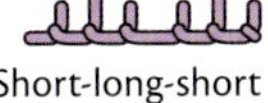

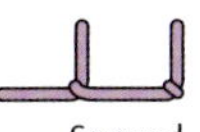
Spaced

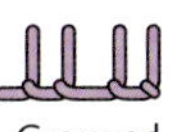
Grouped

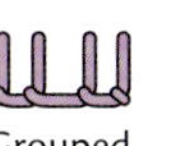
Short-long

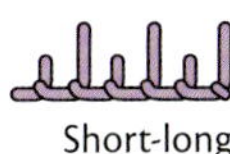
Short-long-short

Blanket Stitch Angled

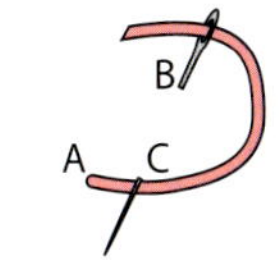

1. Come up at **A**. Follow Step 1 of the blanket stitch (at left) from *, with the stitch angled.

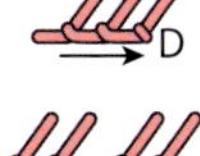
Grouped

2. Repeat from * to finish the row. To end the stitch, go down at **D**.

Variations: *Change the spacing or the pattern of the stitches.*

Short-long

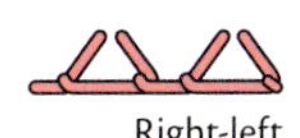
Right-left

Blanket Stitch Up and Down

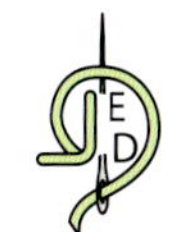

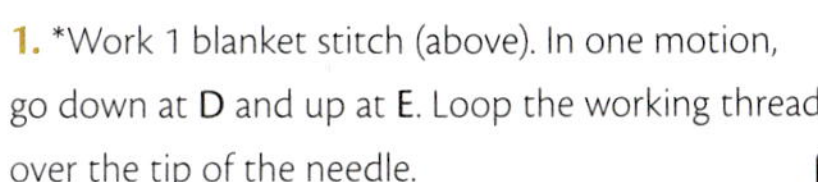

1. *Work 1 blanket stitch (above). In one motion, go down at **D** and up at **E**. Loop the working thread over the tip of the needle.

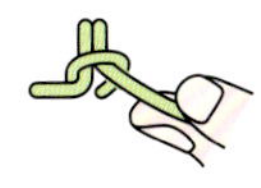

2. Pull the needle through the fabric. Thread the needle under the loop and gently pull the thread to tighten.

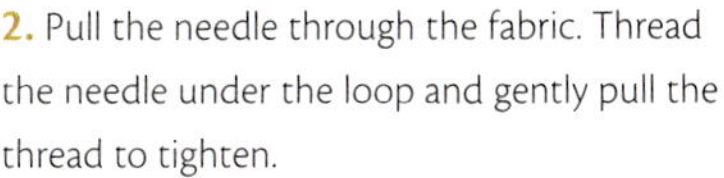

3. Repeat from * to finish the row. To end the stitch, go down at **F**.

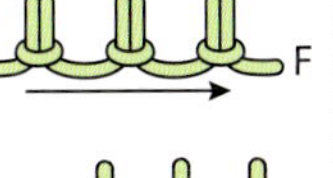
Short-long

Variations: *Change the length or the angle of the stitches.*

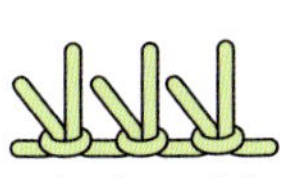
Angle-straight

Blanket Stitch Closed

Follow the directions for the blanket stitch angled (above).

1. Work 1 stitch angled to the right.

2. Work a second stitch angled to the left, going down at **B** and up at **D**.

Closed-straight

3. Repeat Steps 1 and 2 to finish the row. To end the stitch, go down at **E**.

Straight-angle

Variations: *Change the spacing or add in additional stitches.*

Angle-long-angle

Angle-straight, straight

Blanket and Chain Stitches

1. Work 1 blanket stitch (page 55) or 1 set of grouped blanket stitches. Work 1 chain stitch (page 52), going down at **D** and up at **E**.

Blanket stitch with chain stitch

2. Repeat Step 1 to finish the row. To end the stitch, go down at **F** after a blanket stitch or chain stitch.

Blanket stitch grouped with chain stitch

Blanket Stitch Looped

1. Come up at **A**. *In one motion, go down at **B** and up at **C**. Wrap the working thread under the eye and the tip of the needle and back to the base of the stitch. Pull the needle through the fabric.

2. Go down at **D**, to catch the loop. Come up at **E**.

3. Repeat from * to finish the stitch. To end the stitch, go down at **F**.

Variations: *Change the length, spacing, or number of stitches in a pattern.*

Blanket Stitch Crossed

1. *Work 1 blanket stitch angled (page 55) to the right. Work a second stitch angled to the left, going down at **D** and up at **E**, and crossed over the previous stitch.

2. Repeat from *, to finish the row. To end the stitch, go down at **F**.

Variation: *Change the length of the stitches.*

Blanket Stitch with Loose Knot

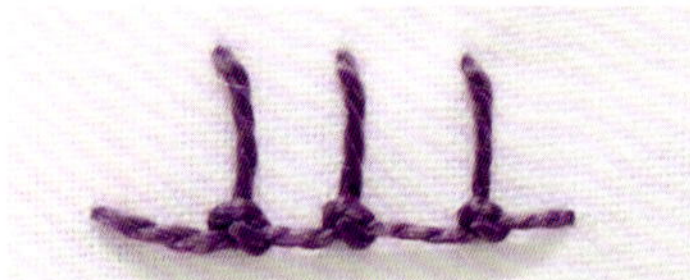

1. *Work 1 blanket stitch (page 55). Go under the base stitch only; wrap the working thread under the tip of the needle. Pull the thread firmly around the base stitch.

2. Repeat from * to finish the row. To end the stitch, go down at **D**.

Variations: *Add this knot to any of the blanket stitch directions.*

Chain and Cross Stitches

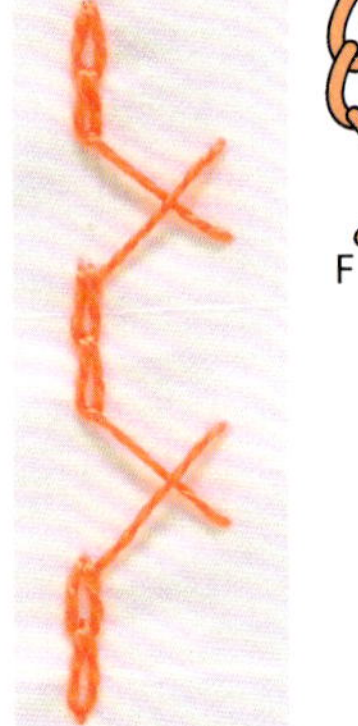

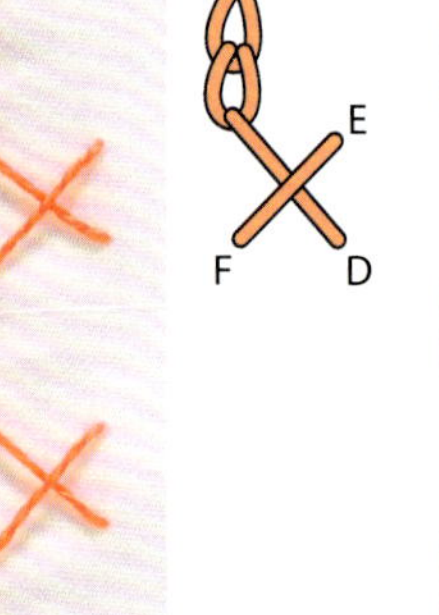

1. *Work 2 chain stitches (page 52). Go down at **D**. Come up at **E** and go down at **F**.

2. Repeat from * to finish the row. To end the stitch, go down at **F** or **G**.

Snail Trail Stitch

1. Come up at **A**. *In one motion, go down at **B** and up at **C**.

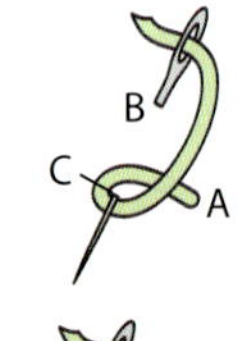

2. Wrap the working thread over the needle and under the tip. Place your thumb over the loop and pull the needle through the fabric.

3. Repeat from * to finish the row a short distance away from the previous stitch. To end the stitch, go down at **D**.

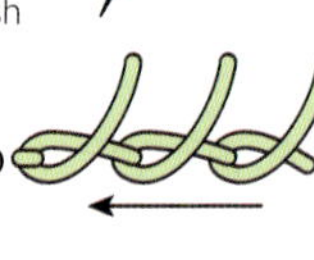

Fly Stitch Chain Link

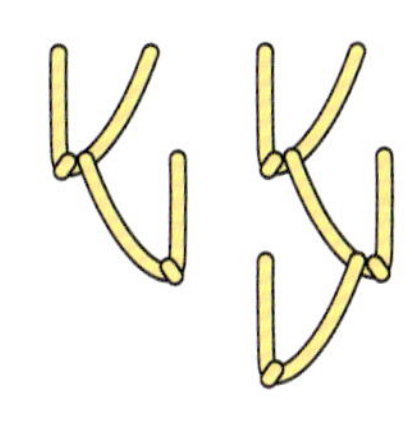

1. Work 1 fly stitch with straight edge (page 67).

2. Work the next stitch in the opposite direction, with Point **B** worked into the previous stitch.

3. Repeat Steps 1 and 2 to finish the row, working the stitches below and into the previous stitch.

Fishhook Stitch

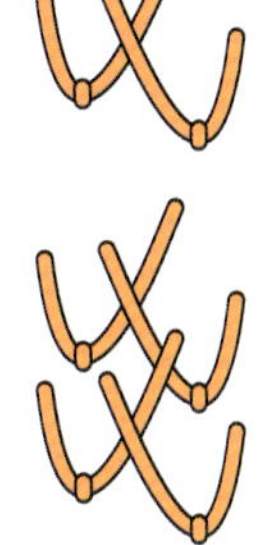

1. Work 1 fly stitch (page 67) angled to the right, with **B** above **A**.

2. Work the next stitch angled in the opposite direction, with point **B** crossed over the previous stitch and even with point **A** of the stitch.

3. Repeat Steps 1 and 2 to finish the row, working the stitches below and into the previous stitch.

Cross Stitch Row

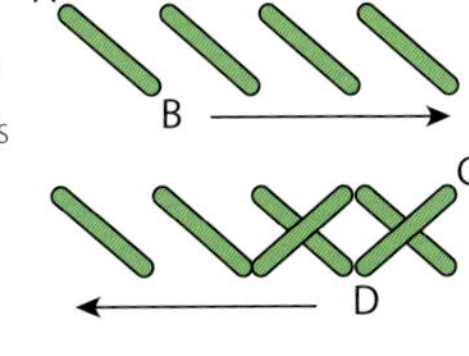

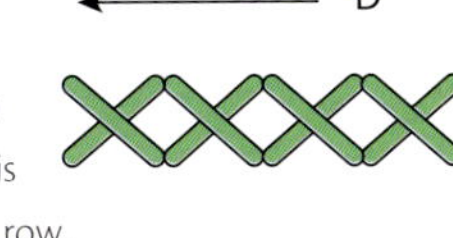

1. Come up at **A** and go down at **B**. Repeat this step across the row.

2. Come up at **C** and go down at **D**. Repeat this step across the row.

Variations: *Change the length and/or height of the stitches or substitute a different color of thread in Step 2.*

Cretan Stitch

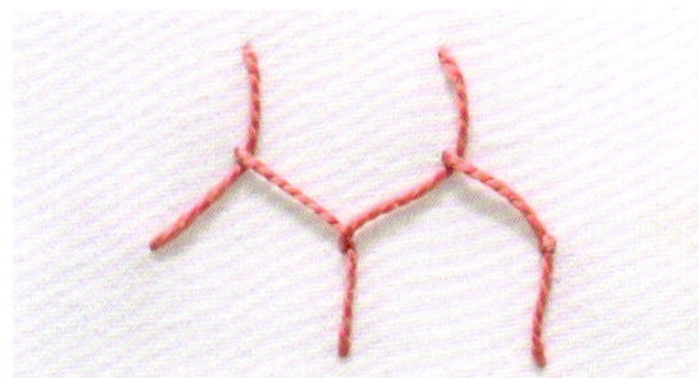

1. Come up at **A** on line 2. *In one motion, go down at **B** on line 4 and up at **C** on line 3. Wrap the working thread under the tip of the needle. Pull the needle through the fabric.

2. In one motion, go down at **D** on line 1 and up at **E** on line 2. Wrap the working thread under the tip of the needle. Pull the needle through the fabric.

3. Repeat from * to finish the row. To end the stitch, go down at **F**, either after Step 1 or Step 2.

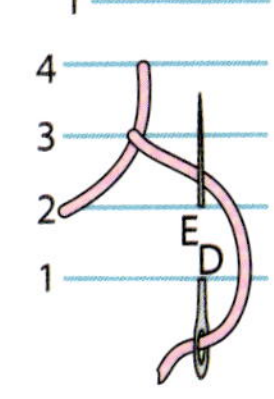

Note: *This stitch can be worked between 4 horizontal rows.*

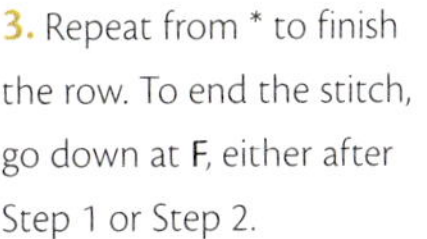

Cretan Stitch with Knot Tip

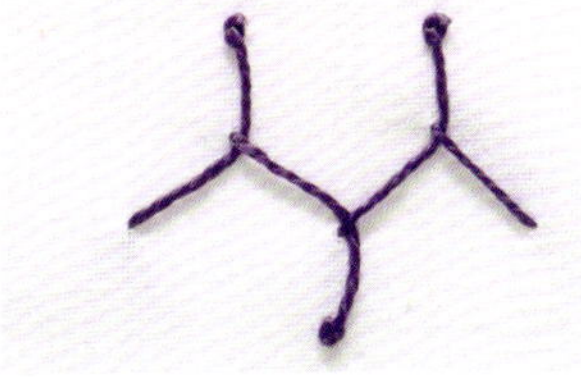

1. Come up at **A**. *Loop the thread over your finger and place the loop next to the fabric. Backstitch the needle in one motion down at **B**, through the loop, and up at **C**.

Pull the thread tightly; then pull the needle through the fabric.

2. In one motion, go down at **D** and up at **E**; repeat Step 1 from *. **E** now becomes **A**.

3. Repeat Steps 1 and 2 to finish the row. To end the stitch, go down at **F**.

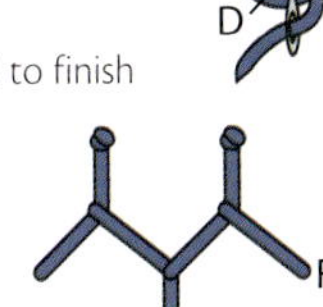

Cretan Stitch Looped

1. Come up at **A**. In one motion, go down at **B** and up at **C**. *Wrap the working thread under the eye and the tip of the needle and back to the base of the stitch. Pull the needle through the fabric. Go down at **D**.

2. Come up at **E**. In one motion, go down at **F** and up at **G**. Repeat from *. Go down at **H**.

3. Repeat Steps 1 and 2 to finish the row. To end the stitch, go down at **I**.

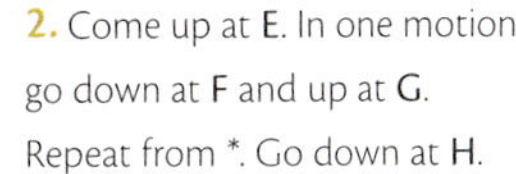

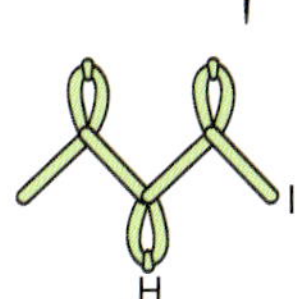

Note: *The stitches on this page are worked with seed beads in a variety of sizes.*

Beaded Vine Stitch

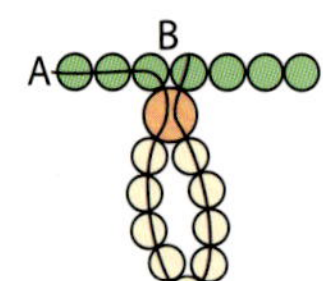

1. Work a row of continuous bead stitches (page 53) using size 11° seed beads.

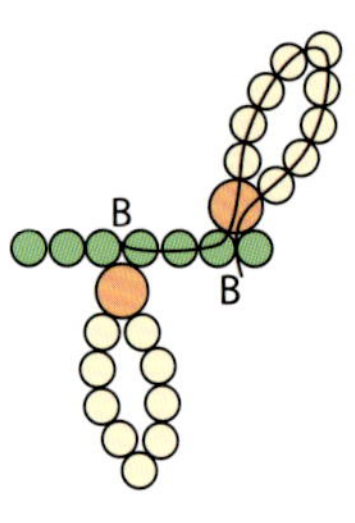

2. Come up at **A** and go through the first 3 beads at the beginning of the row. *Thread 1 size 8° and 9 size 11° seed beads onto the needle. Thread the needle back through the size 8° seed bead and down through the fabric at **B**. Knot the thread.

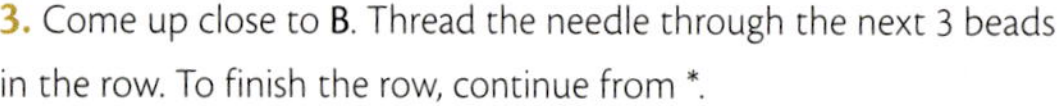

3. Come up close to **B**. Thread the needle through the next 3 beads in the row. To finish the row, continue from *.

Variation: *Follow Step 2 of the lazy daisy stitch (beaded) (page 69) to tack the loop in place.*

Blanket Stitch Even (Beaded)

1. Work a row of continuous bead stitches (page 53).

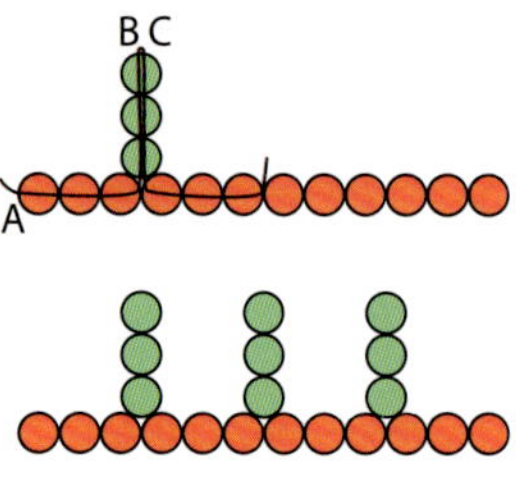

2. Come up at **A** and go through the first 3 beads at the beginning of the row. ***Spoke:** Thread 3 size 11° seed beads onto the needle; lay the beads flat against the fabric. Go down at **B**. Knot the thread.

3. Come up at **C**, thread the needle back through the spoke, and go through the next 3 beads in the row. To finish the row, continue from *.

Variations: *Increase the number of beads for the spoke in Step 2, angle the direction of the spokes, or work the spokes on either side of the row.*

Blanket Stitch Frilled (Beaded)

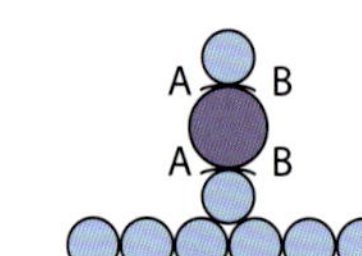

Spoke: 1 size 11°, 1 size 8°, and 1 size 11° seed beads

Follow the directions for the blanket stitch even (beaded) (above), using these suggestions.

Note: *Follow the couching directions in Step 2 of the bead combination stitch (page 71).*

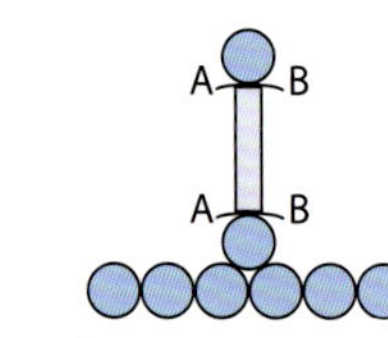

Spoke: 1 size 11°, 1 bugle bead, and 1 size 11° seed bead

Blanket Stitch Fancy (Beaded)

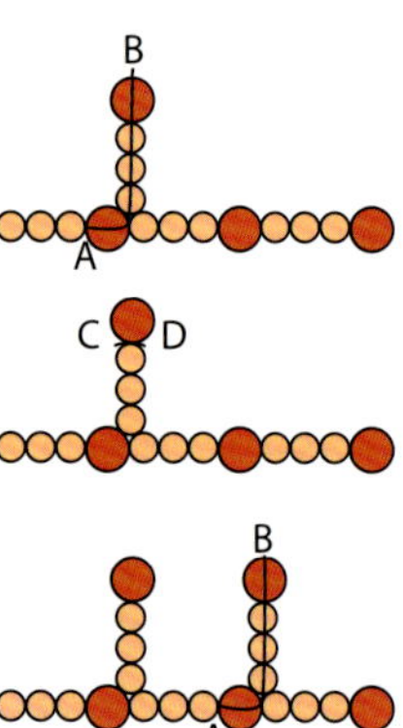

1. Work a row of continuous bead stitch fancy (page 53).

2. *Come up at **A** next to the size 8° seed bead in the row and go through it. **Spoke:** Thread 3 size 11° and 1 size 8° seed beads onto the needle; lay the beads flat against the fabric. Go down at **B**. Knot the thread.

3. Come up at **C**, between the 11° and 8° beads, and go down at **D** to couch the bead thread.

4. To finish the row, continue from *.

Note: *The stitches on this page are worked with seed beads in a variety of sizes.*

Cross Stitch Long Arm Row (Beaded)

1. Come up at **A**. Thread 1 size 8°, *3 size 11°, 1 size 8°, 3 size 11°, and 1 size 8° seed beads onto the needle. See **Note 1**. Go down at **B**. Knot the thread.

2. Come up at **C**. Thread 1 size 8° and **3 size 11 seed beads onto the needle. See **Note 1**. Pass the needle through the size 8° bead in the previous row. See **Note 2**. Thread 3 size 11° and 1 size 8° seed beads onto the needle. See **Note 1**. Go down at **D**. Knot the thread.

3. Come up at **E** and pass the needle through the size 8° bead in the previous row. See **Note 2**. Follow Step 1, threading beads from * onto the needle.

4. To complete the stitch, come up at **F**, then go through the size 8° bead. Follow Step 2, threading beads from ** onto the needle.

Note 1: *Lay the beads flat against the fabric.*

Note 2: *This changes the direction of the bead.*

Herringbone Stitch (Beaded)

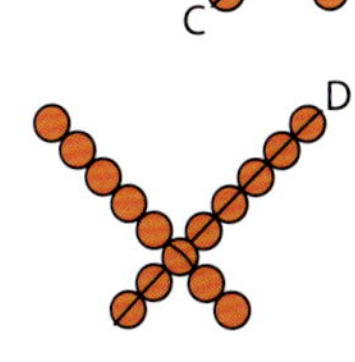

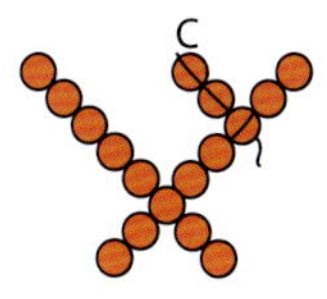

1. Come up at **A**. Thread 8 size 11° seed beads onto the needle; lay the beads flat against the fabric. Go down at **B**. Knot the thread.

2. *Come up at **C**. Thread 2 size 11° seed beads onto the needle; lay the beads flat against the fabric. Pass the needle from either top or bottom through the third bead in the previous row.

Note: *This changes the direction of the bead.*

3. Thread 5 size 11° seed beads onto the needle; lay the beads flat against the fabric. Go down at **D**. Knot the thread.

4. To finish the row, repeat from *.

Serpentine Stitch V Shape(Beaded)

1. Come up at **A**. Thread 1 size 8°, 3 size 11°, and 1 size 8° seed beads onto the needle; lay the beads flat against the fabric. Go down at **B**. Knot the thread.

2. *Come up at **C**. Pass the needle through the size 8° bead in the previous row.

Note: *This changes the direction of the size 8° bead.*

3. Thread 3 size 11° and 1 size 8° seed beads onto the needle; lay the beads flat against the fabric. Go down at **B**. Knot the thread.

4. Repeat Steps 2 and 3 to finish the row.

Variation: *Increase the number of size 11° seed beads.*

Serpentine Stitch Fancy (Beaded)

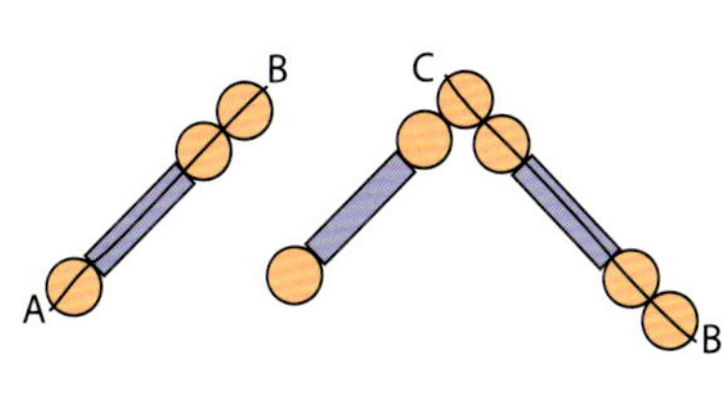

1. Come up at **A**. *Thread 1 size 11° seed bead, 1 bugle bead, and 2 size 11° seed beads onto the needle; lay the beads flat against the fabric. Go down at **B**. Knot the thread.

2. Come up at **C**. Pass the needle through the second size 11° bead in the previous row.

Note: *This changes the direction of the size 11° bead.*

3. To finish the row, repeat from *.

Variations: *Increase the number of size 11° seed beads by 1 or change the bugle bead to a size 8° or 6° seed bead.*

BORDER ROW STITCHES FOR MEDIUM SEAMS OR MEDIUM SPACES

BORDER ROW STITCHES FOR LONG SEAMS OR WIDE SPACES

Feather Stitch

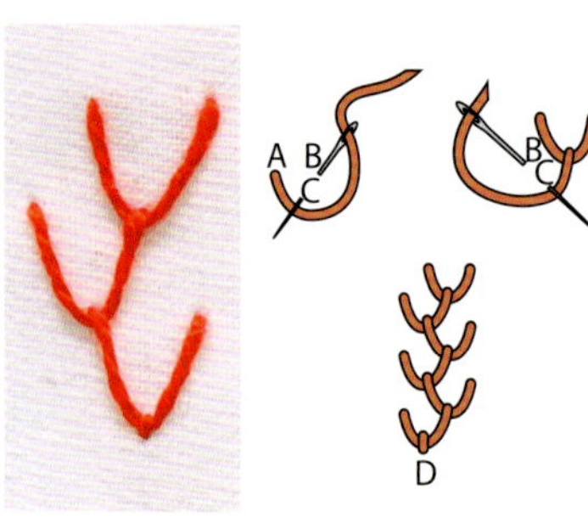

1. Come up at **A**. *In one motion, go down at **B** and up at **C**. Wrap the working thread under the tip of the needle. Pull the needle through the fabric.

2. Repeat Step 1 from *, working the next stitch below and in the opposite direction.

3. Repeat Steps 1 and 2 to finish the row. To end the stitch, go down at **D**.

Feather Stitch Double

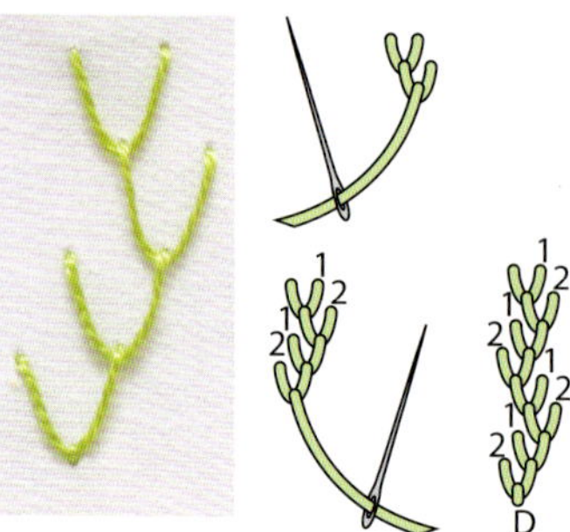

1. Follow Step 1 of the feather stitch (at left). Work a second stitch below and in the same direction.

2. Follow Step 2 of the feather stitch. Work a second stitch below and in the same direction.

3. Repeat Steps 1 and 2 to finish the row. To end the stitch, go down at **D**.

Feather Stitch with Chain Stitch Center

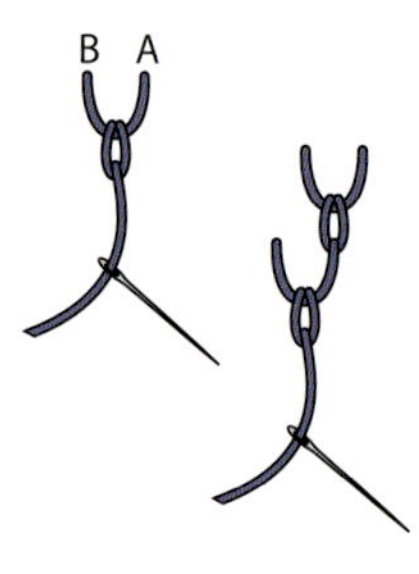

1. Work 1 feather stitch (at left). Work a chain stitch (page 52) inside the loop and below the feather stitch.

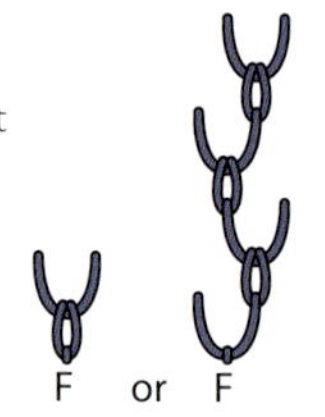

2. Repeat Step 1 to finish the row, working the next group of stitches below and in the opposite direction. To end the stitch, go down at **F**, after the feather or chain stitch.

Feather Stitch Straight Side

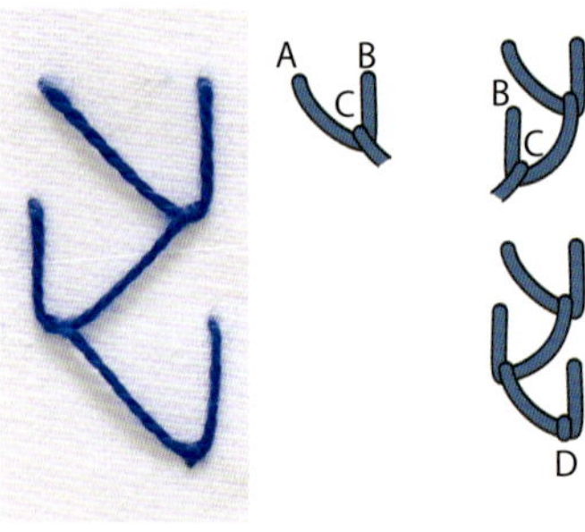

1. Come up at **A**. *In one motion, go down at **B** and up at **C**, with **C** directly below **B**. Wrap the working thread under the tip of the needle. Pull the needle through the fabric.

2. Repeat Step 1 from *, working the next stitch below and in the opposite direction.

3. Repeat Steps 1 and 2 to finish the row. To end the stitch, go down at **D**.

Note: *This stitch can be worked between two vertical lines or over a length of ribbon.*

Feather Stitch Looped

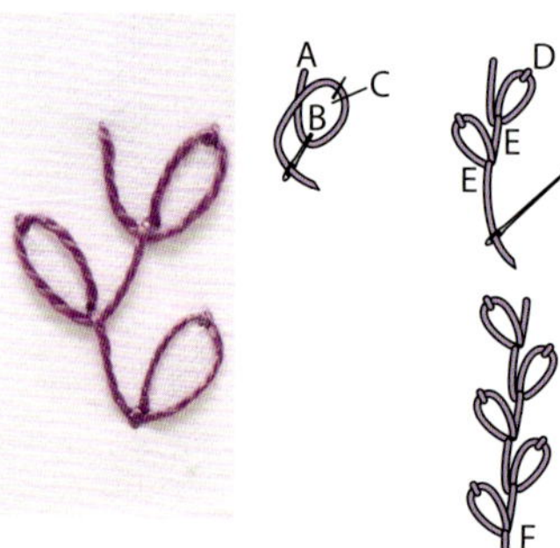

1. Come up at **A**. *In one motion, go down at **B** and up at **C**. Wrap the working thread under the eye and the tip of the needle and back to the base of the stitch. Pull the needle through the fabric. Go down at **D** to catch the loop. Come up at **E**.

2. Repeat Step 1 from *, working the next stitch below and in the opposite direction.

3. Repeat Steps 1 and 2 to finish the row. To end the stitch, go down at **F**.

Feather Stitch Variations

Evenly spaced

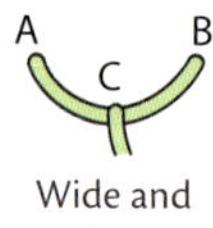

Wide and short

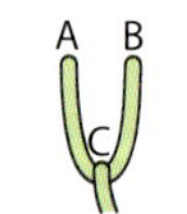

Narrow and long

The feather stitch can vary dramatically by changing the distance between points **A**, **B**, and **C**.

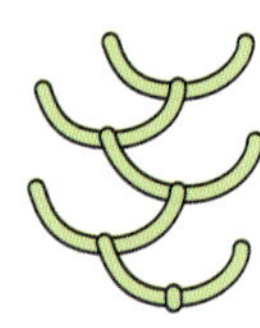
Wide and short

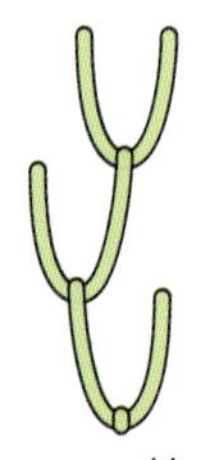
Narrow and long

Fishnet Stitch

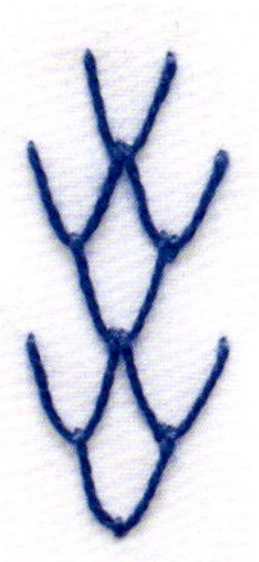

First Row: Follow Step 1 of the feather stitch double (page 60). Go down at **D** to end the row.

Second Row: Follow the directions for the First Row, working the first 2 stitches into the previous row and 1 more stitch below and in the same direction. Go down at **D** to end the row.

Last Row: Follow the directions for the First Row, working the stitches into the previous row. Go down at **D** to end the row.

Herringbone Stitch

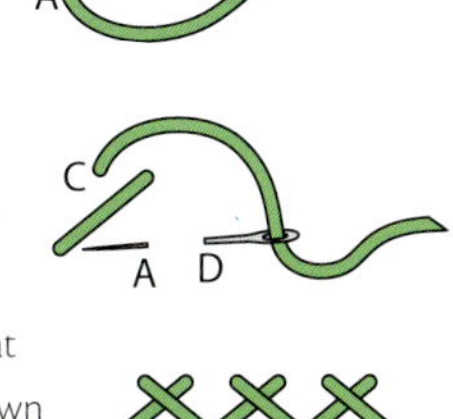

1. Come up at **A**. *Backstitch the needle in one motion down at **B** and up at **C**. Pull the needle through the fabric. Repeat from *, going down at **D** and up at **A**.

2. Repeat Step 1 to finish the row. To end the stitch, go down at **B** or **D**.

Variation: *This stitch can be worked over a length of ribbon.*

Herringbone Long Arm Stitch

1. Come up at **A**; go down at **B**. Come up at **C**; go down at **D**.

2. Repeat Step 1 to finish the row.

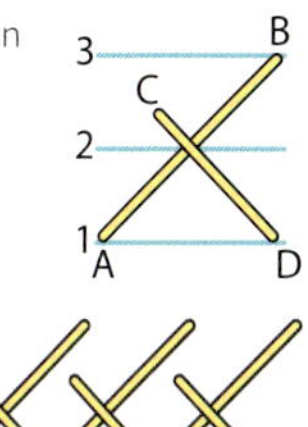

Herringbone Stitch with Details

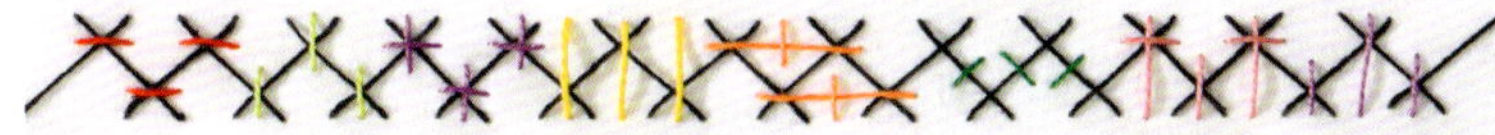

1. Stitch a row of herringbone stitches (above).

2. With a different color of thread, stitch straight stitches (page 70) in any number of patterns shown.

Chevron Stitch

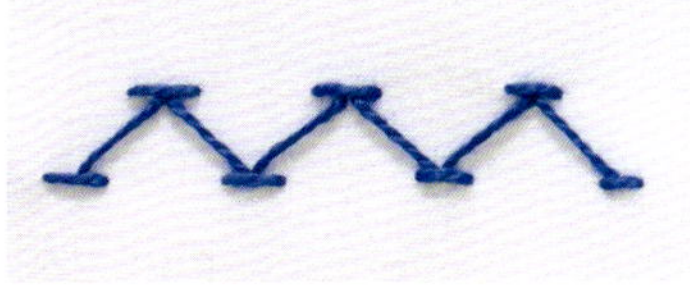

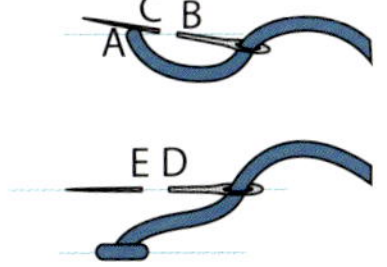

1. Come up at **A**. Backstitch in one motion down at **B** and up at **C**. Pull the needle through the fabric.

2. Backstitch in one motion down at **D** and up at **E**. Pull the needle through the fabric.

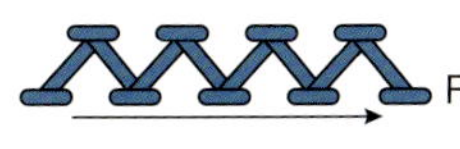

Backstitch in one motion down at **F** and up at **D**.

3. Repeat Step 2 to finish the row, alternating the direction of the stitches. To end the stitch, go down at **F**.

Variation: *This stitch can be worked over a length of ribbon.*

Sawtooth Stitch

1. Follow Steps 1 and 2 of the chevron stitch (at left), working the stitch positions in this pattern: angled, then straight.

2. Repeat Step 1 to finish the row.

Note: *The stitches on this page are worked with seed beads in a variety of sizes.*

Feather Stitch (Beaded)

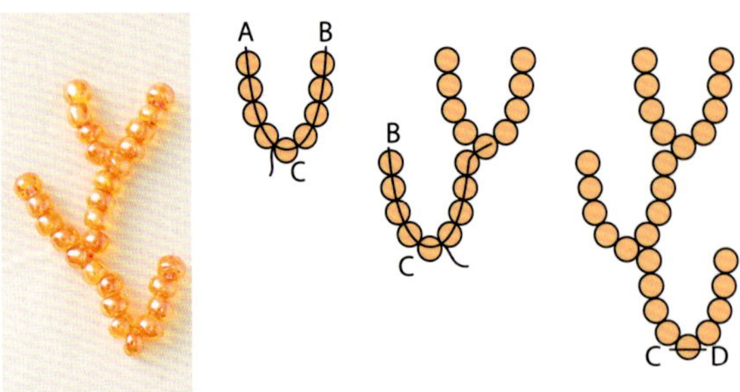

1. Come up at **A**. *Thread 9 size 11° seed beads onto the needle and lay the beads flat against the fabric. Go down to the right at **B**. Knot the thread. Come up at **C**; stitch through the middle bead, from right to left.

2. Follow Step 1 from *. Go down to the left at **B**. When you come up at **C**, stitch through the middle bead, from left to right.

3. To finish the row, alternate stitches to the right and to the left. To end the stitch, come up at **C**, stitch through the middle bead, and go down at **D**. Knot the thread.

Variation: *To make a longer stitch, increase the number of beads by 4.*

Feather Stitch Single (Beaded)

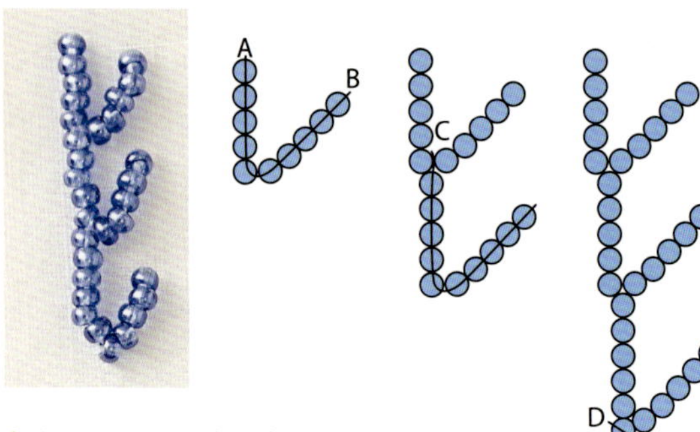

1. Come up at **A**. *Thread 10 size 11° seed beads onto the needle and lay the beads flat against the fabric. Go down to the right at **B**, slightly below **A**. Knot the thread.

2. To finish the row, come up at **C**. Follow Step 1 from *, laying the thread between the fifth and sixth beads of the previous stitch.

3. To end the stitch, follow Step 1 from *, but with 11 size 11° seed beads. Come up at **D**, stitch through the middle bead, and go down through the fabric at **E**. Knot the thread.

Variation: *This stitch can be worked with the tips facing right or left.*

Feather Stitch Fancy (Beaded)

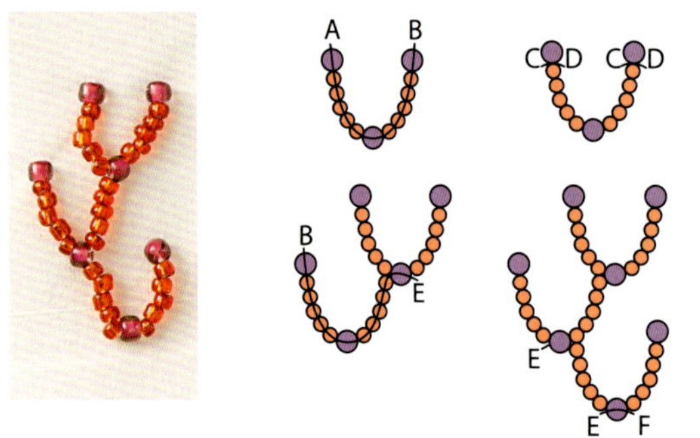

1. Come up at **A**. *Thread 1 size 8°, 5 size 11°, 1 size 8°, 5 size 11°, and 1 size 8° seed beads onto the needle and lay the beads flat against the fabric. Go down to the right at **B**. Knot the thread.

2. Come up at **C**, between the size 8° and 11° beads, and go down at **D** to couch the bead thread. Knot the thread.

3. Come up at **E**; stitch through the size 8° bead from right to left. Thread 5 size 11°, 1 size 8°, 5 size 11°, and 1 size 8° seed beads onto the needle and lay the beads flat against the fabric. Go down to the left at **B**. Knot the thread. Follow Step 2.

4. To finish the row, alternate stitches to the right and to the left, passing the needle through the size 8° bead in the direction of the next stitch. To end the stitch, come up at **E**, stitch through the size 8° bead, and go down at **F**. Knot the thread.

Variation: *To make a longer stitch, increase the number of all size 11° beads by 2 each time.*

Cretan Stitch Fancy (Beaded)

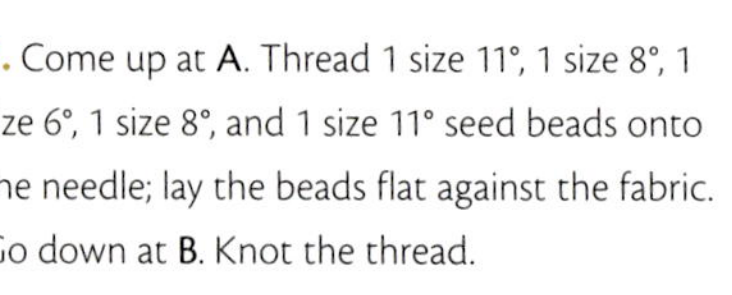

1. Come up at **A**. Thread 1 size 11°, 1 size 8°, 1 size 6°, 1 size 8°, and 1 size 11° seed beads onto the needle; lay the beads flat against the fabric. Go down at **B**. Knot the thread.

2. *Come up at **C**. Pass the needle through the size 11° bead in the previous row. Thread 3 size 15° seed beads onto the needle; lay the beads flat against the fabric. Pass the needle back through the size 11° bead.

Note: *This changes the direction of the size 11° bead.*

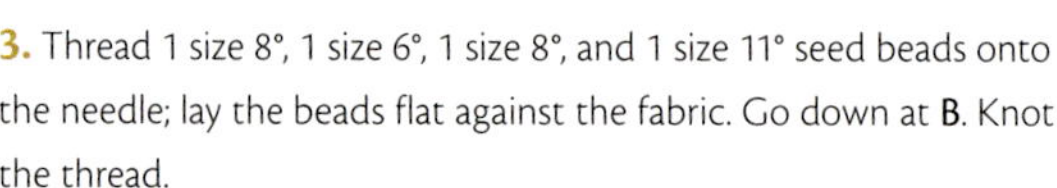

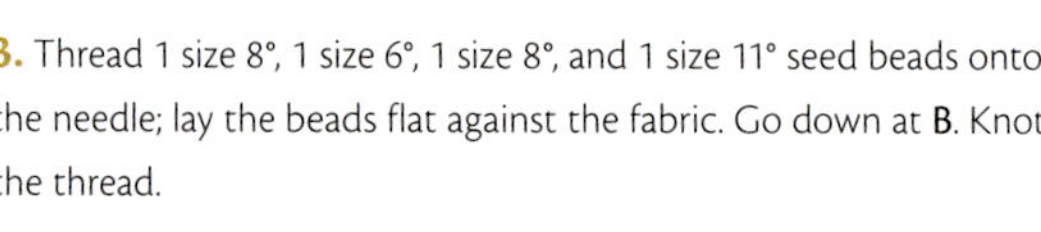

3. Thread 1 size 8°, 1 size 6°, 1 size 8°, and 1 size 11° seed beads onto the needle; lay the beads flat against the fabric. Go down at **B**. Knot the thread.

4. Repeat Steps 2 and 3 to finish the row.

VINES AND STALKS

Vines

Stem stitch vine

1. Draw the image with an air-erasable pen.

2. Embroider over the lines, working the vine and branches with the same stitch or different stitches.

Suggested stitches: *backstitch, couched stitch, stem stitch, outline stitch, or running stitch (page 51)*

Stalks

Straight stitch stalk

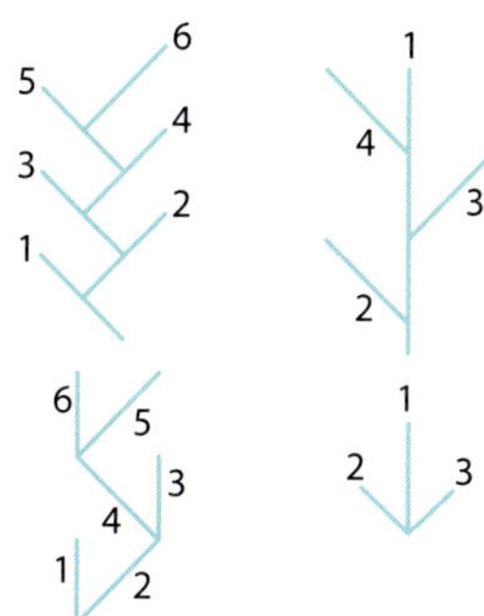

1. Draw the image with an air-erasable pen.

2. Embroider over the lines, working the stitches in the order they are shown.

Suggested stitches: *straight or pistil stitches (page 70), lazy daisy (page 65) or fly stitches (page 67)*

Blanket Stitch Stalk or Row

STALK

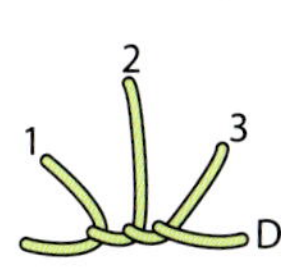

1. *Work 1 blanket stitch (page 55), angled to the left. Work 1 blanket stitch, straight. Work 1 blanket stitch, angled to the right.

2. To end the stitch, go down at D.

ROW

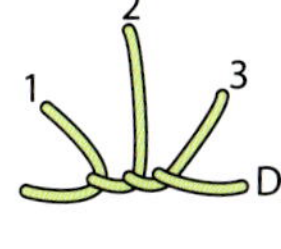

Follow Step 1 above, continuing the next pattern a short distance away. To finish the row, follow Step 2.

Leaves and Stem Stalk or Row

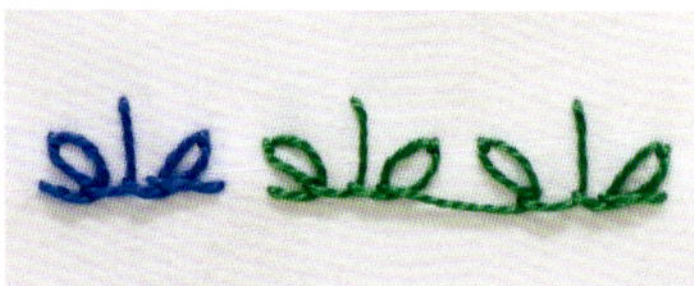

STALK

1. Work 1 blanket stitch looped (page 56), angled to the left.
Work 1 straight blanket stitch (page 55). Work 1 blanket stitch looped, angled to the right.

2. To end the stitch, go down at H.

ROW

Follow Step 1, continuing the next pattern a short distance away. To finish the row, follow Step 2.

Looped Petal Row

1. Work 1 blanket stitch looped (page 56), angled to the left. Work a second stitch, straight, and a third stitch, angled to the right.

2. To finish the row, repeat Step 1 a slight distance away from the previous pattern. To end the stitch, go down at F.

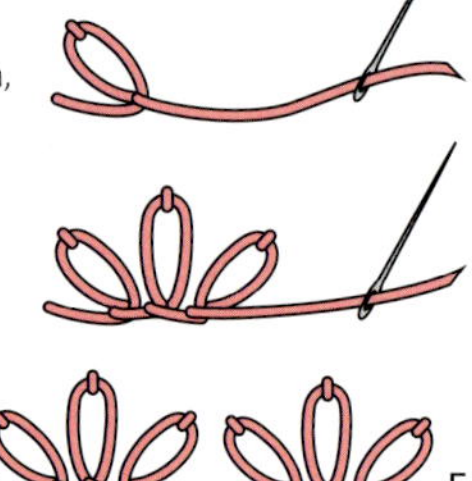

Shell Stitch Row

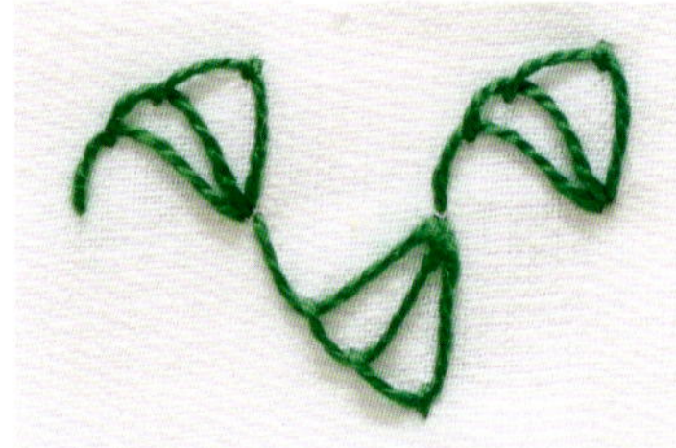

1. Draw or follow a quarter circle; follow Step 1 of the blanket stitch (page 55), with A and C on the curved line.

2. Work a second stitch and a third stitch along the curved line. To end the stitch, go down at D.

3. Work a second stitch upside down and to the right, with A of the new stitch close to B of the previous stitch.

4. Repeat Steps 1–3 to finish the row.

Fern Stitch Modern

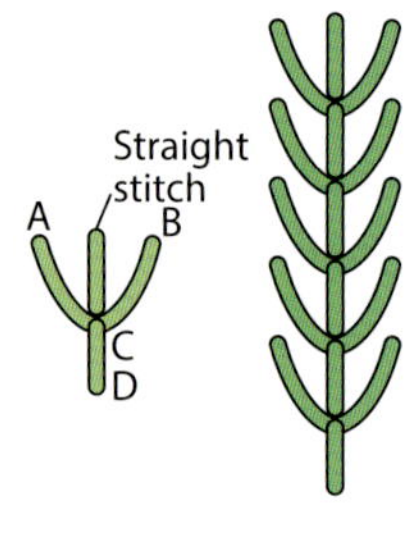

1. Draw a line with an erasable pen or follow a seam line.

2. Work a straight stitch (page 70) on the line. *Work 1 fly stitch with a long tail (page 67); the tail is the beginning of the next stitch with D on the line.

3. Repeat from * to finish the row.

Thorn Stitch

1. Stitch a row of backstitches (page 51) or long straight stitches (page 70).

2. Come up at A and go down at B. Come up at C and go down at D.

3. Repeat Step 2 to finish the row.

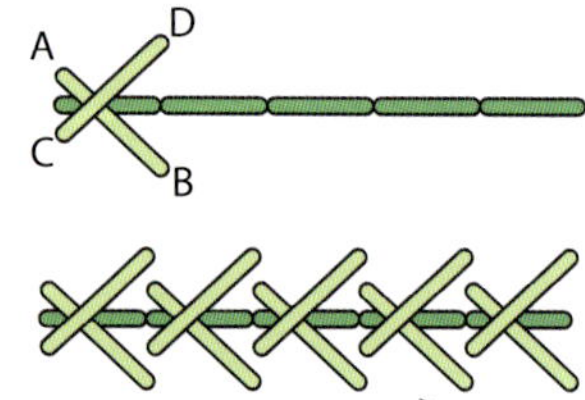

DECORATIVE STITCHES

Lazy Daisy Stitch

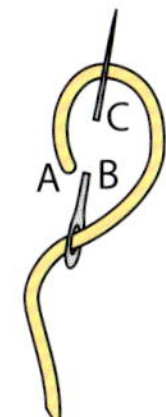

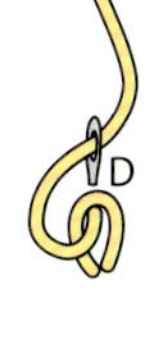

1. Come up at **A**. In one motion, go down at **B** and up at **C**. Wrap the working thread under the tip of the needle. Pull the needle through the fabric.

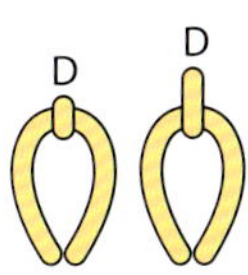

2. To end the stitch, go down at **D** or a short distance away for a long arm stitch.

Lazy Daisy Square Tip Stitch

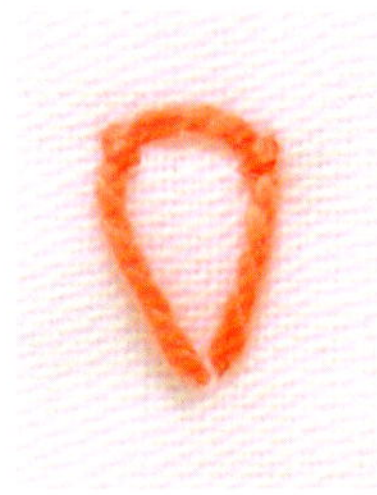

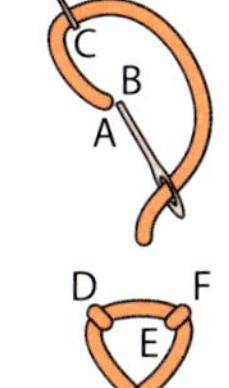

1. Come up at **A**. In one motion, go down at **B** and up at **C**. Wrap the working thread under the tip of the needle. Gently, pull the needle through the fabric, leaving a slight loop. Go down at **D** to catch one edge of the loop.

2. To end the stitch, come up at **E** and go down at **F** to catch the other edge of the loop.

Lazy Daisy with French Knot Stitch

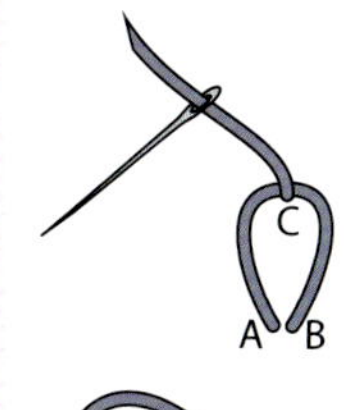

1. Follow Step 1 of the lazy daisy stitch (at left).

2. Holding the needle close to the fabric, wrap the thread 1–3 times around the needle. Go down at **D**. Pull the needle through the wrapped stitches and fabric.

Lazy Daisy with Bullion Tip Stitch

C
A
B
D

1. Come up at **A**. In one motion, go down at **B** and up at **C**, but do not pull the thread through the fabric. Wrap the thread around the needle 2 or 3 times.

2. Pull the needle through the fabric. To end the stitch, go down at **D**, just beyond the wraps.

Lazy Daisy Tulip Stitch

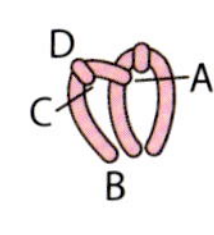

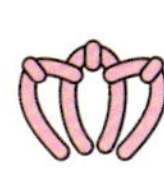

Center: Work 1 lazy daisy stitch (above).

Sides: Come up at **A**; in one motion, go down at **B** and up at **C**, pulling the needle through the fabric. To end the stitch, go down at **D**. Repeat for the other side.

Lazy Daisy Piggyback Stitch

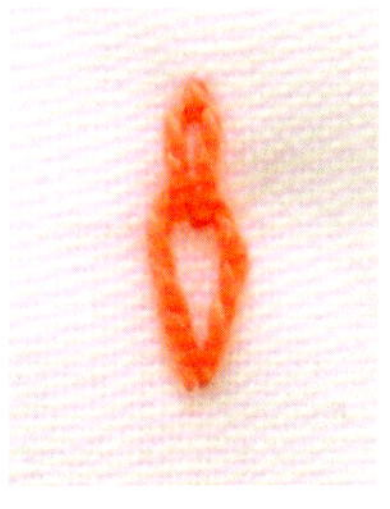

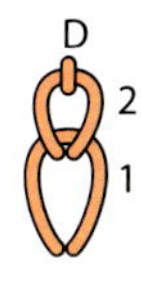

Follow Step 1 of the lazy daisy stitch (above). Work a smaller stitch above the first stitch. To finish the stitch, go down at **D**.

Barb Stitch

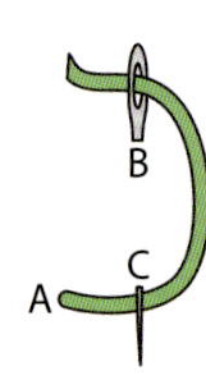

1. Come up at A. In one motion go down at B and up at C. Wrap the working thread under the tip of the needle. Pull the needle through the fabric.

D D

2. To end the stitch, go down at D or a short distance away.

Fleet Stitch

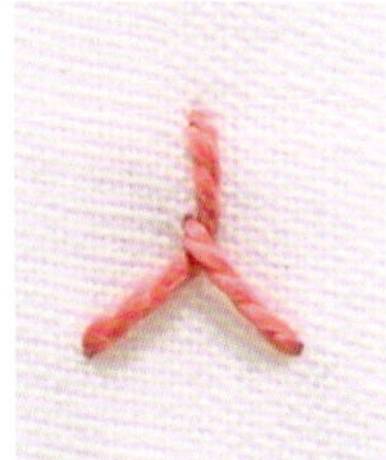

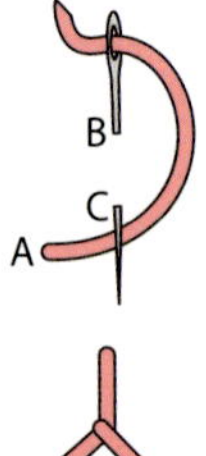

1. Come up at A. In one motion, go down at B and up at C. Wrap the working thread under the tip of the needle. Pull the needle through the fabric.

2. To end the stitch, go down at D.

Cross Stitch

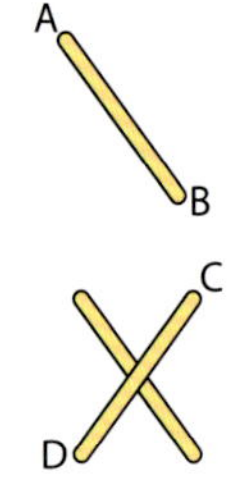

1. Come up at A and go down at B.

2. Come up at C and go down at D, crossing over the first stitch.

Elongated horizontally

Variations: *Change the length or height of the stitches.*

Elongated vertically

Cross Stitch with Details

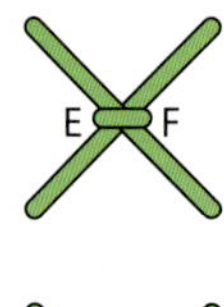

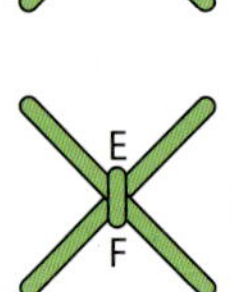

1. Stitch 1 cross stitch (above).

2. Stitch 1 short straight stitch (page 70) from E to F, crossing over the middle of the first stitch.

Note: *In Step 2, use the same color thread or a different color thread.*

Cross Stitch Doubled

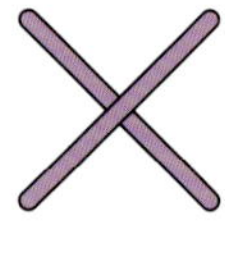

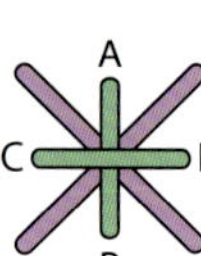

1. Stitch 1 cross stitch (above).

2. Stitch a second stitch vertically over the first stitch, using a different color thread.

Crossed Lazy Daisy Stitch

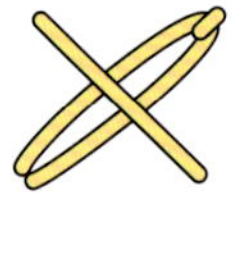

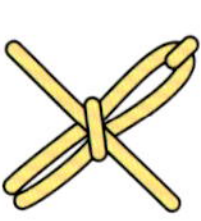

1. Stitch 1 lazy daisy stitch (page 65).

2. Stitch 1 straight stitch (page 70) the same length and width over the stitch.

3. Stitch 1 short straight stitch, crossing over the middle of the crossed section.

Fly Stitch

1. Come up at **A**. In one motion, go down at **B** and up at **C**. Wrap the working thread under the tip of the needle. Pull the needle through the fabric.

2. To end the stitch, go down at **D** or a short distance away for a long tail.

Fly Stitch Offset

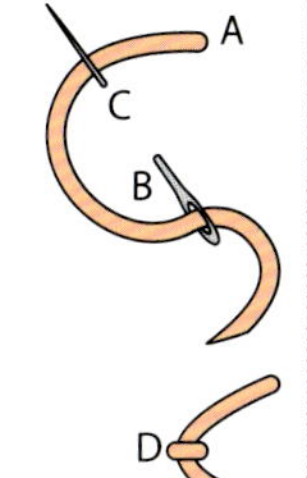

1. Come up at **A**. In one motion, go down at **B** and up at **C**. Wrap the working thread under the tip of the needle. Pull the needle through the fabric.

2. To end the stitch, go down at **D**.

Note: *A and B can be even or one shorter; C can be in the center or off to one side.*

Fly Stitch with Straight Edge

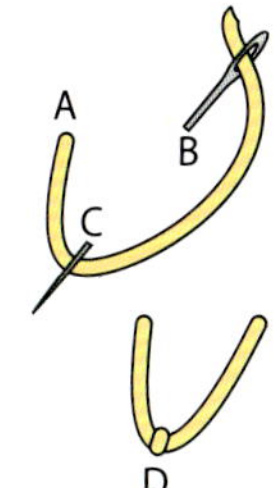

1. Come up at **A**. In one motion, go down at **B** and up at **C**, with **C** directly below **A**. Wrap the working thread under the tip of the needle. Pull the needle through the fabric.

2. To end the stitch, go down at **D**.

Fly Stitch with French Knot Stitch

1. Follow Step 1 of the fly stitch (above).

2. Holding the needle close to the fabric, wrap the thread 1–3 times around the needle. Go down at **D**. Pull the needle through the wrapped stitches and fabric.

Fly Stitch with Lazy Daisy Stitch

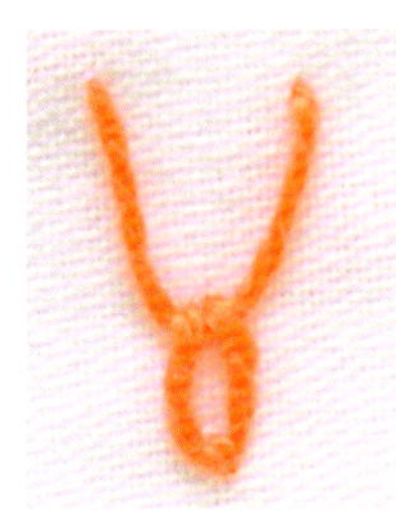

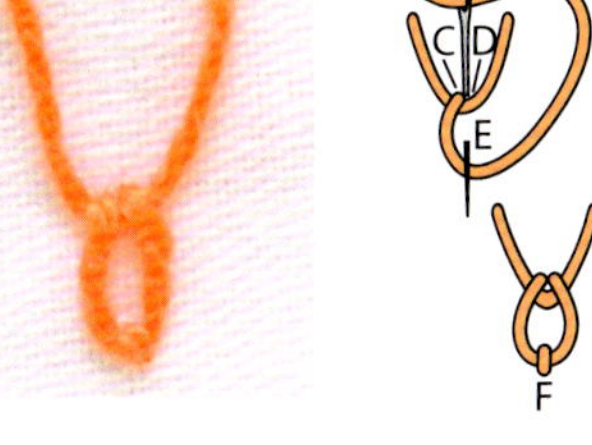

1. Follow Step 1 of the fly stitch (above). In one motion, go down at **D** and up at **E**. Wrap the working thread under the tip of the needle. Pull the needle through the fabric.

2. To end the stitch, go down at **F**.

Fly Stitch with Loop

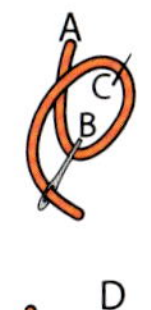

1. Come up at **A**. In one motion, go down at **B** and up at **C**. Loop the working thread under the eye and the tip of the needle and back to the base of the stitch. Pull the needle through the fabric. Go down at **D**.

2. To end the stitch, come up at **E** and go down at **F**.

Note: *The stitches on this page are worked with silk embroidery ribbon.*

Padded Straight Stitch

1. Work 1 straight stitch (page 70).

2. Work a second stitch over and slightly longer than the first.

Ribbon Stitch

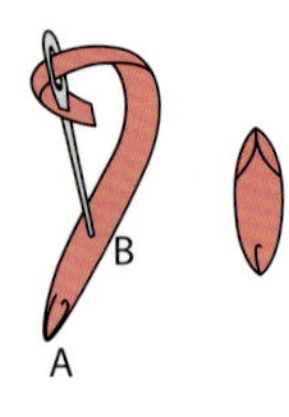

1. Come up at A. Hold the ribbon flat against the fabric. Go down at B, through the ribbon.

2. Form a curved tip by gently pulling the ribbon through the stitch.

Ribbon Loop Stitch

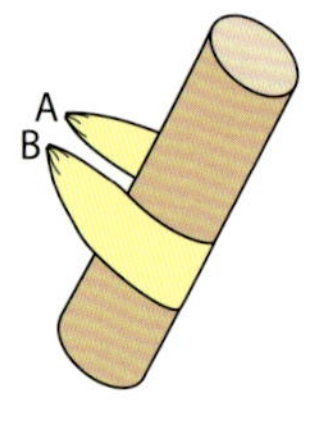

1. Come up at A and go down at B.

2. Insert a porcupine quill or straw into the center of the loop. Pull the ribbon through the fabric to the desired length.

French Knot Bud Stitch

1. Come up at A. Twirl the needle to the right to twist the ribbon. Wrap the ribbon around the needle loosely 5 times.

2. Go down close to A, arranging the wraps down the needle and against the fabric, with the last wrap forming the outer ring and the first wrap as the center.

3. Pull the needle through the fabric. Knot the tail of ribbon.

4. Tackstitch around the outer ring with sewing thread.

Ruched Rose Stitch

1. Come up through the fabric. Hold the needle a short distance away from the fabric. Wrap the ribbon around the needle 2–3 times.

2. Gather stitch the needle down the length of the ribbon.

3. Stitch through the end of the ribbon and through the fabric, pulling the ribbon gently to form the petals.

Pointed Petal Stitch

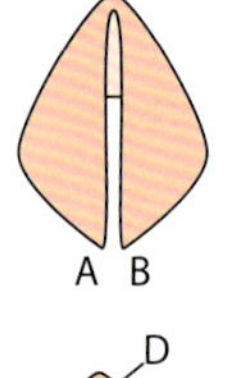

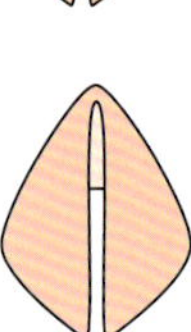

1. Come up at A and go down at B. Pull the ribbon through the fabric to form a point at the tip. Set the needle aside.

2. Thread a needle with sewing thread. Come up at C through the ribbon; go down at D at the tip of the ribbon. Knot and cut both the thread and ribbon.

Note: *The stitches on this page are worked with seed beads in a variety of sizes.*

Lazy Daisy Stitch (Beaded)

1. Come up at **A**. Thread 10 size 11° seed beads onto the needle and lay beads flat against the fabric. Take the needle back through the first bead. Go down at **B**. Knot the thread.

2. Come up at **C**, stitch through the middle bead, and go down at **D**. Knot the thread.

Variation: *To make a longer stitch, increase the number of all size 11° beads by 4. A different color or size of bead can be used for the middle bead in the loop.*

Lazy Daisy Stitch Fancy (Beaded)

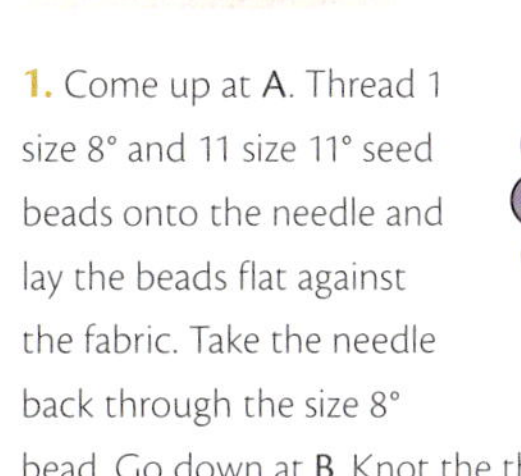

1. Come up at **A**. Thread 1 size 8° and 11 size 11° seed beads onto the needle and lay the beads flat against the fabric. Take the needle back through the size 8° bead. Go down at **B**. Knot the thread.

2. Come up at **C**, stitch through the middle bead, and go down at **D**. Knot the thread.

Variation: *To make a longer stitch, increase the number of all size 11° beads by 4.*

Fly Stitch (Beaded)

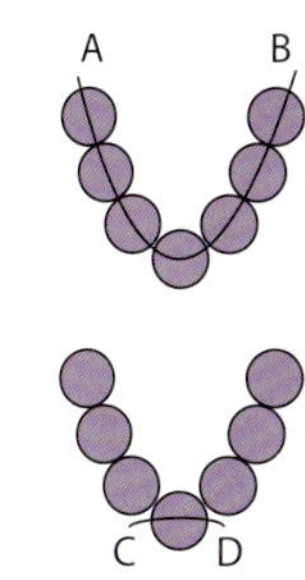

1. Come up at **A**. Thread 7 size 11° seed beads onto the needle and lay the beads flat against the fabric. Go down at **B**. Knot the thread.

2. Come up at **C**, stitch through the middle bead, and go down at **D**. Knot the thread.

Variation: *To make a longer stitch, increase the number of all size 11° beads by 4. A different color or size of bead can be used for the middle bead in the loop.*

Fly Stitch Fancy (Beaded)

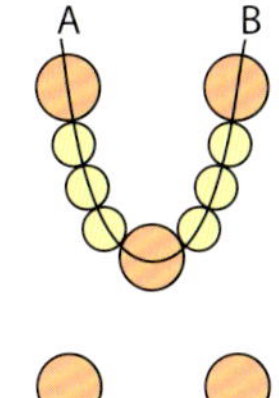

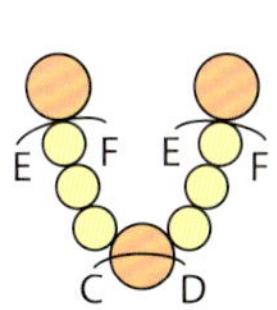

1. Come up at **A**. Thread 1 size 8°, 3 size 11°, 1 size 8°, 3 size 11°, and 1 size 8° seed beads onto the needle and lay the beads flat against the fabric. Go down at **B**. Knot the thread.

2. Come up at **C**, stitch through the middle bead, and go down at **D**. Knot the thread.

3. Come up at **E**, between the 8° and 11° beads, and go down at **F** to couch the bead thread. Knot the thread.

Variation: *To make a longer stitch, increase the number of size 11° beads by 2 each time.*

Cross Stitch (Beaded)

Single

Cross Stitch Row (beaded): Work a series of single stitches.

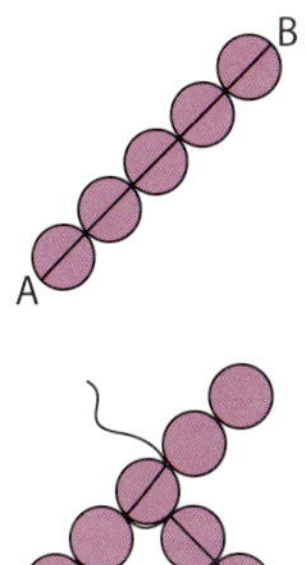

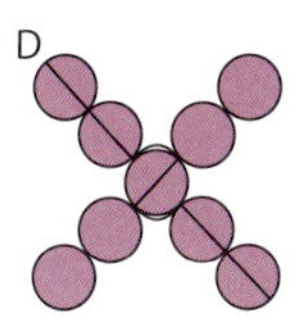

1. Come up at **A**. Thread 5 size 11° seed beads onto the needle and lay the beads flat against the fabric. Go down at **B**. Knot the thread.

2. Come up at **C**. Thread 2 size 11° seed beads onto the needle and lay the beads flat against the fabric. Pass the needle from bottom to top through the middle bead in the previous row.

Note: *This changes the direction of the bead.*

3. Thread 2 size 11° seed beads onto the needle and lay the beads flat against the fabric. Go down at **D**. Knot the thread.

Variation: *Increase the number of beads to 7 in Step 1 and to 3 in Steps 2 and 3.*

DETAIL STITCHES

Straight Stitch

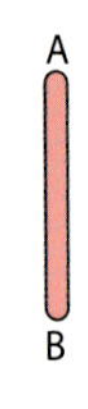

Come up at **A** and go down at **B**.

Stamen Stitch

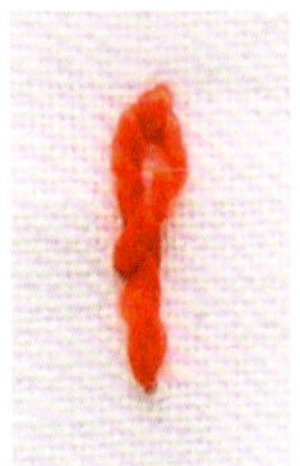

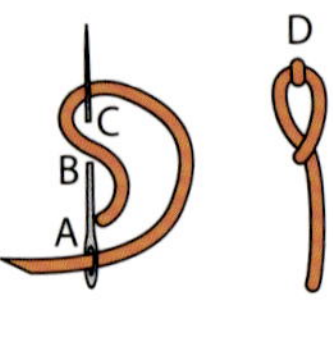

1. Come up at **A**. In one motion, go down at **B** and up at **C**; wrap the working thread over the needle and under the tip.

2. Pull the needle through the fabric. To finish the stitch, go down at **D**.

Pistil Stitch

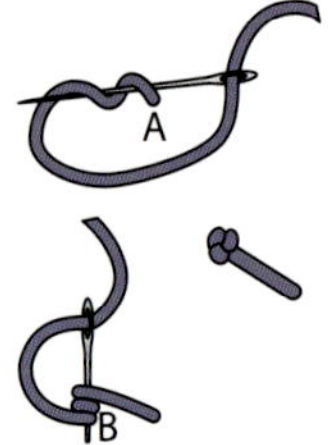

1. Come up at **A**. Holding the needle a short distance away and close to the fabric, wrap the thread 1–3 times over the needle.

2. Go down at **B**. Pull the thread tight around the needle and pull the needle through the fabric.

French Knot Stitch

1. Come up at **A**. Holding the needle close to the fabric, wrap the thread around the needle 1–5 times.

2. Go down at **B**. Pull the thread tight around the needle, and hold the end of the tail of thread with your thumb. Pull the needle through the fabric.

Seed Stitch

Stitch 2 straight stitches (above), grouped together. Repeat, randomly filling in the section.

Knotted Seed Stitch

Stitch 3 French knot stitches (at left) in a group. Work the stitch off a border row, to fill in a space, or repeat randomly, filling in a section.

Note: *The stitches on this page are worked with seed beads in a variety of sizes.*

Single Bead Stitch

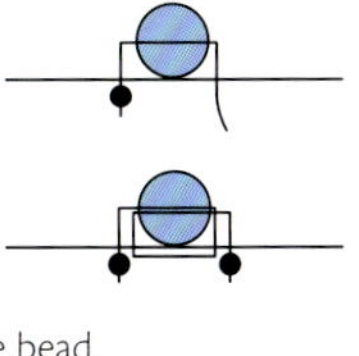

1. Come up and thread 1 seed bead onto the needle. Lay the bead flat against the fabric. Go down beyond the edge of the bead.

2. Come up and pass the needle through the bead a second time, and go down. Knot the thread after every 4 stitches.

Note: *When using this stitch for larger beads, knot the thread each time.*

Grouped Bead Stitch

Follow the directions for the single bead stitch (at left), but with 2 or 3 of the same size and type of seed bead. Knot the thread after every 2 stitches.

Note: *When using this stitch through the holes of a button, knot the thread when the stitch is complete.*

Bead Combination Stitch

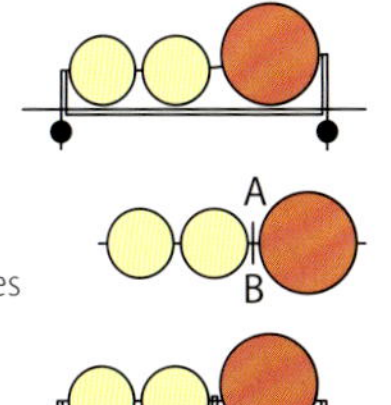

1. Follow the directions for the single bead stitch (at left), but with a group of different sizes or shapes of beads.

2. Come up at **A**, between the large and small beads, and go down at **B** to couch the thread. Knot the thread after every 2 stitches.

Stacked Bead Stitch

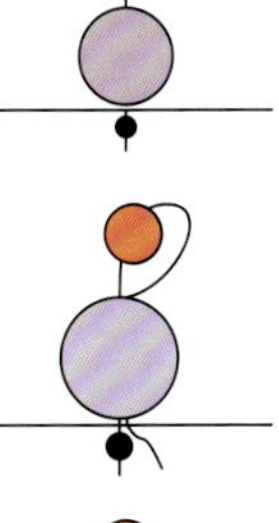

Base bead: Come through a large bead, sequin, or other object.

Stopper bead: Thread 1 smaller bead onto the needle. Holding on to the last bead, pass the needle back down through the base bead and the fabric. Knot the thread.

Picot Tip Stitch (Beaded)

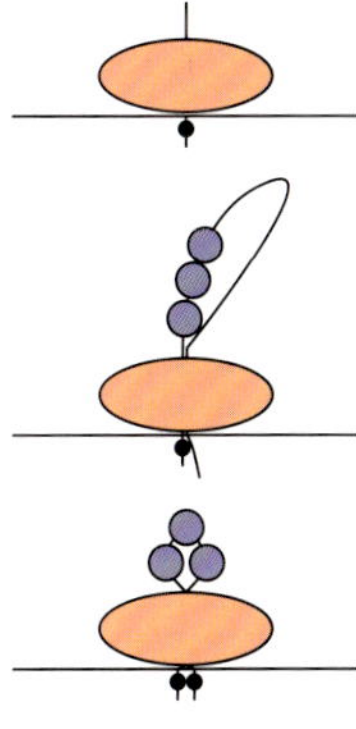

Base bead: Come up through a large bead, sequin, or other object.

Picot tip: Thread 3 smaller beads onto the needle. Holding on to the last beads, pass the needle back down through the base bead and the fabric. Knot the thread.

Bead Cascade Stitch

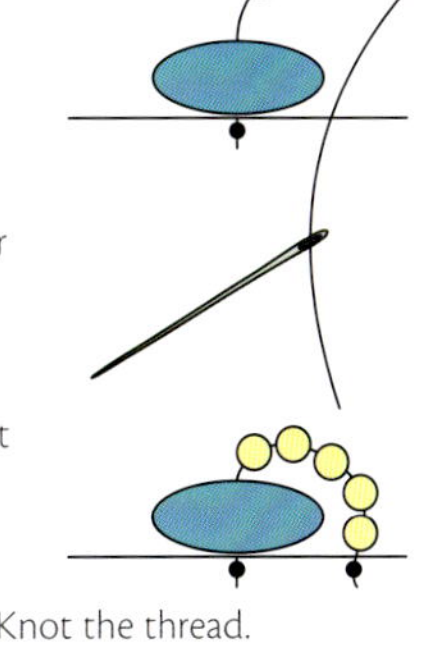

Base bead: Come up through a large bead, sequin, or other object.

Cascade: Thread 3 or more smaller beads onto the needle; go down just beyond the edge of the larger bead. Knot the thread.

Note: *The stitches on this page are worked with seed beads in a variety of sizes and other materials.*

Beaded Pistil Stitch

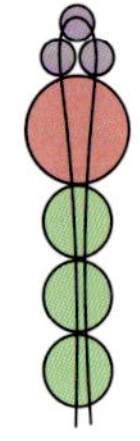

1. Come up and thread 3–5 size 11° seed beads, 1 size 8° seed or larger bead, and 1–3 size 15° seed beads onto the needle.

2. Holding onto the last bead/s, pass the needle through the remaining beads and go down. Knot the thread.

Stem and Flower Stitch (Beaded)

1. Come up and thread 3 size 11° seed beads, a flower or rondelle bead, and 1–3 size 11° or 15° seed beads onto the needle.

2. Holding onto the last bead/s, pass the needle through the remaining beads and go down. Knot the thread.

Front-to-Back Hole Charm Stitch (Beaded)

Come up through the hole in the charm, add 1 seed bead, and go down through the hole. Knot the thread.

Or come up through the hole of the charm, add 3 seed beads, and go down beyond the hole of the charm. Knot the thread.

Top-to-Bottom Hole Charm Dangle Stitch

1. Come up and thread a group of beads ranging in size from small-medium-large-medium-small, ending with 1 size 11° or 3 size 15° seed beads.

2. Holding onto the last bead/s, pass the needle back through the remaining beads in the row, and go down. Knot the thread.

Snap and Hook Decorative Stitches

Stitch a dome snap, hook, or eye with a straight stitch (page 70), lazy daisy stitch (page 65), or bead cascade stitch (page 71).

Sequin Decoration Stitches (Beaded)

Stitch a sequin, or group of sequins, with a single bead stitch (page 71), stacked bead stitch (page 71), or bead cascade stitch (page 71).

Note: *The stitches on this page are worked with a variety of materials.*

FLOWERS

Flower Templates

Draw in the lines for the template.

Stitch Suggestions: for lazy daisy, fly, or straight stitch flowers, use perle cotton, cotton floss, or silk embroidery ribbon. For straight beaded petals, use a variety of seed beads.

Option: *Stitch a French knot (page 70) in the center of the flower, or a size 11° seed bead.*

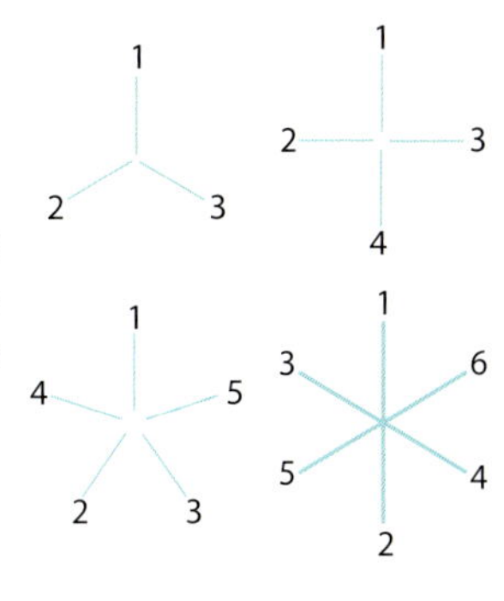

Silk Ribbon Petal Stitches

Suggested stitches: pointed petal stitch (page 68), ribbon stitch (page 68).

Lazy Daisy Stitch Flowers

Suggested stitches: lazy daisy stitch (page 65), lazy daisy with French knot stitch (page 65), lazy daisy with bullion tip stitch (page 65).

Additional stitches: lazy daisy stitch (beaded) (page 69), lazy daisy stitch fancy (beaded) (page 69).

Fly Stitch Flowers

Suggested stitches: fly stitch (page 67), fly stitch with French knot stitch (page 67).

Additional stitches: fly stitch (beaded) (page 69), fly stitch fancy (beaded) (page 69).

Note: *Work the stitch on either side of the drawn line.*

Straight Stitch Flowers

Suggested stitches: straight stitch (page 70), pistil stitch (page 70), stamen stitch (page 70), padded straight stitch (page 68).

Flowers with Straight Petals (Beaded)

Suggested centers: stacked bead stitch (page 71), picot tip stitch (beaded) (page 71).

Suggested petals: grouped bead stitch (page 71), bead combination stitch (page 71).

Note: *The stitches on this page are worked with a variety of materials.*

French Knot Stitch Flowers

Use perle cotton, cotton floss, or silk embroidery ribbon.

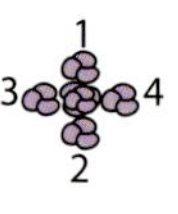
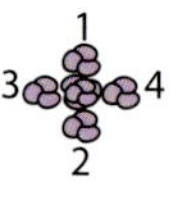

Center: Work a 3-wrap French knot (page 70).

Petals: Work 2 wrap knots around the center in the order as shown.

Variation: *Stitch size 8° or 11° seed beads with the single bead stitch (page 71).*

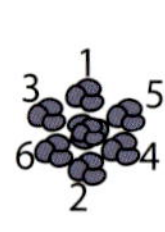

Flower with Petite Petals (Beaded)

Suggested stitch: stacked bead stitch (page 71).

Additional stitches: Use any of the sequin decoration stitches (page 72) for the petals.

Note: *Use the French knot flower (at left) illustrations for a placement guide.*

Silk Ribbon Flower Stitch

1. Draw the short lines of the flower.

2. Work the petals with the ribbon loop stitch (page 68), using silk embroidery ribbon.

Option: *Work a French knot stitch (page 70) into the center.*

Button Bezel Stitch (Beaded)

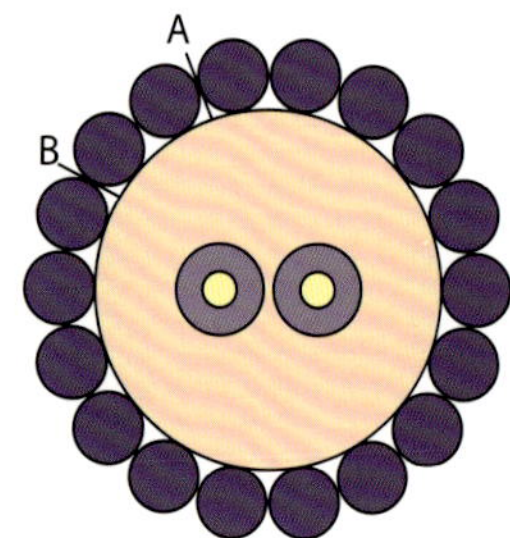

1. Stitch the center of the button in place with a buttonhole decoration stitch (page 81).

2. Come up at **A**. Thread 4 size 11° seed beads onto the needle. Follow the directions for the continuous bead stitch (page 53), coming back through the last 2 beads.

3. Continue to add beads, with the last group of beads flush with the first bead. Pass the needle through the entire row of beads. Go down at **B**. Knot the thread.

Button Flower with Petals Stitch (Beaded)

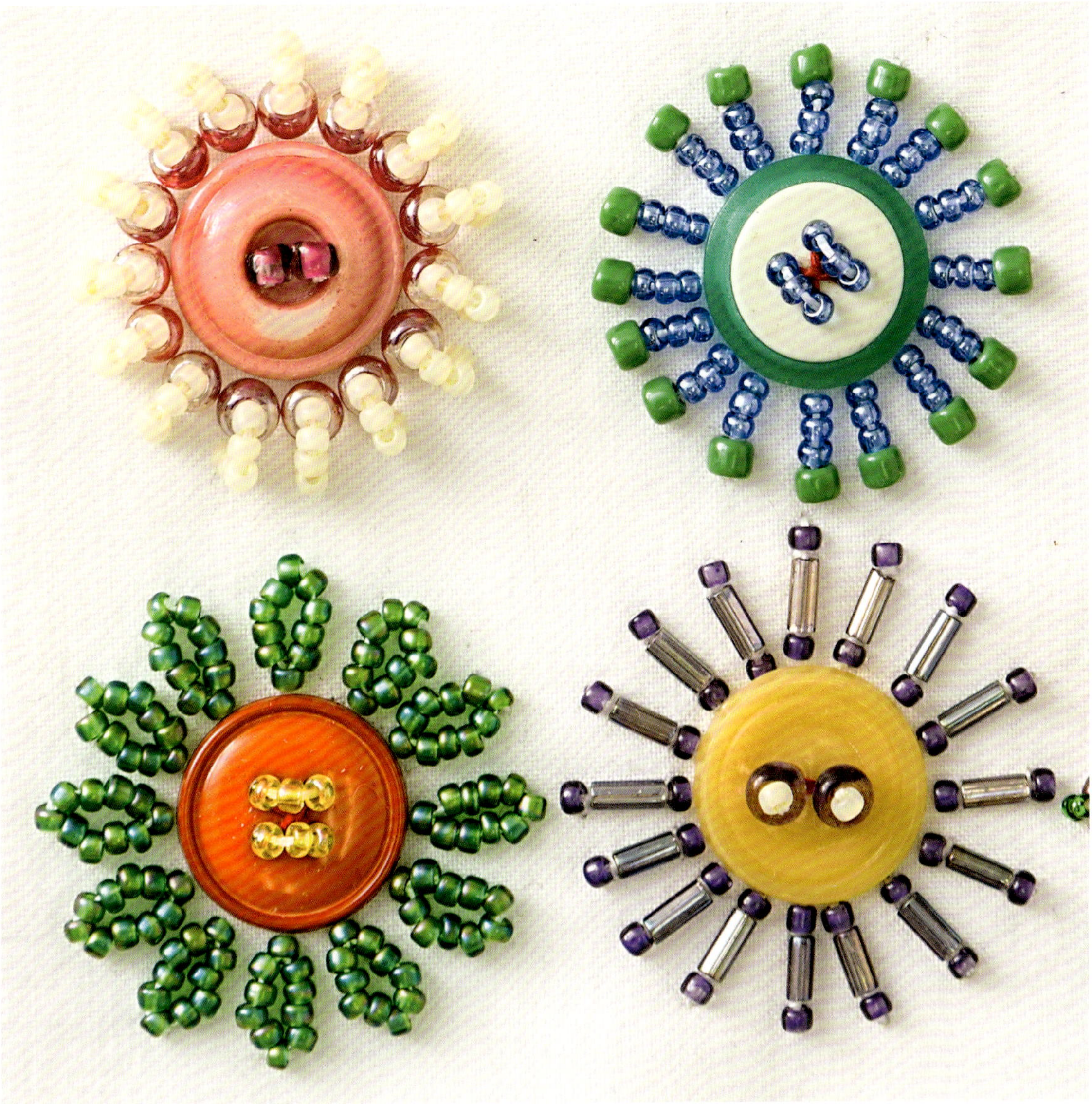

Center: Stitch the center with a buttonhole decoration stitch (page 81).

Suggested petal stitches: bead cascade stitch (page 71), bead combination stitch (page 71), lazy daisy stitch (beaded) (page 69).

Floret Stitch (Beaded)

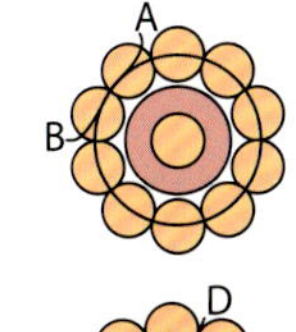

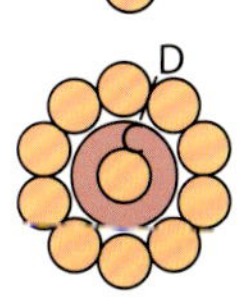

1. **Center:** Work a stacked bead stitch (page 71) with 1 size 6° and 1 size 11° seed beads. Come up at A.

2. **Bezel:** Thread enough size 11° seed beads (10–12 beads) to wrap around the center. Pass the needle through the entire row of beads. Go down at B. Knot the thread.

3. Come up at C, between 2 beads, and go down at D to couch the bead thread. Repeat this step every 2 beads in the row.

Bell Flower Stitch

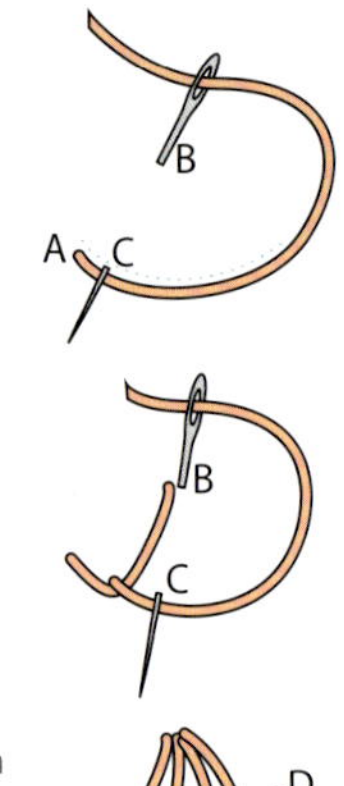

1. Draw a half circle and mark the center. Follow Step 1 of the blanket stitch (page 55), *with **B** as the center point and **A** and **C** on the curved line.

2. Repeat from *, working the stitches around the curve. To end the stitch, go down at **D**.

Buttonhole Circle Stitch

1. Draw a circle and mark the center point. Follow Step 1 of the blanket stitch (page 55), * with point **B** as the center of the stitch and points **A** and **C** on the curved line.

2. Repeat from *, working the stitches around the circle. To end the stitch, go down next to the first stitch.

Spiderweb Rose Stitch and Variation

Options: *Work with single thread or a blend of 2 or more threads. See Note below.*

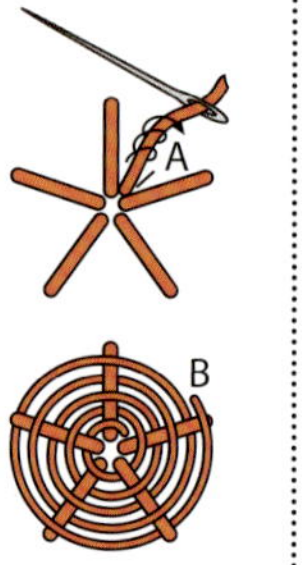

1. Draw a circle, then draw 5 equally spaced spokes. Work straight stitches (page 70) from the outer edge of the circle to the center. Knot and cut the thread.

2. Thread a chenille needle with 30″ (76.2cm) of the same or heavier weight thread. Come up at **A**.

3. Weave the needle and thread over and under the spokes counterclockwise, pulling the thread through the spokes. To end the stitch, go down at **B**.

Note: *When working with a blend of threads, twirl the needle to the right to twist the threads.*

Woven Rose Stitch and Variation

Variation: *Weave a center with one color and the remaining petals with another color.*

1. Thread a needle with perle cotton; follow Step 1 for the spiderweb rose (at left).

2. Thread a needle with silk embroidery ribbon; come up at **A**, and twist the ribbon slightly clockwise.

3. Weave the needle and ribbon over and under the spokes counterclockwise, pulling the ribbon through the spokes. To end the stitch, go down at **B**.

FILLER SHAPES

Looped Tendril Stitch

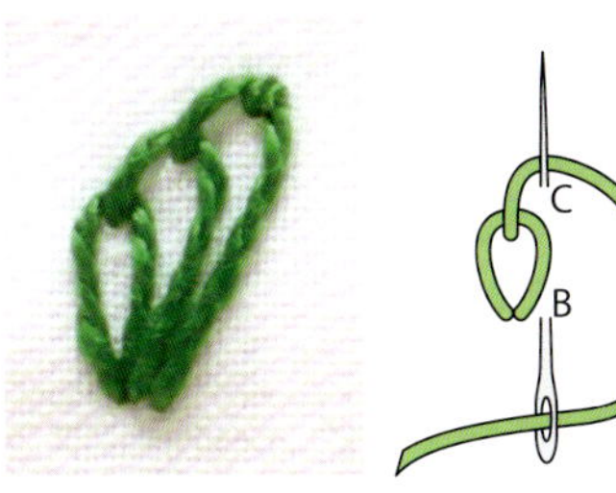

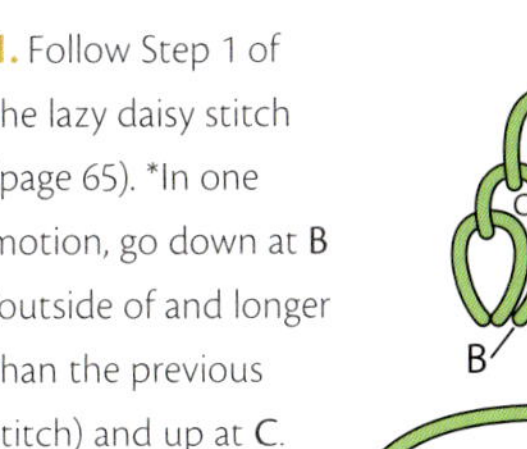

1. Follow Step 1 of the lazy daisy stitch (page 65). *In one motion, go down at **B** (outside of and longer than the previous stitch) and up at **C**.

2. Repeat from *, stitching a third loop longer than the previous stitch. To end the stitch, go down at **D**.

Whip-Stitch Star

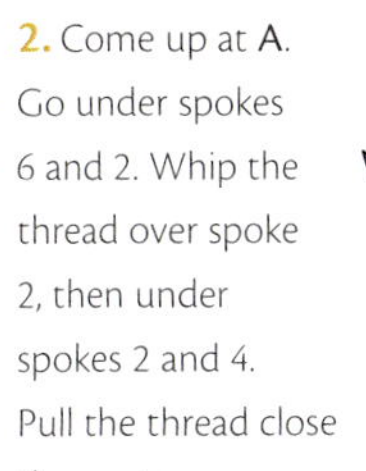

1. Work 3 straight stitches (page 70). Stitch a short stitch across the center of the stitches.

2. Come up at **A**. Go under spokes 6 and 2. Whip the thread over spoke 2, then under spokes 2 and 4. Pull the thread close to the center.

3. Continue whipping the thread over a spoke and then under the same spoke and the next spoke. To end the stitch, go down at **B** after the last spoke is covered.

Crossed Triangle Stitch

1. Following Steps 1 and 2 of the blanket stitch (page 55), work 2 stitches angled to the right to points 1 and 2.

2. Work 2 stitches angled to the left to points 3 and 4, crossing over the previous stitches. To end the stitch, go down at **D**.

Fly Stitch Stacked

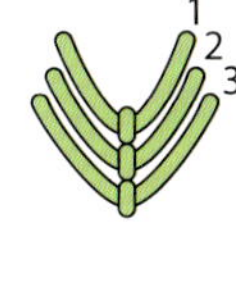

Work 1 fly stitch (page 67). Work the next 2 stitches below and around the previous stitch.

Variation: *Work the stitch in different colors or substitute a different fly stitch.*

Crosshatch Stitch

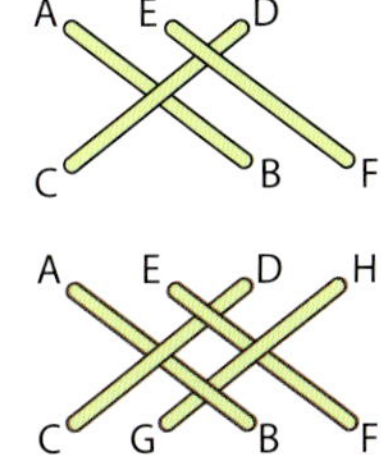

1. Work 1 cross stitch (page 66) elongated horizontally. Come up at **E** between **D** and **A**, and go down at **F**.

2. Come up at **G** below **E**; thread the needle under the stitch, and then over the previous stitch, go down at **H**.

Herringbone and Cross Stitch Single

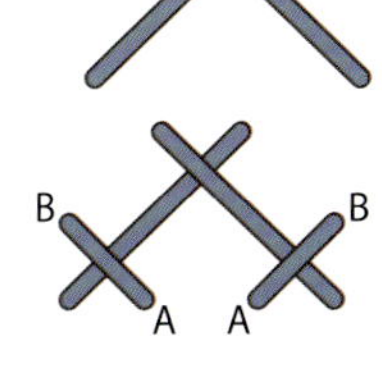

1. Stitch 1 set of herringbone stitches (page 61).

2. Work 2 straight stitches (page 70) from **A** to **B** across the bottom portion of the stitch.

Variation: *Work the straight stitches in a different color of thread.*

BzzyBee Stitch

Draw in the lines. Use silk embroidery ribbon for the body and the wings

Body: Stitch 1 lazy daisy with French knot stitch (page 65).

Wings: Stitch 4 ribbon stitches (page 68).

Butterfly Stitch

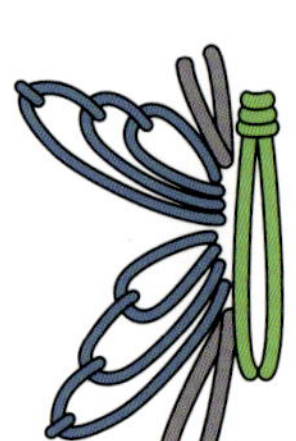

Body: Stitch 1 lazy daisy with bullion tip stitch (page 65).

Wings: Stitch 2 looped tendril stitches (page 77).

Antennae and Legs: Stitch 2 straight stitches (page 70) for each.

Sideview Butterfly Stitch

Draw in the lines. Use silk embroidery ribbon for the body and the wings and perle cotton for the antennae.

Body: Stitch 1 padded straight stitch (page 68).

Wings: Stitch 2 lazy daisy stitches (page 65).

Antennae: Stitch 2 straight stitches (page 70).

Curved Wing Butterfly Stitch

Draw the template; mark the center.

Wings: Stitch 2 looped tendril stitches (page 77) in opposite directions.

Body and Antennae: Stitch 2 pistil stitches (page 70), slightly angled. Couch with straight stitches (page 70).

Legs: Stitch 2 straight stitches.

Dragonfly Stitch

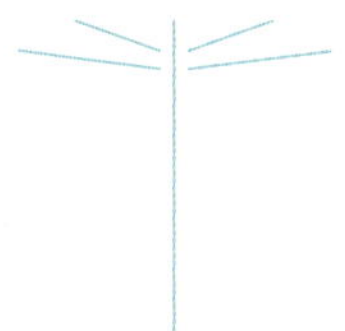

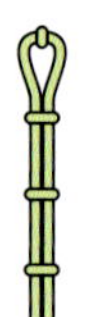

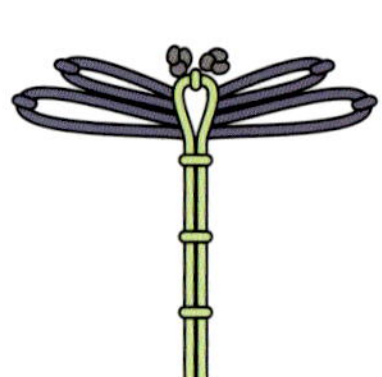

Draw the lines for the body and the wings.

Body: Stitch 1 lazy daisy stitch (page 65). Stitch 3 straight stitches (page 70) across the body as shown.

Wings: Stitch 4 lazy daisy stitches.

Eyes: Stitch 2 French knot stitches (page 70).

Steampunk Bugs

Choose from a variety of bodies and embroidery stitches to create these fun creepy crawlers!

Body: safety pins, dome snaps, hooks, or eyes.

Suggested Stitches

Wings: looped tendril stitch (page 77), lazy daisy stitch (page 65), fly stitch (page 67).

Antennae and legs: straight stitch (page 70), fly stitch offset (page 67).

Eyes: French knot stitch (page 70).

Spiderwebs: Corner and Round

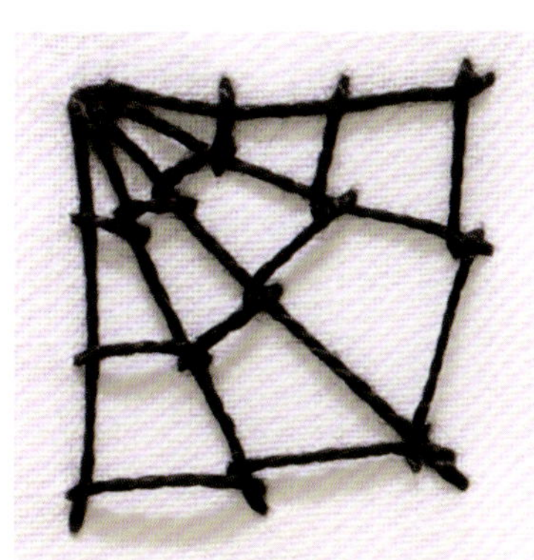

Corner

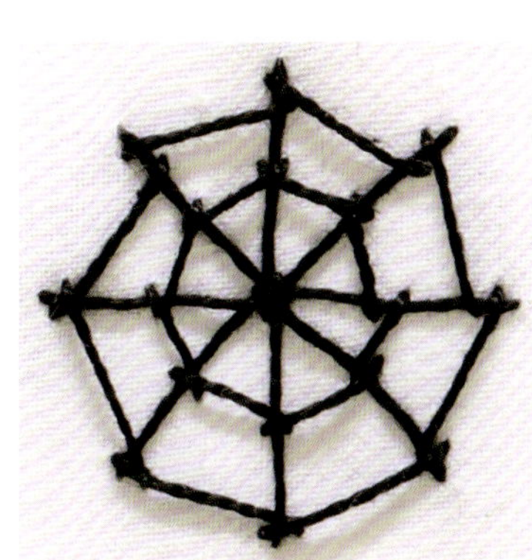

Round

Spokes: Work each straight stitch (page 70) in the order listed.

Web: Begin at the outer edge and work long stem stitches (page 51) in rows or a continuous spiral back to the center of the web.

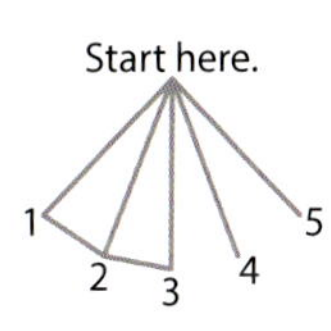

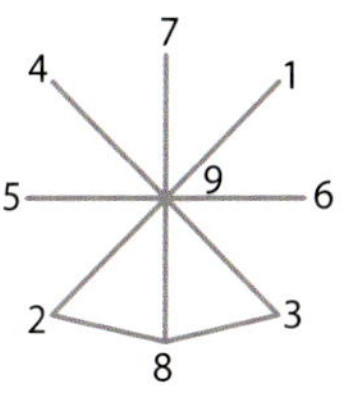

Blanket Stitch Cobweb

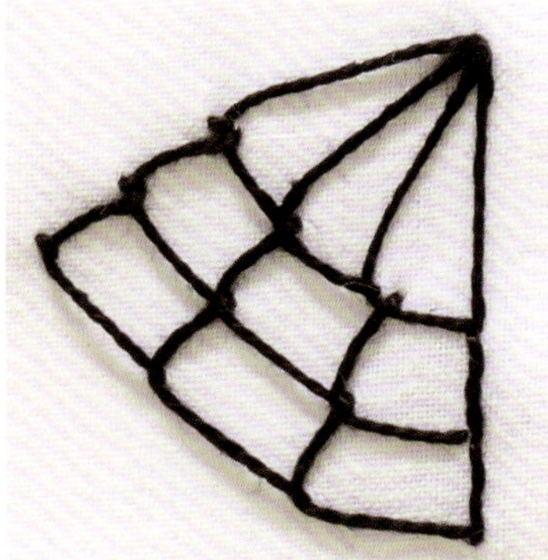

1. Follow Steps 1 and 2 of the shell stitch row (page 64).

2. Draw a line slightly above the curve of the previous row. Follow Step 1 of the blanket stitch (page 55), with **A** and **C** on the drawn line and **B** inside the stitch of the previous row. Work a second and third stitch; to end the stitch, go down at **D**.

3. Repeat Step 2 to finish the web.

4. Work a straight stitch (page 70) at the beginning of each row of stitches.

Spiderweb Stitch (Beaded)

Draw 5 lines for the spokes.

Center: Stitch a stacked bead stitch, with 1 size 6° and 11° seed beads (page 71).

Spokes: Stitch each spoke with a continuous bead stitch, using size 11° seed beads (page 53).

Web: Work continuous bead stitches (page 53), using size 11° seed beads between each spoke.

Button Spider Stitch

Head and body: 1 large, 1 small button.

Legs: fly stitch offset (page 67).

Bead Spider Stitch

Head and body: single bead stitch (page 71), 1 small, 1 large bead.

Legs: fly stitch offset (page 67).

Button Bug Stitch

Body: 1 4-hole button.

Wings: lazy daisy stitches (page 65).

Antennae and legs: pistil stitch (page 70).

BUTTON EMBELLISHMENT STITCHES

Buttons, Who's Got the Buttons?

The holes of the button can be straightstitched with perle cotton in a variety of patterns. The buttons can also be clustered, stacked, or grouped into a cascade.

A. 2-hole buttons.

B. 4-hole buttons.

C. Stacked: Stack and stitch a smaller button on top of a larger button.

D. Clustered: Stitch a group of buttons, slightly overlapping each other.

E. Button cascade: Stitch a group of buttons in a straight or curved row, slightly overlapping each other.

Buttonhole Decoration Stitches

Stitch the button in place with perle cotton.

Suggested stitches: single bead stitch (page 71), stacked bead stitch (page 71), grouped bead stitch (page 71), bead cascade stitch (page 71).

Button Flower

Stitch a leaves and stem stalk (page 64). Stitch a button at the top of the stalk.

Buttons with Embroidery Stitches

The embroidery stitches can be worked with perle cotton, through the holes of the button and around the outer edge of the button. See Embroidered Buttons (page 83) for more examples.

Embroidered Buttons

Sew buttons in place with perle cotton. Work the embroidery stitches in the same color or choose additional colors.

Suggested stitches: barb stitch (page 66), bell flower stitch (page 76), blanket stitch (page 55), chain stitch (page 52), fly stitch (page 67), fly stitch stacked (page 77), French knot stitch (page 70), lazy daisy stitch (page 65), lazy daisy piggyback stitch (page 65), pistil stitch (page 70), straight stitch (page 70).

Fly and straight stitches

French knot stitches

Barb stitch, straight stitch

Blanket stitch rows

Lazy daisy stitch, French knot stitches

Fly stitch, straight stitch

Chain stitch, French knot stitches

Bellflower stitch, lazy daisy stitch

Lazy daisy piggyback stitch, French knot stitches

Pistil stitch, straight stitch, French knot stitches

Fly stitch stacked, straight stitch

Bellflower stitch, French knot stitches

Straight stitch, French knot stitches

Lazy daisy stitch, French knot stitches

Straight stitch, lazy daisy stitch, French knot stitches

Ivory and Pastel

This sewing caddy is an example of a crazy-pieced pattern, broken up into sections by adding ribbon down the length of each section. Six different fabrics were used, A–F, cut in a variety of strip and wedge shapes. The base diagram could be used to create a wall hanging by embroidering each section individually or by embroidering each seam individually, as was done for *Crazy Colorful* (page 46) and *Primarily Crazy for Kevin* (page 47).

CQ- Sewing Caddy project, beaded embroidery stitching

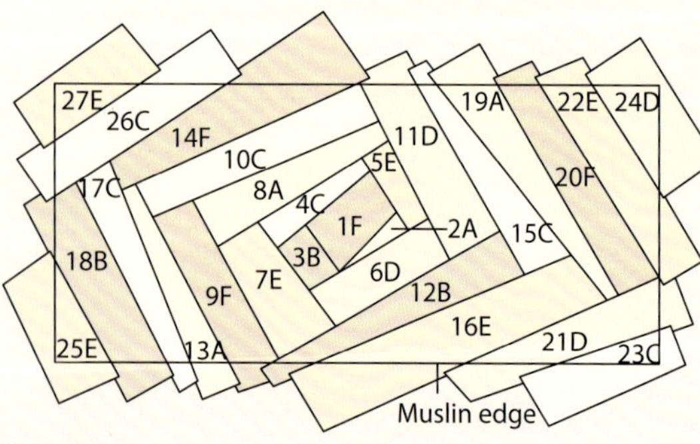

Base diagram

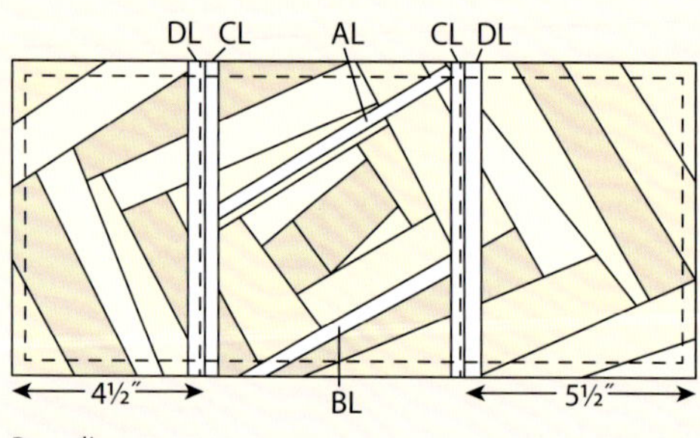

Base diagram

Embroidery by Design

Sweet Summer Stitching

Size: 14½" x 14½" (36.8 × 36.8cm)

Project: Hand Embroidery Basics and Beyond, Creative Spark Online Learning

I constructed this Crazy-Pieced Block with borders from cotton batik fabrics. The center is an example from my class Hand Embroidery Basics and Beyond on the Creative Spark Online Learning platform. The embroidery stitches are worked in perle cotton, cotton floss, and silk embroidery ribbon. A novelty ribbon is used for the sashing (page 37). Embellishments are novelty-shaped, and two- and four-hole buttons. See Crazy-Pieced Block (page 170) and Foundation-Pieced Border, option B (page 39) for ideas.

Design Diagram Take a photograph of your pieced base, and print the image so that you can draw in and "audition" the stitches and embellishments that you want to add in.

STITCHING INSPIRATION

Let me share my simple approach to creating a project, from the color choices and design of the base to the embroidery and embellishments used.

I suggest starting with a fabric that has an interesting print or a batik that will offer a selection of colors to choose from. Then, gather additional fabrics and other components, such as ribbons, trims, laces, threads, beads, buttons, and anything else you want to incorporate.

Once all the components have been selected, the next step is to determine the best pieced design for the embroidery and embellishment stitches. For ideas, refer to Strip, Patch, or Get Crazy (page 24) and Custom Design Ideas (page 101).

Choosing a Color Palette

Select your fabrics, then choose your trimmings, embroidery materials, and embellishments in the same colors or in lighter or darker tones.

Fabrics: Start with a print or batik with a variety of colors; choose additional fabrics that coordinate.

Trimmings: Select 1 or more colors to complement your fabrics.

Perle cotton: Choose the same number as your fabrics.

Stranded floss: Choose the same number as your fabrics.

Silk embroidery ribbon: Choose a selection of colors.

Beads: Choose a variety of sizes in the same number of colors as your fabrics.

Embellishments: Choose a selection of colors.

Note: *For further reading, see* *Getting It Together (page 17).*

Additional Accent Colors

In addition to the color selections below, you can introduce more colors for added interest, such as metallics or neutrals.

Gold or antique gold: Choose for a warm color palette.

Silver or antique silver: Choose for a cool color palette.

Copper, antique copper, or brass: Choose for a warm color palette.

Black or white: Choose for a cool color palette.

Brown or cream: Choose for a warm color palette.

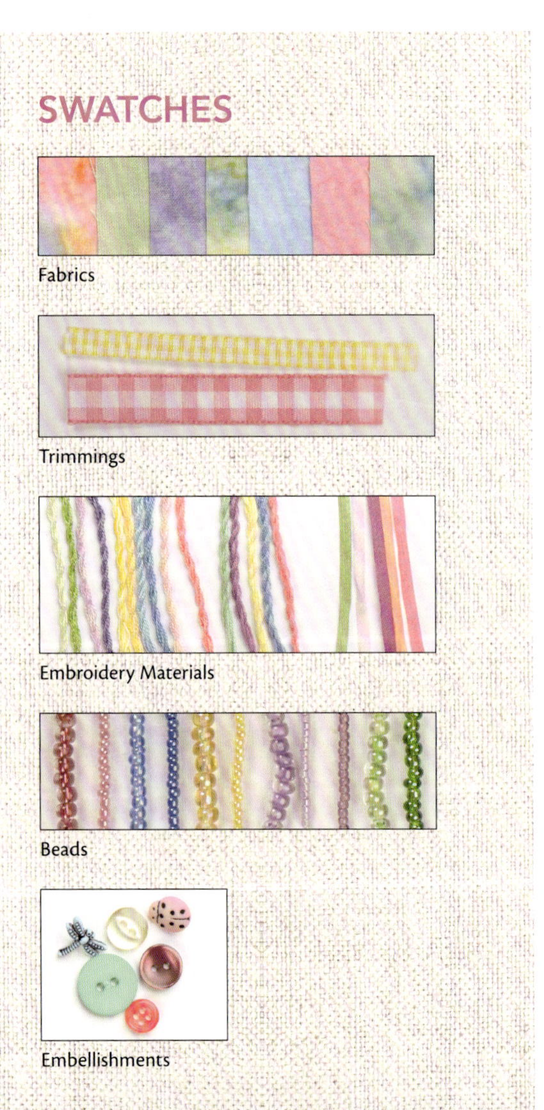

EMBROIDERY OPPORTUNITIES

Understanding the size and shape of the pattern pieces and sections of the block will help to determine where the stitches can be worked. The embroidery and embellishment stitches can be worked along a seam and within the open space of fabric between seams.

Pattern Shapes and Block Sections

Strip or rectangle: the width of the pattern piece is the same along the length of the section.

Triangle: the width of the pattern piece is narrow at one point and then widens to the final two points.

Wedge: the width of the pattern piece is angled from wide to narrow.

Center: the square, rectangular, or five-sided section of fabric in the center of the block.

Corner section: a triangular section of fabric, adjacent to two sections of fabric or a block edge.

Open space: the space between seams.

Vignette intersection: a section where two or more seams meet.

Seam Descriptions

The length of the seam and the space around the seam will help to determine what stitches will look best where. Work stitches on the seam or on either side of the seam.

Short seams or narrow spaces: Select a stitch from Border Row Stitches for Short Seams or Narrow Spaces (page 51).

Medium seams or medium spaces: Select a stitch from Border Row Stitches for Medium Seams or Medium Spaces (page 55).

Long seams or wide spaces: Select a stitch from Border Row Stitches for Long Seams or Wide Spaces (page 60).

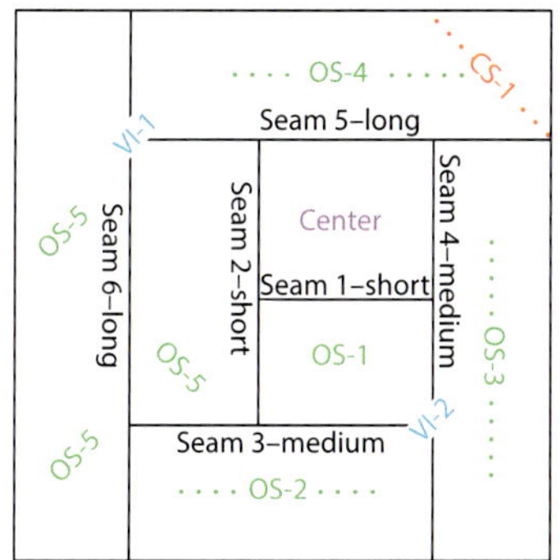

Strip-Pieced Block Diagram (page 168), with rectangular-shaped pattern pieces (In the above diagram, CS is corner section, OS is open space, VI is vignette intersection)

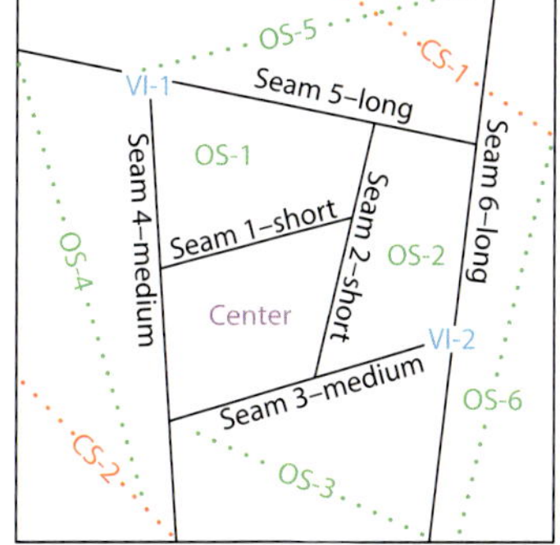

Wedge-Pieced Block Diagram (page 169), with wedge-shaped pattern pieces (In the above diagram, CS is corner section, OS is open space, VI is vignette intersection)

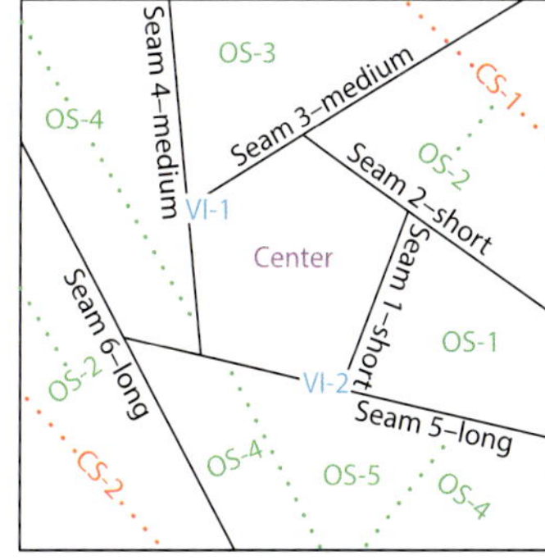

Crazy-Pieced Block Diagram (page 170), with wedge- and triangular-shaped pattern pieces (In the above diagram, CS is corner section, OS is open space, VI is vignette intersection)

WHICH STITCHES WHERE?

Think of each row as an opportunity for your creativity to shine!

1. **Border rows**, such as a continuous stitch, repeated individual stitch, vine, or stalk, are stitched along a seam, a line drawn in the open spaces between seams, or over a length of trim.

2. **Decorative stitches,** such as individual stitches, flowers, and filler shapes, are stitched off the border rows.

3. **Detail stitches** are stitched off or around the border rows and decorative stitches.

4. **Embellishment stitches** are stitched off or around the previous stitches.

5. Center, corner section, open space, and vignette intersection: Hand-quilted stitches, additional border rows, flowers, filler shapes, and embellishment stitches can be stitched in the open spaces between seams, or in sections where seams meet.

Note: *Refer to the Visual Guide for suggested stitches (page 6).*

Working the Stitches

1. First, stitch in any trims or large components that are on a seam.

2. **Border row:** Embroider a continuous or individual stitch along a seam or line.

3. **Decorative stitch/es:** Embroider 1 stitch or a combination of stitches off the tips of the **border row**, in the open areas, and in spaces between stitches.

4. **Detail stitches:** Embroider 1 stitch or several stitches on the **border row**, or add to the **decorative stitch/es**.

5. **Embellishment stitches:** Embroider 1 stitch or several stitches on the **border row**, or add to the **decorative stitch/es**.

6. Center, corner section, open space, and vignette intersection: Embroider and embellish the remaining sections.

SAVVY STITCHING

- *Work the stitches in one type of material or a combination of materials.*
- *A second border row, like the chain or stem stitch, can be worked below a stitch with a continuous edge.*
- *The tips of a continuous stitch can be worked with the same combination of decorative and detail stitches, or two or more combinations of stitches can be alternated on the tips.*
- *Stitches like the feather, cretan, herringbone, or chevron stitches have a tip on either side of the seam; these can be worked in the same combination of stitches, alternated between two or more combinations, or each side can be worked in separate combinations.*
- *Continue to stitch the tips of a border row, unless there is not enough room to finish the pattern; then embroider whatever portion of the pattern will fit in the remaining space.*
- *When working the stitches with embroidery threads or silk embroidery ribbon, begin with the shorter seams. When working with beaded embroidery stitches, begin with the longer seams.*
- *Do not work beaded embroidery stitches or buttons ¾" (1.9cm) from the raw edges.*

EMBROIDERY AND EMBELLISHMENT EXAMPLES

Refer to the Visual Guide (page 6) and Embroidery and Embellishment Stitches (page 46) for individual stitch instructions or for more stitch options.

Seam Design Ideas

DIAGRAM EXAMPLE CODE

A: Tip of a stitch

B: Open area between stitches

C: Spaces between two stitches

D: Additional areas: crossed section, or the bottom edge

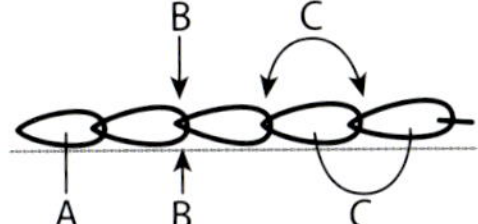

Border row: Chain Stitch Opportunities

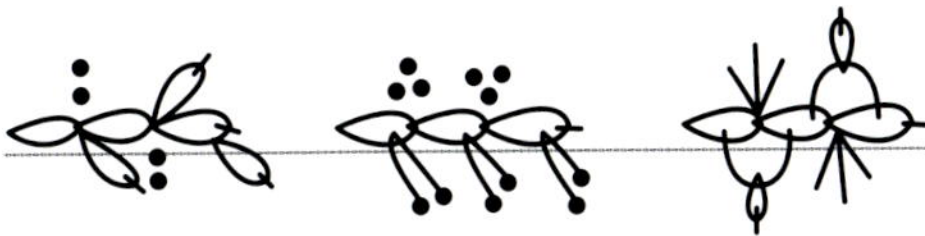

Decorative stitches: lazy daisy stitch, fly stitch with lazy daisy stitch

Detail stitches: French knot stitch, knotted seed stitch, pistil stitch, straight stitch

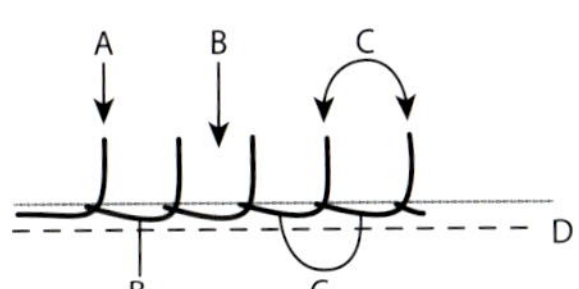

Border row: Blanket Stitch Opportunities

Additional border row: chain stitch, stem stitch

Decorative stitches: lazy daisy stitch, fly stitch, lazy daisy stitch with French knot stitch

Detail stitches: French knot stitch, straight stitch, knotted seed stitch

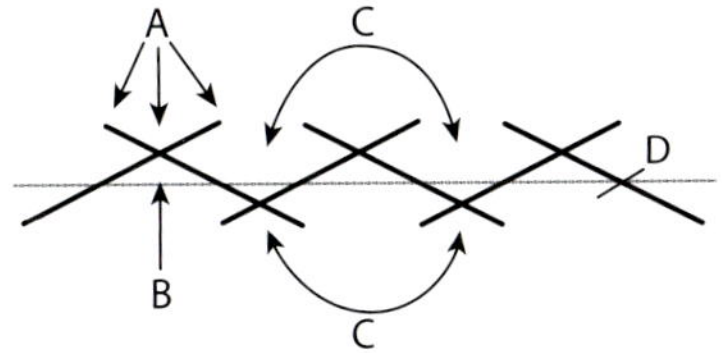

Border row: Herringbone Stitch Opportunities

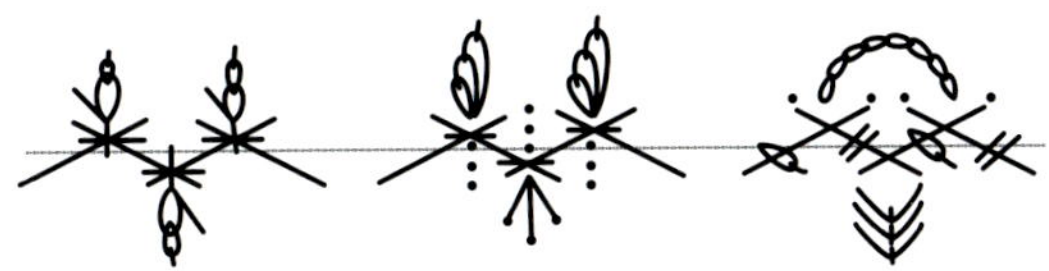

Decorative stitches: lazy daisy piggyback stitch, looped tendril stitch, fly stitch stacked, chain stitch, lazy daisy stitch

Detail stitches: straight stitch, pistil stitch, French knot stitch

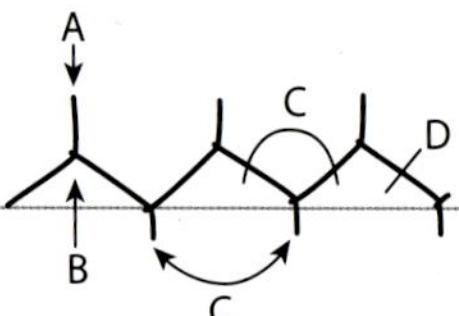

Border row: Cretan Stitch Opportunities

Decorative stitches: lazy daisy stitch, fly stitch, cross stitch with details, fly stitch with lazy daisy stitch

Detail stitches: French knot stitch, knotted seed stitch

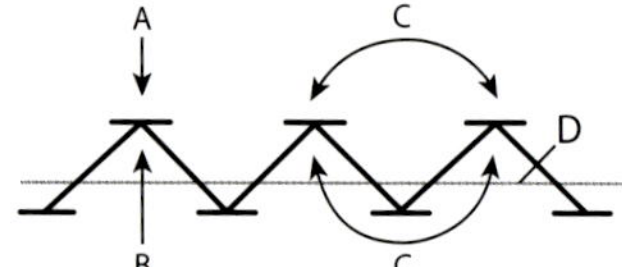

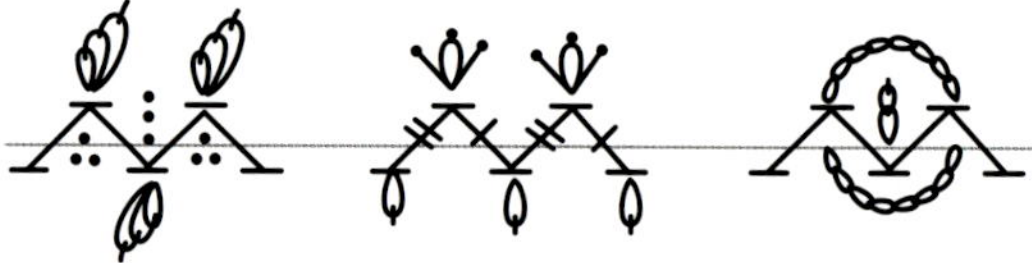

Border row: Chevron Stitch Opportunities

Decorative stitches: looped tendril stitch, lazy daisy with French knot stitch, lazy daisy stitch, chain stitch, lazy daisy piggyback stitch

Detail stitches: French knot stitch, knotted seed stitch, pistil stitch, straight stitch

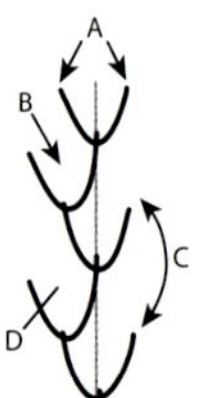

Border row: Feather Stitch Opportunities

Decorative stitches: lazy daisy stitch, looped tendril stitch, chain stitch

Detail stitches: pistil stitch, French knot stitch, knotted seed stitch

Vignette and Filler Shapes

These stitches can be used to fill in the center of a block, the corner sections, or the open spaces between seams.

Refer to the Visual Guide (page 6) and Embroidery and Embellishment Stitches (page 46) for the individual stitch instructions or for more stitch options.

Center: fabric square filled with embroidery stitches, following the pattern of fabric

Vignette intersection: ribbon buttons, group of 3 stacked bead stitches, shank button

Vignette intersection: fabric circle, novelty button, charm

Vignette intersection: group of woven roses, lazy daisy stitches, pistil stitches, French knot stitches, beads

Center: fabric yo-yos, stacked bead stitch, sequins

Open space: group of buttons, sequins, floret stitches (beaded)

Center: group of 3 whip-stitch roses, lazy daisy stitches, French knot stitches, chain stitch, continuous bead stitch

Center: large button focal point

Corner section: single and groups of buttons

Corner section: group of 3 mod hexies, buttons, charm

Open space: button spider stitch, charms, buttons

Embellished Trims

RIBBON

Embroidery stitches can be worked over the edge of the ribbon, through the ribbon, or on the outer edges of the ribbon.

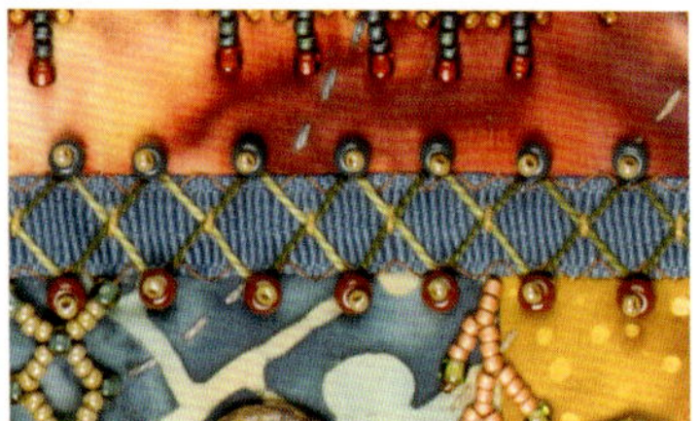

Cross stitch, straight stitch, stacked bead stitch

Chain stitch zigzag, French knot stitch, stacked bead stitch

Two ribbons layered with button embellishments

LACE

Embroidery stitches can be worked into the open areas of the lace pattern along the outer edge of the lace.

Ribbon and lace, blanket and chain stitches, French knot stitch, straight stitch

Ribbon: cross stitch, straight stitch, lazy daisy stitch, French knot stitch

Lace: French knot stitch, straight stitch, stacked bead stitch, single bead stitch

TRIMS

Embroidery stitches can be worked over the trim or between the curved wave edges of the trim.

Leaf trim: straight stitch, lazy daisy stitch, fabric yo-yos, spiderweb rose, bellflower stitch, French knot stitch, single bead stitch, grouped bead stitch, buttons

Rickrack trim: straight stitch, fly stitch modern, French knot stitch, mod hexies, buttons, steampunk bugs

EMBROIDERY DIAGRAMS

On the following pages you will see how the concepts covered in this chapter can be used on three of the block patterns.

Strip-Pieced Block

The strip- and rectangle-shaped pattern pieces of this block offer simple seam lines for embroidery and embellishment. See the Strip-Pieced Block Diagram (page 87); choose pattern piece 1 or 2 for the center of the block.

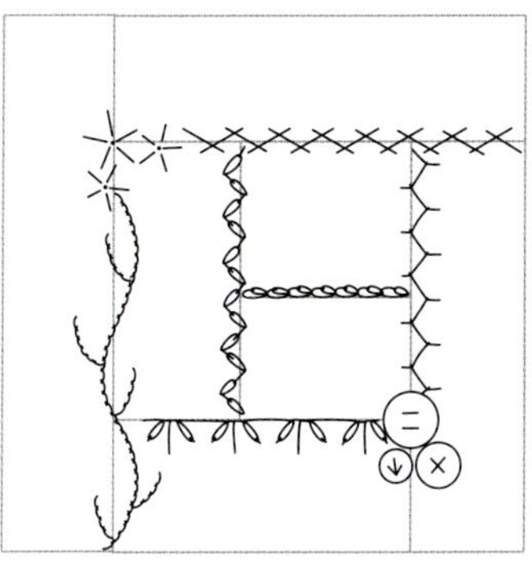

STEP 1

Stitch in any large components, then embroider the seams with a **border row**.

Vignette intersection **1:** 3 woven rose stitch bases

Vignette intersection **2:** button cluster

Seam 1, **border row:** chain stitch double

Seam 2, **border row:** chain stitch feathered

Seam 3, **border row:** leaves and stem row

Seam 4, **border row:** cretan stitch

Seam 5, **border row:** herringbone stitch

Seam 6, **border row:** stem stitch vine

STEP 2

Embroider the **decorative stitches** and **detail stitches**.

Vignette intersection **1:** 3 woven rose stitches

Vignette intersection **2:** group of 3 straight stitches

Seam 1, **detail stitch:** French knot stitch

Seam 2, **decorative stitches:** first side—alternate between 5 and 6 petal French knot stitch flowers, second side—lazy daisy stitch, fly stitch; **detail stitch:** French knot stitch

Seam 3, **decorative stitch:** 5-petal lazy daisy stitch flower; **detail stitches:** French knot stitch, pistil stitch

Seam 4, **decorative stitches:** first side—French knot bud stitch, lazy daisy stitch; **detail stitches:** French knot stitch, second side—fly stitch with lazy daisy stitch

Seam 5, **decorative stitches:** first side—alternate between looped tendril stitch, pistil stitch, knotted seed stitch, second side—lazy daisy stitch; **detail stitch:** straight stitch

Seam 6, **decorative stitches** and **detail stitches:** lazy daisy stitch, French knot stitch, knotted seed stitch

STEP 3

Embroider any additional stitches, the **embellishment stitches**, and any additional components.

Seam 2, **embellishment stitches:** stacked bead stitch, size 6° and 11° seed beads

Seam 3, **embellishment stitches:** stacked bead stitch, 8mm and size 15° seed beads

Seam 4, **embellishment stitches:** stacked bead stitch, size 6° and 11° seed beads

Seam 5, **embellishment stitches:** stacked bead stitch, size 8° and 15° seed beads

Seam 6, **embellishment stitches:** stacked bead stitch, 10mm rondelle and 11° seed beads

Center: stem stitch stalk, lazy daisy stitch, 6-petal lazy daisy stitch flower, pistil stitch

Corner section: spiderweb corner

Open space 1: button spider stitch

Open space 2 and open space 4: hand-quilted row, embroidered buttons: French knot stitch

Open space 3 and open space 5: hand-quilted row, sideview butterfly stitch

Wedge-Pieced Block

The wedge-shaped pattern pieces of this block offer a variety of angled seam lines and open spaces for embroidery and embellishment; see the Wedge-Pieced Block Diagram (page 87).

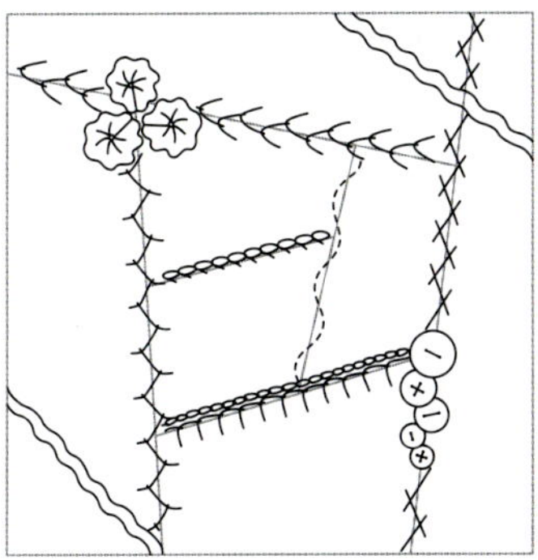

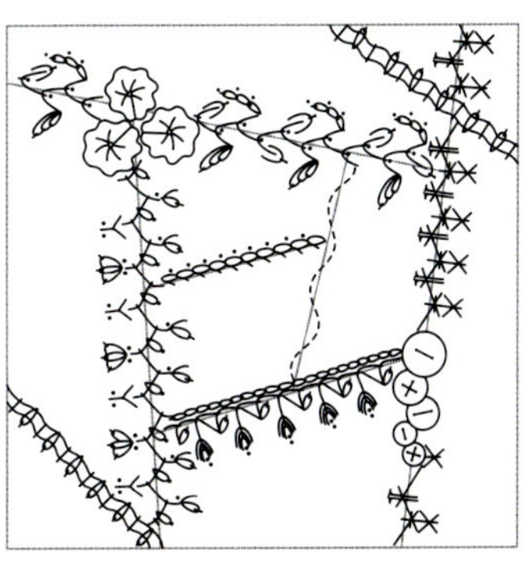

STEP 1

Stitch in any large components, then embroider the seams with a **border row**.

Vignette intersection **1:** 3 rosettes

Vignette intersection **2:** button cascade

Corner section **1** and corner section **2:** rickrack trims

Seam 1, **border row:** chain stitch spiny

Seam 2, **border row:** backstitch vine

Seam 3, **border row:** blanket stitch, chain stitch

Seam 4, **border row:** cretan stitch

Seam 5, **border row:** feather stitch

Seam 6, **border row:** herringbone stitch

STEP 2

Embroider the **decorative stitches** and **detail stitches**.

Seam 1, **detail stitch:** French knot stitch

Seam 3, **decorative stitches:** alternate between fly stitch stacked and lazy daisy stitch; **detail stitches:** alternate between French knot stitch and straight stitch

Seam 4, **decorative stitches:** first side—alternate between lazy daisy tulip stitch and fleet stitch, second side—fly stitch with loop (beaded); **detail stitches:** lazy daisy stitch, French knot stitch

Seam 5, **decorative stitches:** outer tips—alternate between chain stitch and looped tendril stitch, remaining tips—fly stitch with French knot stitch; **detail stitch:** French knot stitch

Seam 6, **decorative stitches:** first side—cross stitch with details, second side—barb stitch; **detail stitch:** straight stitch

Corner section **1** and corner section **2:** lazy daisy stitch, straight stitch

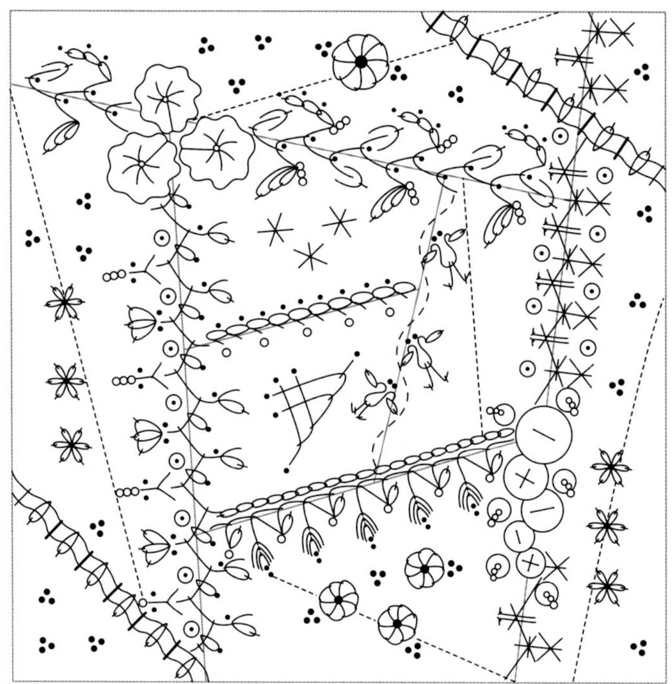

STEP 3

Embroider any additional stitches, the **embellishment stitches**, and any additional components.

Seam 1, **embellishment stitch:** single bead stitch, size 11° seed bead

Seam 2, **embellishment stitch:** steampunk bugs

Seam 3, **embellishment stitch:** single bead stitch, size 11° seed bead

Seam 4, **embellishment stitch:** stacked bead stitch, size 6° and 11° seed beads, grouped bead stitch, size 11° seed beads

Seam 5, **embellishment stitch:** grouped bead stitch, size 11° seed beads

Seam 6, **embellishment stitch:** stacked bead stitch, size 6° and 11° seed beads

Center: crossed triangle stitch, French knot stitch

Vignette intersection **1:** single bead stitch, size 6° seed bead

Vignette intersection **2:** bead cascade stitch, size 6° and 11° seed beads

Open space **1:** whip-stitch star stitch

Open space **2:** hand-quilted row

Open space **3** and open space **5:** hand-quilted row, buttonhole circle stitch, knotted seed stitch

Open space **4** and open space **6:** hand-quilted row, 6-petal lazy daisy flower, knotted seed stitch

Crazy-Pieced Block

The 5-sided center and wedge- and triangle-shaped pattern pieces of this block offer a variety of seam lines and open spaces for embroidery and embellishment; see the Crazy-Pieced Block Diagram (page 87).

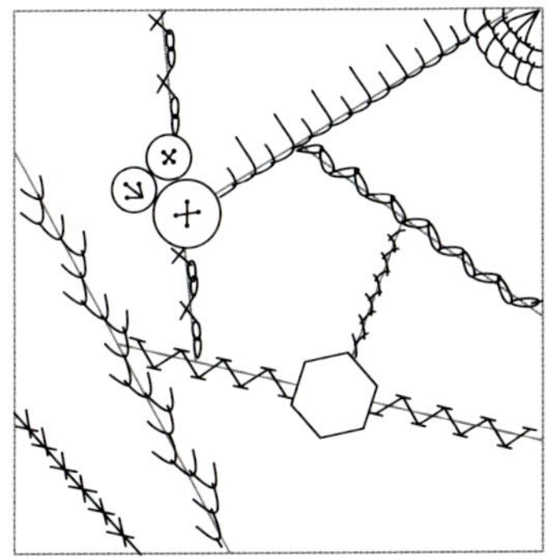

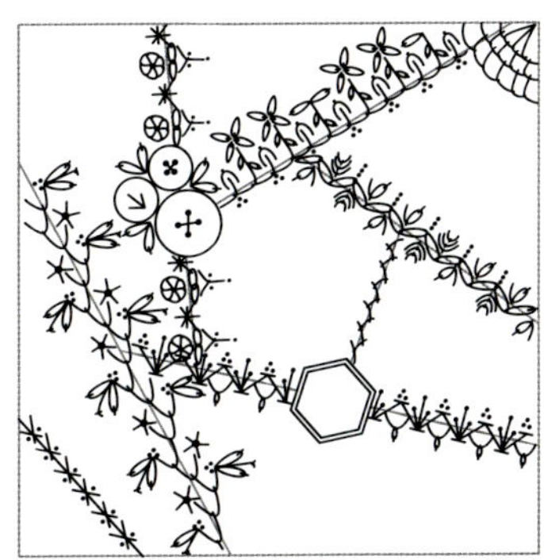

STEP 1

Stitch in any large components, then embroider the seams with a **border row**.

Vignette intersection **1:** button cluster

Vignette intersection **2:** mod hexie

Seam 1, **border row:** stem/outline fern stitch

Seam 2, **border row:** chain stitch zigzag

Seam 3, **border row:** blanket stitch short-long

Seam 4, **border row:** chain and cross stitch

Seam 5, **border row:** chevron stitch

Seam 6, **border row:** feather stitch double

Corner section **1:** blanket stitch cobweb

Corner section **2:** thorn stitch

STEP 2

Embroider the **decorative stitches** and **detail stitches**.

Seam 2, **decorative stitches:** alternate between fly stitch stacked and fly stitch with loop (beaded); **detail stitch:** French knot stitches

Seam 3, **decorative stitches:** long tip—alternate between 4-petal lazy daisy stitch flowers and lazy daisy stitches, short tip—fly stitch with French knot stitch; **detail stitches:** lazy daisy stitch, knotted seed stitch

Seam 4, **decorative stitches:** first side—buttonhole circle stitch, second side—fleet stitch; **detail stitches:** straight stitch, French knot stitches

Seam 5, **decorative stitches:** fly stitch with lazy daisy stitch; **detail stitches:** pistil stitch, knotted seed stitch

Seam 6, **decorative stitches:** long tip—lazy daisy stitch, barb stitch; **detail stitches:** knotted seed stitch, short tip—5-petal straight stitch; **detail stitch:** French knot stitch

Vignette intersection **1:** 2 lazy daisy stitches between each button

Vignette intersection **2:** backstitch

Corner section **2:** French knot stitch

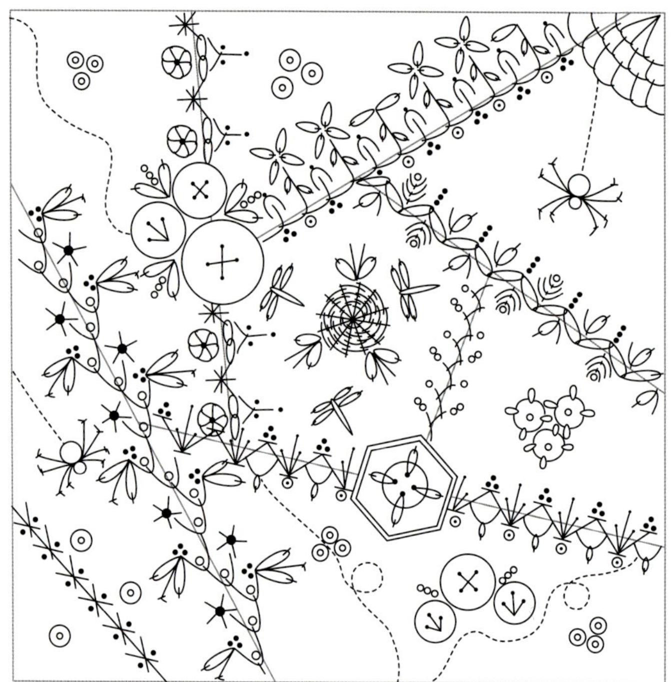

STEP 3

Embroider any additional stitches, the **embellishment stitches**, and any additional components.

Seam 1, **embellishment stitches:** alternate between grouped bead stitch and single bead stitch, size 11° seed beads

Seam 2, **embellishment stitch:** single bead stitch, size 11° seed bead

Seam 3, **embellishment stitches:** single bead stitch, size 11° seed bead, stacked bead stitch, size 8° and 15° seed beads

Seam 5, **embellishment stitch:** stacked bead stitch, size 8° and 15° seed beads

Seam 6, **embellishment stitch:** single bead stitch, size 11° seed bead

Center: woven rose stitch, lazy daisy stitch, straight stitch, 3 dragonfly stitches

Corner section **2:** stacked bead stitch, 10mm rondelle and 11° seed beads

Open space **1:** group of 3 dome snaps, lazy daisy stitch

Open space **2:** hand-quilted row, bead spider stitch

Open space **3:** stacked bead stitch, 10mm rondelle and 11° seed beads

Open space **4:** hand-quilted row, stacked bead stitch, size 6° and 11° seed beads

Open space **5:** button cluster, grouped bead stitch, size 11° seed beads

EVEN MORE STITCHING IDEAS

Saltwater Taffy Trimmings

Size: 23″ × 18½″ (58.4 × 47cm)

This is a project that I created from leftover strip- and patch-pieced sections combined with ribbons and rickrack trims. I showcased buttons in many of the open sections; for ideas on embellishing see Embroidered Buttons (page 83). For more ideas on using ribbon, see my book *Creative Embroidery, Mixing the Old with the New* by C&T Publishing.

Even More Stitches! For a myriad of stitch choices, you can dive into *Hand Embroidery Dictionary* and *Beaded Embroidery Stitching* by C&T Publishing.

Base diagram

Tropical Illusion

Size: 21½" x 21½" (54.6 × 54.6cm)

This is an example of four different Crazy-Pieced Blocks, made from two different fabric combinations, with embroidery thread combinations in a range of light, medium, and dark colors. For extra dimension, I worked the stitches in perle cotton #5, #8, and #12, with the cotton floss worked in 2, 3, or 6 strands. See Crazy-Pieced Block (page 170), the base diagram (below), Fabric or Ribbon Sashing (page 37), and Border-Edge Assembly (page 42) for ideas to create your own base.

Adding Interest and Dimension

As a design exercise, each block started with a group of border rows and their variations. The decorative and detail stitches were worked on each block, using different variations and combinations.

Block 1, color combination A, border rows feather stitch (page 60) and chain stitch (page 52)

Block 2, color combination B, border rows herringbone stitch (page 61) and chevron stitch (page 61)

Block 3, color combination B, border rows cross stitch row (page 57), fern stitch modern (page 64), and cretan stitch (page 57)

Block 4, color combination A, border rows blanket stitch (page 55), outline and stem stitches (page 51)

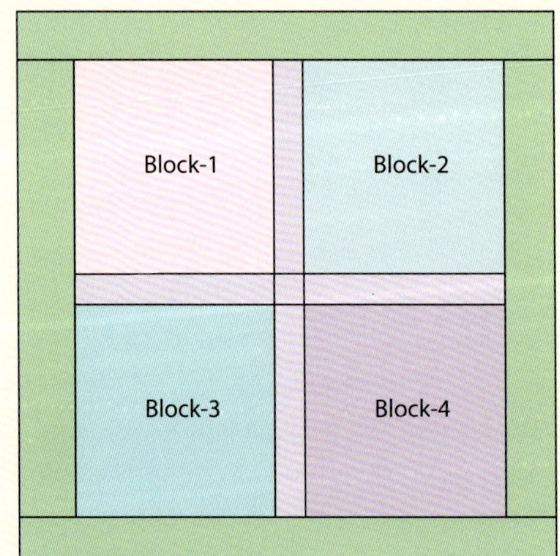

Base diagram

Need Inspiration? Sometimes we all need a little inspiration! I used all three sets of my embroidery stencils (page 22) for imagery and ideas.

Custom Design Ideas

PROJECTS

This chapter introduces twelve projects that use the Block Patterns (pages 168–173) as a single design, repeated in a group, or combined and grouped with other blocks. Creative additions include sashing, borders, and additional bits and pieces. The embroidery and embellishments are worked with a variety of threads, silk ribbons, and beads. Finally, you have several choices for finishing the project and adding extra touches.

Tips for Success

Each project is unique. Print out the block diagrams and blueprints given in each project, and enlarge these so that they are easier to read.

Refer to Getting It Together (page 17) and Choosing a Color Palette (page 86) for materials and color suggestions. Flip back to Embroidery and Embellishment Stitches (page 46) for stitch directions. Embroidery by Design (page 85), Embroidery Opportunities (page 87), and Embroidery and Embellishment Examples (page 89) will remind you where to apply the wide variety of stitches.

Embroider in Stages

Each seam lists the stitches that are used; I suggest you break these into steps. See Savvy Stitching (page 88) for more ideas.

Note: *First stitch in any large components that are on a seam.*

1. Embroider each seam with a **border row**.
2. Embroider the **decorative stitches** and the **detail stitches**.
3. Embroider the **embellishment stitches**.
4. Embroider any additional components.

Jaipur Spring, 15½" x 15½" (39.4 × 39.4cm)

3 Bs: Birds, Butterflies, and Bees, 10" x 10" (25.4 × 25.4cm)

Strip-Pieced Block Wall Hanging

This wall hanging starts with four Strip-Pieced Blocks (page 25) using the seven-fabric combination, with additional pieces added to make the blocks larger. Ribbon is used for the sashing (page 37), with lace and additional ribbon details. Extras include fabric circles (page 31), rosettes (page 32), appliqués, buttons, and beads.

Time for Tea, 17″ x 17″ (43.2 × 43.2cm)

Creative Option Use leftover bits to personalize a label for your project; see Signature Label (page 44).

SWATCHES

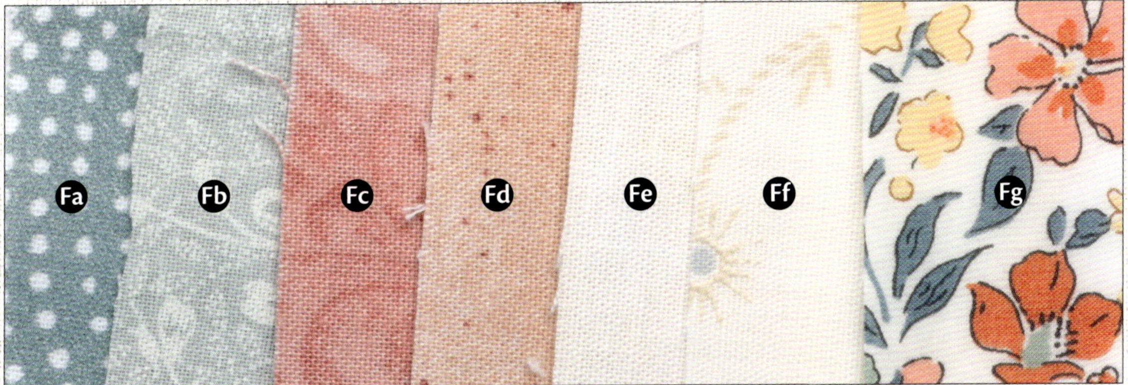

Fabrics

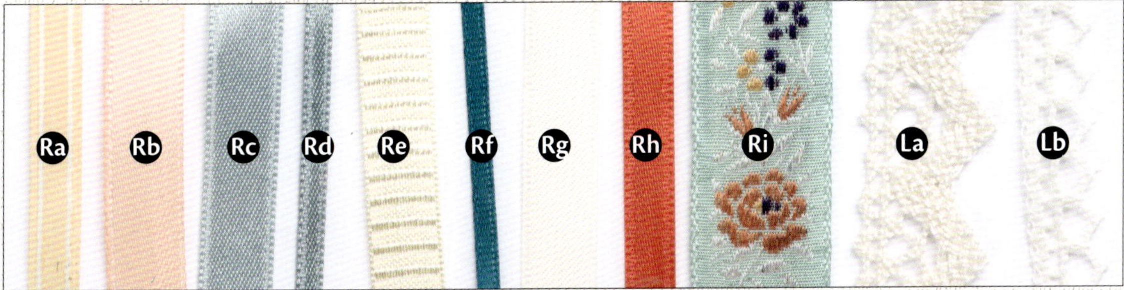

Trimmings

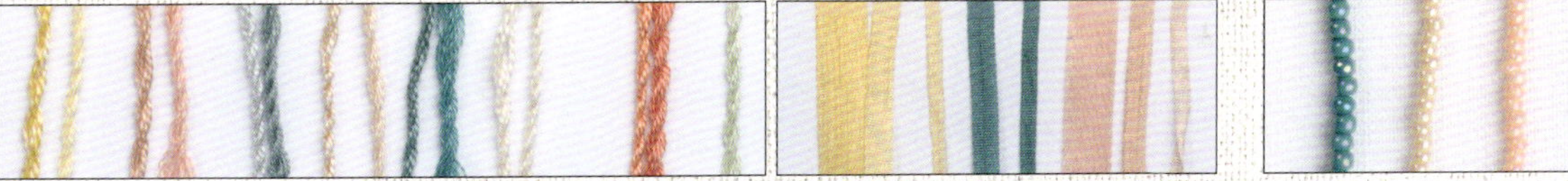

Pearl cotton, cotton floss, silk embroidery ribbons

Seed beads

1. Fabric circle **2.** Rosettes **3.** Appliqués

Embellishments (not all shown)

Materials

FABRICS

Fa, Fb, Fc, Fd: ¼ yard (22.9cm) each

Fe, Ff, Fg: fat quarters or scraps

TRIMMINGS

Ra, Rh: ¼" (6mm) satin ribbon 1 yard (1m) each

Rb, Rc, Rg: ⅜" (10mm) satin ribbon 2 yards (1.9m) each

Rd, Rf: ⅛" (3mm) satin ribbon 1 yard (1m) each

Re: ⅜" (10mm) novelty print satin ribbon 1 yard (1m)

Ri: ¾" (19mm) jacquard ribbon 1⅛ yard (1.1m)

La: ¾" (19mm) lace 1 yard (1m)

Lb: ⅜" (10mm) lace 1 yard (1m)

Appliqués: 2 styles, 4 each

EMBROIDERY MATERIALS IN A VARIETY OF COLORS

Perle cotton (pc): #8

Cotton floss (cf)

Silk embroidery ribbon (ser): 7mm, 4mm, 2mm

Seed beads (sb): size 11°

EMBELLISHMENTS

Buttons

Ba: novelty teapot and teacup, 4 sets

Bb: novelty teacup, 4

Bc: shank, 2 colors, 8

Bd: novelty teapot or teacup, 4

Glass and Metal Components

Angel charm: 4

Butterfly bead 24 × 12mm: 16

Flower rondelle 8mm: 20

Flower rondelle 10mm: 8

Flower rondelle 12mm: 8

Flower rondelle 20mm: 4

Flower button 12mm: 12

Flower bead: 12

8mm bead: 12

Muslin: ¼ yard (22.9cm)

fast2fuse, heavy: 2½" × 10" (6.4 × 25.4cm)

Shape-Flex: ½ yard (45.7cm)

Batting: ½ yard (45.7cm)

Sewing and beading threads: neutral colors

Cutting Instructions

BLOCKS

Follow Steps 1–3 of Pieced Blocks (page 27), with the Strip-Pieced Block pattern (page 168). Refer to the Strip-Pieced Block Wall Hanging Diagram (below).

Cut 4 pieces from each pattern piece and the additional pieces listed below to make 4 blocks.

Pattern piece 1: *Fg*

Pattern piece 2: *Fd*

Pattern piece 3: *Fb*

Pattern piece 4: *Ff*

Pattern piece 5: *Fa*

Pattern piece 6: *Fe*

Pattern piece 7: *Fc*

Pattern piece 8: *Fb*, 1¾″ x 6″ (4.4 × 15.2cm)

Pattern piece 9: *Fd*, 1¾″ x 7¼″ (4.4 × 18.4cm)

Pattern piece 10: *Fg*, 1¾″ x 7¼″ (4.4 × 18.4cm)

Pattern piece 11: *Fa*, 1¾″ x 8½″ (4.4 × 21.6cm)

EXTRAS

Fabric circles (page 31): *Fg*, cut 4 circles 2″ (5.1cm) diameter.

fast2fuse: Cut 4 circles 1¼″ (3.2cm) diameter.

Batting: Cut 4 circles 1⅛″ (2.9cm) diameter.

Rosettes: Cut 12 lengths 6″ (15.2cm), 3 each from *Rb*, *Rc*, and *Rg*.

ADDITIONAL PIECES

Muslin: Cut 4 squares 7″ x 7″ (17.8 × 17.8cm).

Shape-Flex: Cut 4 squares 9″ x 9″ (22.9 × 22.9cm).

Sashing: *Ri*, cut 2 lengths 17″ (43.2cm).

Backing: *Fa* and *Fb*, strip-piece sections together; cut 1 square 17″ x 17″ (43.2 × 43.2cm).

Hanging sleeve: *Fa*, cut 1 rectangle 4″ x 15″ (10.2 × 38.1cm).

Batting: 17″ x 17″ (43.2 × 43.2cm)

Binding 1, vertical seams: *Fd*, cut 2 rectangles 3″ x 17″ (7.6 × 43.2cm).

Binding 2, horizontal seams: *Fc*, cut 2 rectangles 3″ x 18″ (7.6 × 45.7cm).

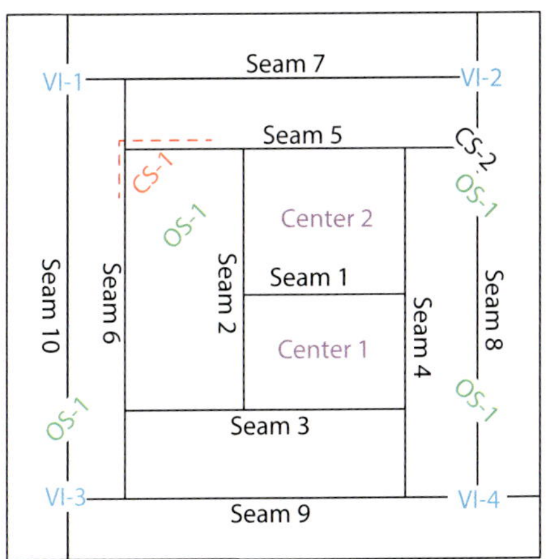

Strip-Pieced Block Wall Hanging Diagram (In diagram, CS is corner section, OS is open space, VI is vignette intersection)

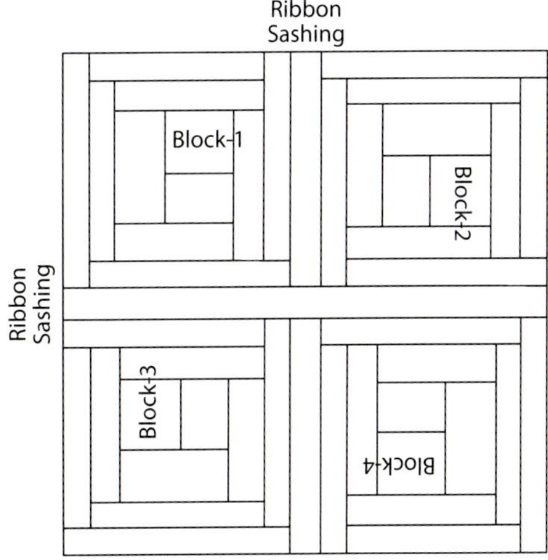

Strip-Pieced Block Wall Hanging Blueprints

SEWING THE BLOCKS AND EXTRAS

1. Follow the directions for Foundation Piecing (page 27), using the pattern pieces and muslin squares. Make 4 blocks. Trim the blocks to 6″ x 6″ (15.2 x 15.2cm).

2. Following the Strip-Pieced Block Wall Hanging Diagram (page 105), stitch pattern pieces 8, 9, 10, and 11 to each block.

3. Stabilize each block with Shape-Flex.

4. Staystitch around the outer edges of each block.

5. Stitch 12 rosettes (page 32).

6. Stitch 4 fabric circles (page 31).

Trimmings and Bits and Pieces

Refer to the Strip-Pieced Block Wall Hanging Block Diagram (page 105) and follow these directions for each block.

1. Cut the ribbon to fit the seam or section of the block; hand stitch in place.

Note: *The raw edge of a ribbon or lace is covered by the following lengths.*

- **Seam 2:** *Rc*
- **Seam 5:** *Rd*
- **Seam 7:** *La, Rh extending over pattern piece 9*
- **Seam 8:** *Re*
- **Seam 9:** *Lb, Rf*
- **Seam 10:** *Rb, Ra*

2. Stitch 1 fabric circle in the vignette intersection **1** position.

3. Stitch a group of 3 rosettes in the vignette intersection **3**.

4. Stitch 1 group of appliqués in the vignette intersection **4**.

5. Follow the directions for Embroidery and Embellishment Design (page 107), then Assembly and Finishing (below).

ASSEMBLY AND FINISHING

Refer to Basic Base Instructions (page 36) and the Strip-Pieced Block Wall Hanging Blueprints (page 105).

1. Follow option B under Base Design Options (page 36), with the batting square. Place the blocks in this order: **block 1**, rotate **block 2** 90° to the right, rotate **block 3** 90° to the left, rotate **block 4** 180°.

2. Follow the directions for Fabric or Ribbon Sashing (page 37), stitching the vertical seam, then the horizontal seam, using *Ri*.

3. Stitch the hanging sleeve (page 41) 4″ x 15″ (10.2 x 38.1cm) to the backing 17″ x 17″ (43.2 x 43.2cm).

4. Follow the directions for the Bound Edge Assembly (page 41), with the backing square.

- *Vertical seams: 3″ x 17″ (7.6 × 43.2cm)*
- *Horizontal seams: 3″ x 18″ (7.6 × 45.7cm)*

Option: *A vintage decorative bone purse handle can be used as a hanger instead of a hanging sleeve.*

EMBROIDERY AND EMBELLISHMENT DESIGN

Refer to the Strip-Pieced Block Wall Hanging Block Diagram (page 105).

Note: *Use 3 strands of cotton floss.*

Base

Seam 1: border row, chain stitch double in pc; detail stitch, 2-wrap French knot stitch in cf.

Seam 2: border row, chain stitch feathered in pc; decorative stitches, alternate between French knot bud stitch in 7mm ser, fly stitch in 2mm ser, and 3 lazy daisy with French knot stitches in pc, straight stitch in pc, 3-wrap French knot stitch in 4mm ser; detail stitches, group of 3-wrap French knot stitches in cf.

Seam 3: border row, leaves and stem stalk row in pc, chain stitch in pc; decorative stitch, 5-petal straight stitch flower in 4mm ser; detail stitches, pistil stitch in cf, 2-wrap French knot stitch in cf; embellishment stitch, glass flower buttons.

Seam 4: border row, feather stitch in pc; decorative stitches, alternate between looped tendril stitch in pc, lazy daisy stitch in pc, lazy daisy stitch in 2mm ser, and fly stitch in pc; detail stitch, 3-wrap French knot stitch in cf.

Corner section **1:** 3 woven rose stitches in 7mm ser, lazy daisy stitches in 4mm ser, lazy daisy stitches in cf, pistil stitches in cf, 3-wrap French knot stitch in pc.

Seam 5: border row, cretan stitch in pc; decorative stitches, alternate between 5-petal 3-wrap French knot stitch flower in cf, lazy daisy stitch in cf, and fly stitch in pc; detail stitch, 2-wrap French knot stitch in cf.

Seam 6: border row, stem stitch vine in pc; decorative stitch, lazy daisy stitch in cf; detail stitches, group of 3 2-wrap French knot stitches in cf, 2-wrap French knot stitch in cf; embellishment stitch, stacked bead stitch with 8mm flower rondelle and 1 size 11° sb.

Seam 7: border row, cross stitch in pc, straight stitch in cf; decorative stitches, lazy daisy stitch in 4mm ser, straight stitch in 2mm ser; detail stitches, straight stitch in cf, 3-wrap French knot stitch in cf; embellishment stitches, alternate between single bead stitch with glass flower beads and stacked bead stitch with 10mm flower rondelle and 1 size 11° sb.

Seam 8: border row, fly stitch with lazy daisy stitch row in pc; decorative stitch, lazy daisy stitch in pc; detail stitch, 3-wrap French knot stitch in cf.

Seam 9: border row, blanket and chain stitches in pc, 3-wrap French knot stitch in pc; detail stitches, 3-wrap French knot stitch in cf; detail stitches, 3-wrap French knot stitches in pc and cf.

Seam 10: border row, herringbone stitch in pc, straight stitch in cf; decorative stitches, alternate between cross and straight stitches pc and 3-wrap French knot stitch in cf.

Additional Sections

Center **1:** *Ba*, teacup; center **2:** *Ba*, teapot; fabric circle: straight stitches in pc, *Bb*, angel charm; Rosettes: pistil stitch with size 11° sb and 8mm bead; Appliqués: *Bd*; corner section **2:** 1 stacked bead stitch with 12mm flower rondelle and 1 size 11° sb; open space **1:** single bead stitch with butterfly bead; vignette intersection **2:** 2 *Bc*, picot bead stitch with 20mm flower rondelle and 11° sb.

Strip-Pieced and Wedged Crumbles Blocks Table Runner

This table runner incorporates two Strip-Pieced Blocks (page 25) and one Wedged Crumbles Block (page 26), using the four-fabric combination. An additional sashing strip was added to the first and third block, with ribbons, trims, fabric circles (page 31), and fabric yo-yos (page 31).

Melon Parfait, 25½″ x 10″ (64.8 × 25.4cm)

Creative Option Turn this project into a wall hanging by rearranging the blocks vertically and adding a Hanging Sleeve (page 41).

SWATCHES

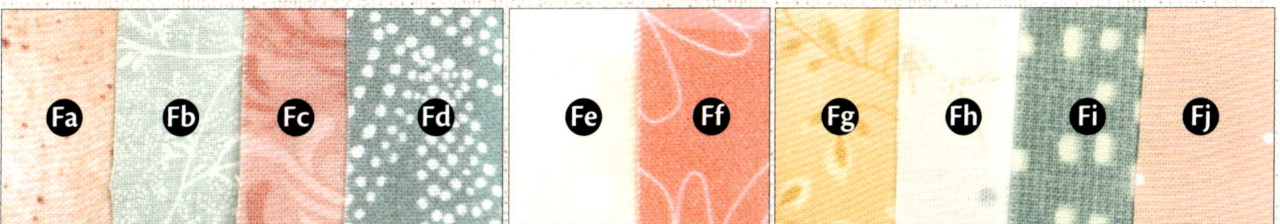

Fabrics

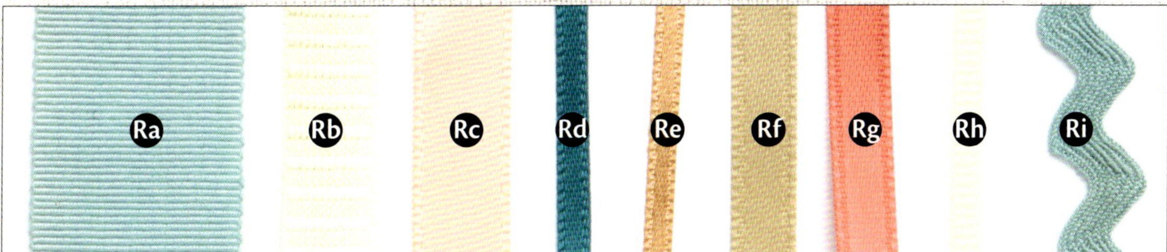

Trimmings

1. Fabric circle **2.** Fabric yo-yos

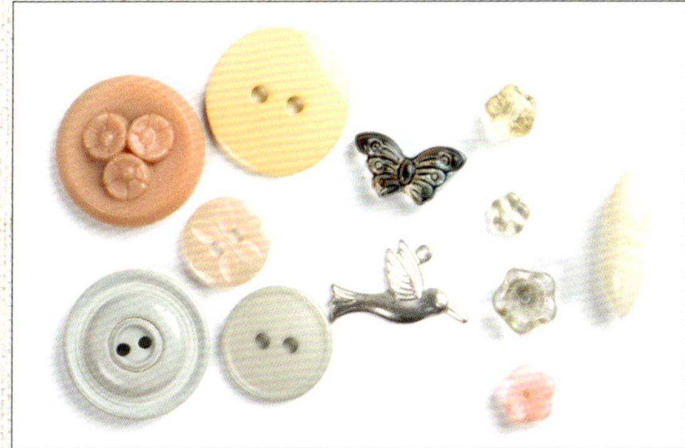

Embellishments (not all shown)

Perle cotton

Seed beads

Materials

FABRICS

Fa, Fb, Fc, Fd: fat quarters

Fe: ⅛ yard (11.4cm)

Ff: ⅜ yard (34.3cm)

Fg: at least 4″ × 6″ (10.2 × 15.2cm)

Fh, Fi, Fj: at least 3″ × 9″ (7.6 × 22.9cm) of each

TRIMMINGS

Ra: ⅞″ (22mm) grosgrain ribbon 2 yards (1.9m)

Rb: ⅜″ (10mm) novelty print satin ribbon 2 yards (1.9m)

Rc: ⅜″ (10mm) satin ribbon 1½ yards (1.4m)

Rd: ⅛″ (3mm) satin ribbon 1½ yards (1.4m)

Re: ⅛″ (3mm) satin ribbon 1 yard (1m)

Rf: ¼″ (6mm) satin ribbon 1 yard (1m)

Rg: ¼″ (6mm) satin ribbon 1 yard (1m)

Rh: ⅛″ (3mm) grosgrain ribbon 1 yard (1m)

Ri: ⅜″ (10mm) rickrack trim 2 yards (1.9m)

Rj: ⅜″ (10mm) satin ribbon (not shown) 1 yard (1m)

EMBROIDERY MATERIALS IN A VARIETY OF COLORS

Perle cotton (pc): #8

Seed beads (sb): sizes 6°, 8°, 11°, 15°

EMBELLISHMENTS

Buttons

Ba: 1½″ (3.8cm) shank, 2

Bb: ⅞″ (2.2cm) toggle button, 6

Note: *The following buttons can be shank, 2-, or 4-hole:*

Bc: ¾″ (1.9cm), 12

Bd: ⅝″ (1.6cm), 11

Be: ½″ (1.2cm), 8

Glass Components

Butterfly bead 24 × 12mm: 9

Flower rondelle 12mm: 4

Flower rondelle 8mm: 17

Flower button 10mm: 9

Tulip 14 × 10mm: 3

Muslin: ¼ yard (22.9cm)

fast2fuse, heavy: 2″ × 8″ (5.1 × 20.3cm)

Shape-Flex: ¼ yard (22.9cm)

Batting: ⅜ yard (34.3cm)

Sewing and beading threads: neutral colors

Cutting Instructions

STRIP-PIECED BLOCK 1

Follow Steps 1–3 of Pieced Blocks (page 27) with the Strip-Pieced Block pattern (page 168). Refer to the Block-1 Strip-Pieced Block Diagram (page 111).

Cut 2 pieces each to make 2 blocks.

Pattern pieces 1, 7: *Fb*

Pattern piece 2: *Fa*

Pattern pieces 3, 5: *Fc*

Pattern pieces 4, 6: *Fd*

Pattern piece 8: *Fa*, 2¼″ x 6″ (5.7 × 15.2cm)

WEDGED CRUMBLES BLOCK 2

Follow Steps 1–3 of Crumbles Blocks (page 28) with the Wedged Crumbles Block pattern (page 172).

Cut 1 pattern piece each to make 1 block.

Pattern piece 1: *Fb, Fa, Fd*

Pattern piece 2: *Fd, Fa, Fb, Fc*

Pattern piece 3: *Fd, Fc, Fb*

BORDERS

Border 1: *Fe*, cut 2 rectangles 2½″ x 20½″ (6.4 × 52.1cm).

Border 2: *Fc*, cut 2 rectangles 3″ x 10″ (7.6 × 25.4cm).

EXTRAS

Fabric circles (page 31): *Fg*, cut 6 circles 2″ (5.1cm) diameter.

fast2fuse: Cut 6 circles 1¼″ (3.2cm) diameter.

Batting: Cut 6 circles 1⅛″ (2.9cm) diameter.

Fabric yo-yos (page 31): *Fh, Fi, Fj*, cut 3 circles 2⅛″ (5.4cm) diameter from each to make 9.

ADDITIONAL PIECES

Muslin: Cut 3 squares 7″ x 7″ (17.8 × 17.8cm).

Backing: *Ff*, cut 1 rectangle 11″ x 25½″ (27.9 × 64.8cm).

Batting: Cut 1 rectangle 10″ x 25½″ (25.4 × 64.8 cm).

Ribbon binding: *Ra, Rb*, cut 2 each 25½″ (64.8cm).

Binding: *Fb*, cut 2 rectangles 3″ x 11″ (7.6 × 27.9cm).

SEWING THE BLOCKS AND EXTRAS

Block 1

1. Follow the directions for Foundation Piecing (page 27), using the pattern pieces and muslin squares. Make 2 blocks. Trim the blocks to 6″ x 6″ (15.2 × 15.2cm).

2. Stitch pattern piece 8 to the right-hand side of each block.

Block 2

1. Follow Steps 4–5 of the Crumbles Blocks (page 28), using the pattern pieces and muslin squares. Make 1 block and trim to 6″ x 6″ (15.2 × 15.2cm).

2. Follow Step 6, with *Rc* over the raw edges of Seam 1 and *Rd* over Seam 2.

Extras

1. Stitch 6 fabric circles (page 31).

2. Stitch 9 fabric yo-yos (page 31).

Option: *28 additional fabric yo-yos can be added to ribbon binding.*

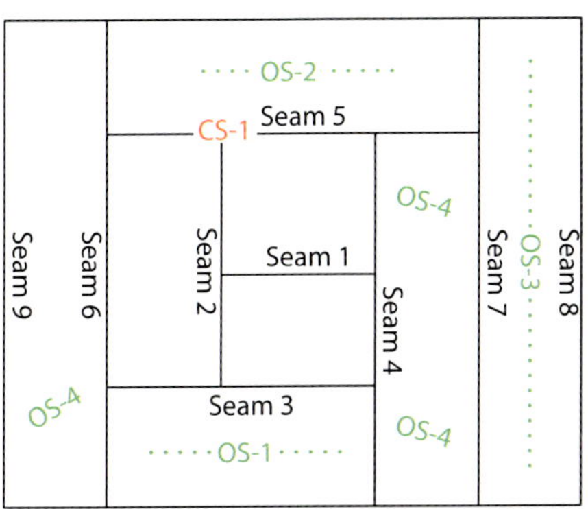

Block 1 Strip-Pieced Block Diagram (In diagram, CS is corner section, OS is open space)

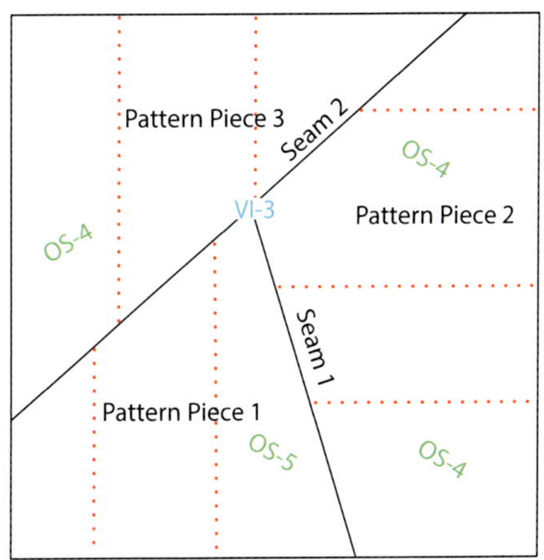

Block 2 Wedged Crumbles Block Diagram (In diagram, OS is open space, VI is vignette intersection)

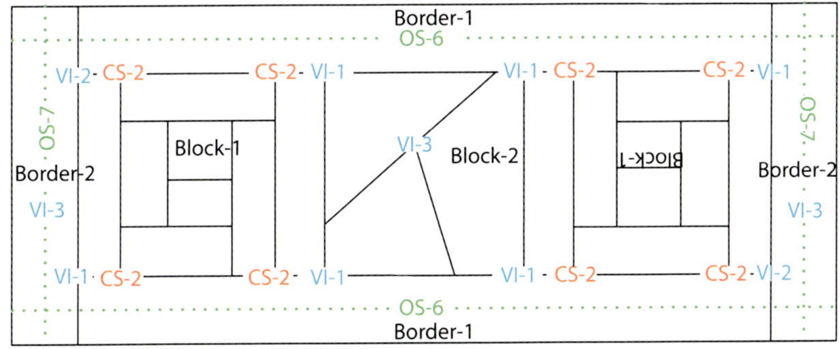

Strip-Pieced and Wedged Crumbles Blocks Table Runner Blueprints (In diagram, CS is corner section, OS is open space, VI is vignette intersection)

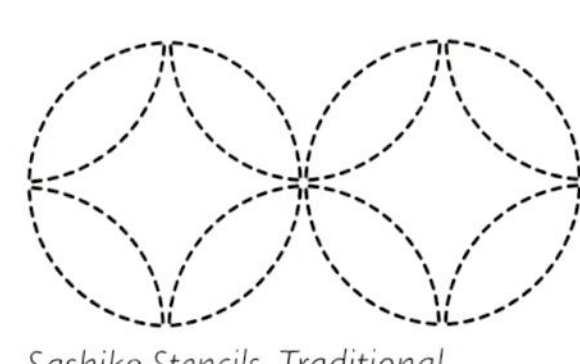

Sashiko Stencils, Traditional Collection, Seven Treasures Variation Sashiko pattern

BASE DESIGN DETAILS

Refer to Basic Base Instructions (page 36).

1. Stitch the blocks together in this order: **Block 1, Block 2, Block 1** (flipped 180°).

2. Follow **Option C** under Base Design Options (page 36) using the rectangle of batting.

3. Follow Step 2 of the Finished Seam Option (page 37), using the 2 **Border 1** rectangles.

4. Follow Step 3, using the 2 **Border 2** rectangles.

5. Staystitch around the outer edges of the base.

Trimmings and Bits and Pieces

Refer to the block diagrams and the Strip-Pieced and Wedged Crumbles Blocks Table Runner Blueprints (page 111).

1. Cut the ribbon to fit the seam or section of the **base**.

Note: *The raw edge of a ribbon is covered by the following length of ribbon or a fabric circle.*

- *Seam 9: Re starting at the edge of* **Block 1,** *continuing over one* **Border 1**.
- *Seam 6: Rh across the width of the base.*
- *Seam 7: Rf across the width of the base.*
- *Seam 5: Rj starting at the edge of* **Border 2,** *continuing over* **Block 1** *and sashing, stopping at seam 8 of* **Block 1**.
- *Seam 8: Rg across the width of the base.*
- *Border 2* open space **6:** *Rc and Rd.*
- *Border 1* open space **6:** *Hand stitch Ri.*

Option: *Hand quilt sections of the base with the pattern (page 111), using perle cotton #12.*

2. Stitch 1 fabric circle in each vignette intersection **1**.

3. Stitch a group of 3 fabric yo-yos in each vignette intersection **3**.

4. Follow the directions for Embroidery and Embellishment Design (below), then Finishing (below).

FINISHING

Refer to the Strip-Pieced and Wedged Crumbles Blocks Table Runner Blueprints (page 111).

1. Stitch 1 25½″ (64.8cm) length each of *Ra* and *Rb* onto the right side of the backing rectangle, overlapping the raw edge ¼″ (6mm).

2. Place the completed base onto the wrong side of the backing rectangle.

3. Fold the backing over to the front of the base. Pin the ribbon in place, covering the vertical edges. Hand stitch in place.

4. Follow the directions for Bound Edge Assembly (page 41), using the 3″ x 11″ (7.6 × 27.9cm) rectangles.

Option: *Hand stitch additional fabric yo-yos to ribbon binding.*

EMBROIDERY AND EMBELLISHMENT DESIGN

Refer to the block diagrams and Strip-Pieced and Wedged Crumbles Blocks Table Runner Blueprints (page 111).

Block 1

Seam 1: border row, blanket stitch stalk; decorative stitches, lazy daisy 6-petal flower, lazy daisy stitch; embellishment stitches, single bead stitch with size 11° sb, stacked bead stitch with 12mm flower rondelle and 1 size 11° sb.

Seam 2: border row, fern stitch modern; decorative stitches, alternate between lazy daisy stitch, straight stitch, and 3-wrap French knot stitch; embellishment stitch, stacked bead stitch with 1 size 8° and 15° sb; corner section **1:** *Bd.*

Seam 3: border row, chevron stitch, straight stitch; decorative stitches, alternate between fly stitch double and 3-wrap French knot stitch; detail stitch, 3-wrap French knot stitch; embellishment stitch, stacked bead stitch with 1 size 8° and 15° sb; open space **1:** 2 *Bd*.

Seam 4: border row, feather stitch; decorative stitches, alternate between 2 lazy daisy stitches, 3-wrap French knot stitch, and 3-wrap French knot stitch; embellishment stitch, stacked bead stitch with 1 size 8° and 15° sb.

Seam 5: *Rj*; border row, fly stitch offset; decorative stitch lazy daisy stitch; detail stitch, 3-wrap French knot stitch; embellishment stitch, stacked bead stitch with 1 size 8° and 15° sb; open space **2:** 1 *Bc* and 2 *Bd*.

Seam 6: *Rh*, border row, herringbone stitch, straight stitch; detail stitch, 3-wrap French knot stitch; embellishment stitch, stacked bead stitch with 1 size 8° and 15° sb.

Seam 7: *Rf*, border row, fly stitch twisted.

Seam 8: *Rg*, border row, cross stitch row; detail stitch, straight stitch; open space **3:** backstitch and straight stitch vine, 8-petal lazy daisy stitch flower, pistil stitch, 3-wrap French knot stitch, 3 *Bd*.

Seam 9: *Re*, border row, blanket and chain stitches; detail stitch, 3-wrap French knot stitch.

Block-2

Seam 1: *Rc*, *Rd* border row, chain stitch.

Seam 2: *Rc*, *Rd* border row, chain stitch.

Pattern Piece 1: border row, snail trail stitch; decorative stitch, fly stitch; detail stitch, 3-wrap French knot stitch; embellishment stitch, stacked bead stitch with 1 size 8° and 15° sb; border row: feather stitch straight center; decorative stitches, 3 chain stitch, fly stitch with lazy daisy stitch; detail stitch, 3-wrap French knot stitch; embellishment stitch, stacked bead stitch with 12mm flower rondelle and 1 size 11° sb.

Pattern Piece 2: border row, blanket stitch angled; decorative stitch, fly stitch with loop; detail stitch, 3-wrap French knot stitch; border row: herringbone long arm stitch, straight stitch; decorative stitches, fly stitch, lazy daisy knot tip; embellishment stitch, stacked bead stitch with 8mm flower rondelle and 1 size 11° sb; border row: cretan and chain stitches; decorative stitch, 5-petal straight stitch flower; embellishment stitches, single bead stitch with size 11° sb, stacked bead stitch with 1 size 8° and 15° sb.

Pattern Piece 3: border row, blanket stitch up and down, backstitch; detail stitches, alternate between 3-wrap French knot stitch and stacked bead stitch with 1 size 8° and 15° sb; border row: chain stitch zigzag; decorative stitch, looped tendril stitch; detail stitch, straight stitch; embellishment stitch, stacked bead stitch with 1 size 8° and 15° sb.

Additional Sections

Corner section **2:** 1 *Be*; open space **4:** single bead stitch, butterfly bead; open space **5:** *Bd*; vignette intersection **1:** fabric circles, straight stitch, *Bb*, *Bc* (in center only); vignette intersection **2:** *Ba*; vignette intersection **3:** fabric yo-yos, single bead stitch size 6° sb, picot tip stitch (beaded) with tulip bead and 15° sb, 3 glass flower buttons.

Border 1: Seam; border row: chain stitch; open space **7:** border row: fly stitch side by side; detail stitches, 3-wrap French knot stitch, stacked bead stitch with 1 size 6° and 11° sb.

Border 2: Border row: chain stitch, blanket stitch, alternate between even straight and looped; detail stitches, alternate between 3-wrap French knot stitch and stacked bead stitch with 1 size 6° and 11° sb.

Wedge-Pieced Block Wall Hanging

For this project, two different four-fabric color combinations are used for the Wedge-Pieced Blocks (page 25) and lined prairie points (page 30). The foundation strip-pieced border (page 39), sashing, and binding are made from additional fabrics. Rickrack trim, grosgrain ribbon, and a variety of buttons add design interest.

Rainbow Gala, 21″ x 21″ (53.3 × 53.3cm)

Creative Option To give this project a different look, make all four blocks using the seven-fabric combination, or substitute some or all of the buttons with ribbon buttons (page 32), large beads, or charms.

SWATCHES

Fabrics

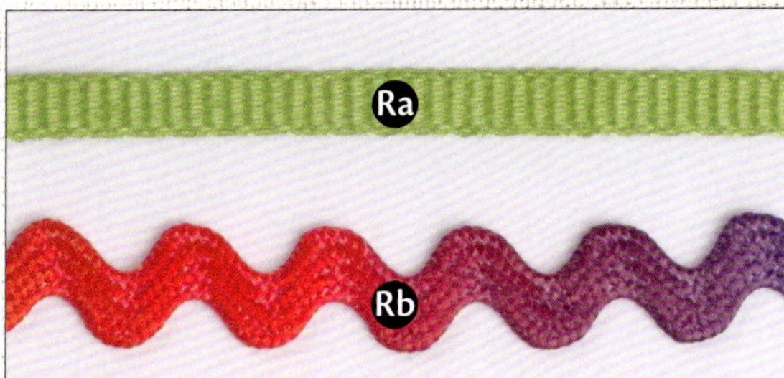

Trimmings

Lined prairie points

Beads and embellishments

Perle cotton

Buttons (not all shown)

Materials

FABRICS

Fa, Fb, Fc, Fd, Fe, Ff, Fg, Fh: ¼ yard (22.9cm) each

Fi: ¾ yard (68.6cm)

Fj: 1 yard (1m)

TRIMMINGS

Ra: rickrack trim 3 yard (2.8m)

Rb: ⅛" (3mm) grosgrain ribbon, 2 yard (1.9m)

EMBROIDERY MATERIALS AND EMBELLISHMENTS IN A VARIETY OF COLORS

Perle cotton (pc): #8, #12

Seed beads (sb): sizes 6°, 11°

Buttons: 127 ranging from ½"–1¼" (1.2 × 3.2cm)

Plastic 12mm flower rondelle: 132

Muslin: ¼ yard (22.9cm)

Shape-Flex: ¾ yard (68.6cm)

Batting: ¾ yard (68.6cm)

Sewing and beading threads: neutral colors

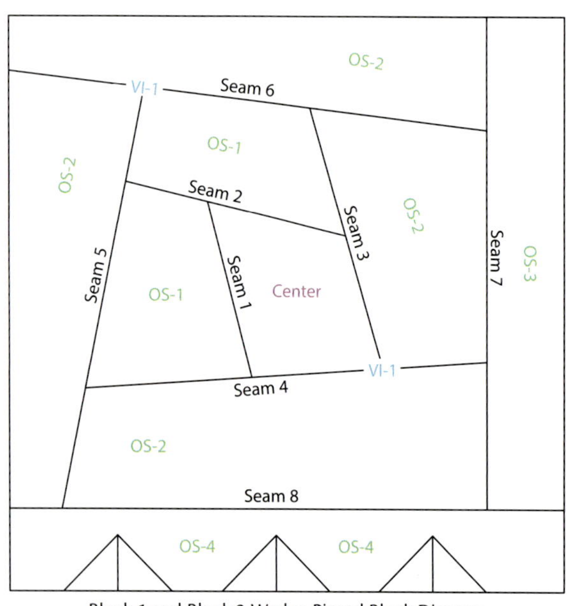

Block 1 and Block 2 Wedge-Pieced Block Diagram
(In diagram, OS is open space, VI is vignette intersection)

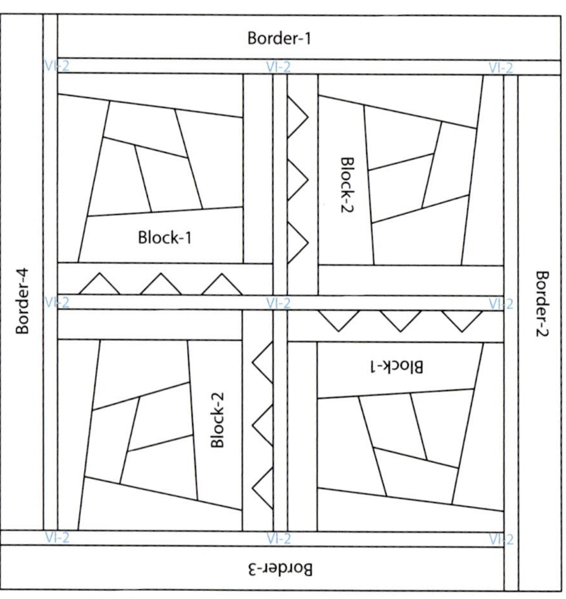

Wedge-Pieced Block Wall Hanging Blueprints
(In diagram, VI is vignette intersection)

Cutting Instructions

BLOCKS

Follow Steps 1–3 of Pieced Blocks (page 27) with the Wedge-Pieced Block pattern (page 169). Refer to the Wedge-Pieced Block Diagram (page 116).

Cut 2 pieces from each pattern piece, and the additional pieces listed in the 2 different color combinations, to make a total of 4 blocks.

Block 1

Pattern piece 1: *Fa*

Pattern pieces 2 and 3: *Fb*

Pattern pieces 4 and 5: *Fd*

Pattern pieces 6 and 7: *Fc*

Pattern piece 8: *Fb*, 2″ x 6″ (5.1 × 15.2cm)

Pattern piece 9: *Fg*, 2″ x 7½″ (5.1 × 19.1cm)

Block 2

Pattern piece 1: *Fg*

Pattern pieces 2 and 3: *Fh*

Pattern pieces 4 and 5: *Ff*

Pattern pieces 6 and 7: *Fe*

Pattern piece 8: *Fh*, 2″ x 6″ (5.1 × 15.2cm)

Pattern piece 9: *Fa*, 2″ x 7½″ (5.1 × 19.1cm)

FOUNDATION-PIECED BORDER

Cut 2 rectangles, each 7″ (17.8cm) x the lengths below.

1¼″ (3.2cm): *Fb, Fd2, Fh*

1½″ (3.8cm): *Fa2, Fe*

1¾″ (4.4cm): *Fa1, Ff, Fg*

2″ (5.1cm): *Fd1*

2½″ (6.4cm): *Fc*

Note: *Or you could create your own pattern to equal 18″ (45.7cm).*

LINED PRAIRIE POINTS

Cut 1 rectangle from each fabric 1¼″ x 40″ (3.2 × 101.6cm): *Fe, Fa*

Cut 1 rectangle from each fabric 2″ x 40″ (5.1 × 101.6cm): *Fd, Fe*

1. Stitch *Fe* and *Fd* together down the length of the rectangles. Press the seam to one side. Repeat for *Fa* and *Fe*.

2. Follow the directions for lined prairie points (page 30) and cut 6 from each rectangle.

ADDITIONAL PIECES

Muslin

Cut 4 squares 7″ x 7″ (17.8 × 17.8cm).

Cut 2 rectangles 7″ x 18″ (17.8 × 45.7cm).

Shape-Flex

Cut 4 squares 7½″ x 7½″ (19.1 × 19.1cm).

Cut 2 rectangles 3″ x 18″ (7.6 × 45.7cm).

Sashing: *Fj*, cut 2 rectangles 1½″ x 15″ (3.8 × 38.1cm).

Sashing: *Fj*, cut 4 rectangles 1½″ x 18″ (3.8 × 45.7cm).

Backing: *Fi*, cut 1 square 21″ x 21″ (53.3 × 53.3cm).

Hanging sleeve: *Fi*, cut 1 rectangle 4″ x 18″ (10.2 × 45.7cm).

Binding vertical seams: *Fj*, cut 2 rectangles 3″ x 21″ (7.6 × 53.3cm).

Binding horizontal seams: *Fj*, cut 2 rectangles 3″ x 22″ (7.6 × 55.9cm).

Batting: 21″ x 21″ (53.3 × 53.3cm)

SEWING THE BLOCKS AND EXTRAS

1. Follow the directions for Foundation Piecing (page 27), using the pattern pieces and muslin squares. Make 4 blocks. Trim the blocks to 6″ x 6″ (15.2 × 15.2cm).

2. Following the Block 1 and Block 2 Wedge-Pieced Block Diagram (page 116), stitch pattern pieces 8 and 9 to each block.

3. Stabilize each block with Shape-Flex.

4. Cut the trim to fit the seam; hand stitch in place.

Note: *The raw edge of a trim is covered by the following length.*

Seam 7: *Ra*

Seam 8: *Rb*

5. Hand stitch the lined prairie points on pattern piece 9, alternating the color combinations.

6. Staystitch around the outer edges of each block.

7. See Quilting Option (at right), then follow the directions for Embroidery and Embellishment Design (below).

Foundation-Pieced Border

1. Stitch each 7″ x 18″ (17.8 × 45.7cm) piece of muslin with this pattern: *Fa1, Fb, Fc, Fd1, Fe, Ff, Fg, Fh, Fa2, Fb, Fc, Fd2, Fe, Ff, Fg.*

2. Cut 2 lengths 3″ x 18″ (7.6 × 45.7cm) from each group.

3. Stabilize each length with Shape-Flex.

4. Cut the trim to fit the seam; hand stitch in place: on *Fb: Ra*, on *Ff: Rb.*

5. See Quilting Option below, then follow the directions for Embroidery and Embellishment Design (below).

QUILTING OPTION

Blocks: Stitch a row of quilted stitches through each fabric section except the **center** with perle cotton #12.

Borders: Stitch randomly across the vertical sections of the border with perle cotton #12.

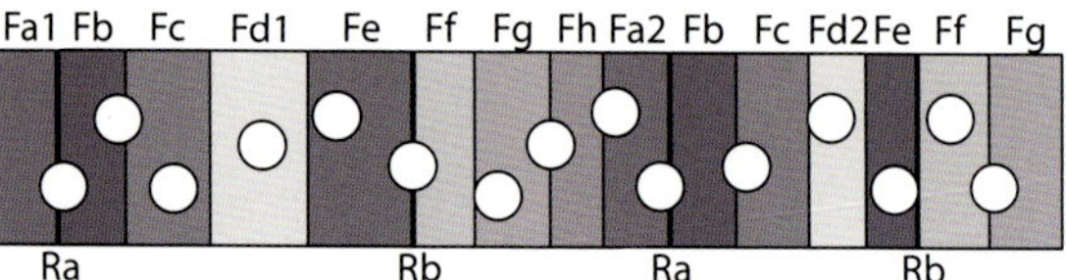

Strip-Pieced Border Diagram

Button embroidery

EMBROIDERY AND EMBELLISHMENT DESIGN

Refer to the Block 1 and Block 2 Wedge-Pieced Block Diagram (page 116) and Wedge-Pieced Block Wall Hanging Blueprints (page 116).

Block 1

Center: cross and straight stitch, group of 3-wrap French knot stitches (fill in stitches as desired).

Seam 1: border row, chain stitch zigzag; decorative stitches, alternate between 3 pistil stitches, 2 straight stitches, and stacked bead stitch with 1 size 6° and 11° sb; detail stitch, 3-wrap French knot stitch.

Seam 2: border row, crossed lazy daisy stitch row; detail stitches, 3-wrap French knot stitch, stacked bead stitch with size 6° and 11° sb.

Seam 3: border row, blanket stitch; decorative stitches, alternate between barb stitch, lazy daisy stitch, and lazy daisy stitch; detail stitch, 3-wrap French knot stitch; embellishment stitch, stacked bead stitch with 1 size 6° and 11° sb.

Seam 4: border row, cretan stitch; decorative stitches, alternate between fly stitch stacked, 2 3-wrap French knot stitch, and fly stitch; detail stitch, lazy daisy stitch; embellishment stitch, stacked bead stitch with 1 size 6° and 11° sb.

Seam 5: border row, feather stitch double; decorative stitches, chain stitch vine, 3 3-wrap French knot stitches, alternate between 3 lazy daisy stitches, straight stitches, and lazy daisy with French knot stitch, fly stitch; detail stitch, 3-wrap French knot stitch; embellishment stitch, stacked bead stitch with 1 size 6° and 11° sb.

Seam 6: border row, herringbone stitch, straight stitch; decorative stitches, alternate between fly stitch with loop with 2 3-wrap French knot stitches, and 2 lazy daisy stitches, 1 pistil stitch; embellishment stitch, stacked bead stitch with 1 size 6° and 11° sb.

Seam 7: *Ra*; border row, fly stitch; detail stitch, 3-wrap French knot stitch.

Seam 8: *Rb*; border row, straight stitch; detail stitch, 3-wrap French knot stitch; embellishment stitch, stacked bead stitch with 1 size 6° and 11° sb.

Block 2

Center: running stitch, 3-wrap French knot stitch (fill in stitches as desired).

Seam 1: border row, chain stitch zigzag; decorative stitches, alternate between fly stitch offset stacked, lazy daisy stitch, and stacked bead stitch with 1 size 6° and 11° sb; detail stitch, 3-wrap French knot stitch.

Seam 2: border row, cross stitch row, straight stitch; detail stitches, alternate between 3-wrap French knot stitch and stacked bead stitch with 1 size 6° and 11° sb.

Seam 3: border row, blanket stitch, fly stitch; decorative stitches, alternate between lazy daisy tulip stitch, fly stitch, 3-wrap French knot stitch, and straight stitches, stacked bead stitch with 1 size 6° and 11° sb.

Seam 4: border row, cretan stitch; decorative stitches, alternate between looped tendril stitch, 2 lazy daisy stitches, 2 straight stitches, and 6 petal French knot flower, fly stitch, 3-wrap French knot stitch; embellishment stitch, stacked bead stitch with size 1 6° and 11° sb.

Seam 5: border row, feather stitch double; decorative stitches, alternate between 3 lazy daisy piggyback stitches, 2 pistil stitches, 2 3-wrap French knot stitches, and lazy daisy stitch, straight stitch; embellishment stitch, stacked bead stitch with 1 size 6° and 11° sb.

Seam 6: border row, herringbone stitch, straight stitch; detail stitches, alternate between fly stitch offset and fly stitch with lazy daisy stitch; detail stitch, 3-wrap French knot stitch; embellishment stitch, stacked bead stitch with 1 size 6° and 11° sb.

Seam 7, see Block 1.

Seam 8, see Block 1.

Additional Sections

Open space **1:** 2 stacked bead stitches with 12mm flower rondelle and 1 size 11° sb; open space **2:** 3 stacked bead stitches with 12mm flower rondelle and 1 size 11° sb; open space **3:** 2 buttons, 3-wrap French knot stitch, 3 stacked bead stitches with 12mm flower rondelle and 1 size 11° sb; open space **4:** 1 button, 3-wrap French knot stitch; vignette intersection **1:** 3 buttons, spray of straight stitches.

Strip-Pieced Borders

Refer to Strip-Pieced Border Diagram (page 118).

1. Stitch straight stitches over the seams with *Ra* or *Rb*.

2. Stitch the chain stitch down each remaining seam.

3. Stitch buttons in place.

4. Embroider a couched stitch from each button, alternating from one edge to the other.

5. See Embroidered Buttons (page 83), embroidering with these stitches: fly and straight stitches, 3-wrap French knot stitch, barb and straight stitches, blanket stitch rows, lazy daisy stitch and 3-wrap French knot stitch, fly and straight stitches, chain stitch and 3-wrap French knot stitch, bellflower and lazy daisy stitches, lazy daisy piggyback stitch and 3-wrap French knot stitch, pistil and straight stitches and 3-wrap French knot stitch, fly stitch stacked and straight stitch, bellflower stitch and 3-wrap French knot stitch, straight stitch and 3-wrap French knot stitch, lazy daisy stitch and 3-wrap French knot stitch, straight and lazy daisy stitches and 3-wrap French knot stitch.

6. Stitch 1 stacked bead stitch with 12mm flower rondelle and 1 size 11° sb around each button.

ASSEMBLY AND FINISHING

Refer to Basic Base Instructions (page 36) and the Wedge-Pieced Block Wall Hanging Blueprints (page 116).

1. Follow **Option D** under Base Design Options (page 36), with the 21″ x 21″ (53.3 × 53.3cm) batting. Place the blocks in this order: **Block 1**, rotate **Block 2** 90° to the right, rotate the second **Block 1** 90° to the left, rotate the second **Block 2** 180°.

2. See Folded Edge Fabric Strip Sashing (page 37), using *Fj*, 1½″ x 15″ (3.8 × 38.1cm) rectangles, first on the vertical seam, then the horizontal seam.

3. Stitch *Ra* down each seam; embroider with straight stitches.

4. Starting with **Border 1**, place the strip-pieced borders flush with the blocks, referring to the **Option** under Disappearing Seam Border (page 38).

5. Repeat Step 2, using *Fj*, 1½″ x 18″ (3.8 × 45.7cm) rectangles for each border.

6. Embroider the chain stitch along both edges.

7. Vignette intersection **2:** Stitch 3 buttons.

8. Stitch the hanging sleeve (page 41) 4″ x 18″ (10.2 × 45.7cm) to the backing, 21″ x 21″ (53.3 × 53.3cm).

9. Follow the directions for the Bound Edge Assembly (page 41) with backing:

Vertical seams: 3″ x 21″ (7.6 × 53.3cm)

Horizontal seams: 3″ x 22″ (7.6 × 55.9cm)

Wedge-Pieced and Crazed Crumbles Blocks Table Covering

For this wall hanging, the the seven-fabric combination Wedge-Piece Block (page 25) is combined with the reduced-in-size Crazed Crumbles Block (page 26). Additional fabrics were used for the foundation-pieced border (page 39), mock prairie points (page 30), fabric circles (page 31), and fabric yo-yos (page 31). Grosgrain ribbon, buttons, beads, and sequins were used for embellishments.

Kaleidoscope, 15″ x 15″ (38.1 × 38.1cm)

Creative Option When working with space dyed, batiks, or variegated components, take a serendipitous approach and use the colors as they come rather than searching for a perfect match.

SWATCHES

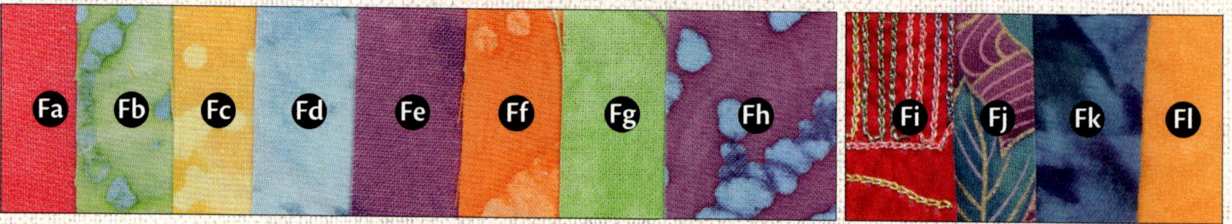

Fabrics

Trimmings

Beads

Buttons and sequins (not all shown)

1. Fabric circle **2.** Fabric yo-yos

Materials

FABRICS

Fa, Fb, Fc, Fd, Fe, Ff, Fg: ¼ yard (22.9cm) each

Fh: ¾ yard (68.6cm)

Fi: at least 3″ × 11″ (7.6 × 27.9cm)

Fj: at least 3″ × 25″ (7.6 × 63.5cm)

Fk: at least 3″ × 23″ (7.6 × 58.4cm)

Fl: at least 3″ × 18″ (7.6 × 45.7cm)

TRIMMINGS

Ra: ⅜″ (10mm) grosgrain ribbon, 1½ yards (1.4m)

Rb: ⅛″ (3mm) grosgrain ribbon, 2 yards (1.9m)

Rc: ¼″ (6mm) grosgrain ribbon, 2½ yards (2.3m)

EMBROIDERY MATERIALS AND EMBELLISHMENTS

Seed beads (sb): sizes 6°, 8°, 11°, 15°

Buttons: 13 ranging from ½″–1¼″ (1.2–3.2cm)

Sequins: a variety of shapes and sizes

Muslin: 7″ x 7″ (17.8 × 17.8cm)

fast2fuse, heavy: 2″ × 7″ (5.1 × 17.8cm)

Shape-Flex: ½ yard (45.7cm)

Batting: ⅝ yard (57.2cm)

Sewing and beading threads: neutral colors

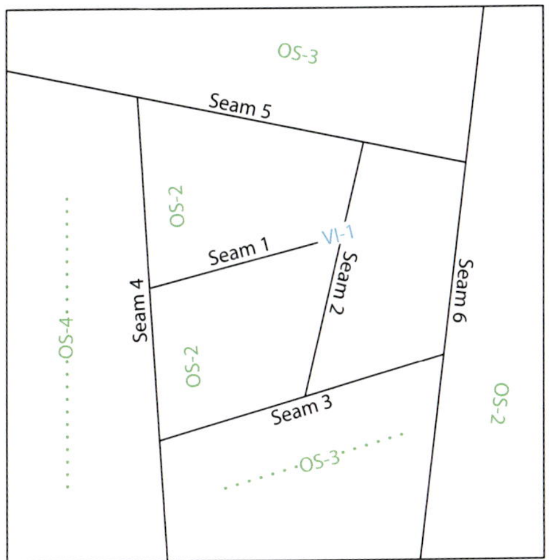

Block 1 Wedge-Pieced Block Diagram
(In diagram, OS is open space, VI is vignette intersection)

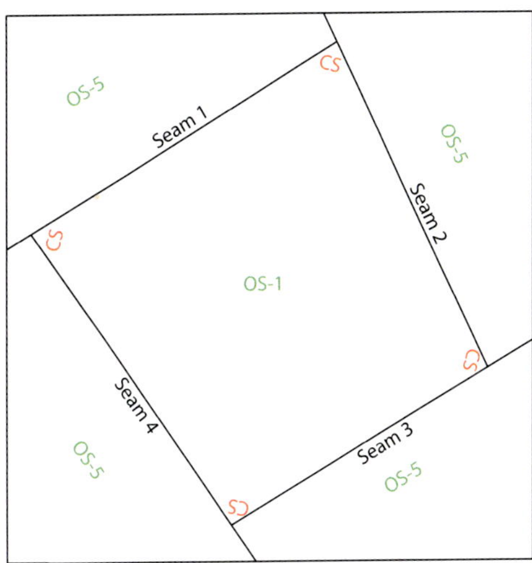

Block 2 A and B Crazed Crumbles Block Diagram
(In diagram, CS is corner section, OS is open space)

Cutting Instructions

BLOCKS

Follow Steps 1–3 of Pieced Blocks (page 27). Refer to the block diagrams.

Wedge-Pieced Block 1

Wedge-Pieced Block pattern (page 169). Cut 1 piece from each pattern piece to make 1 block.

Pattern piece 1: *Fa*

Pattern piece 2: *Fb*

Pattern piece 3: *Fc*

Pattern piece 4: *Fd*

Pattern piece 5: *Fe*

Pattern piece 6: *Ff*

Pattern piece 7: *Fg*

Crazed Crumbles Block 2

Reduce the Crazed Crumbles Block pattern (page 173) to **50%**: *disregard the crumble-pieced lines.*

Block 2A Color A: Cut 3 pieces from each pattern piece to make 3 blocks.

Pattern piece 1: *Fe*

Pattern piece 2: *Ff*

Pattern piece 3: *Fb*

Pattern piece 4: *Fa*

Pattern piece 5: *Fc*

Block 2B Color B: Cut 2 pieces from each pattern piece to make 2 blocks.

Pattern piece 1: *Fa*

Pattern piece 2: *Fd*

Pattern piece 3: *Fc*

Pattern piece 4: *Fg*

Pattern piece 5: *Ff*

MOCK PRAIRIE POINT BORDERS

Borders: Cut 1 rectangle each from *Fh*.

Border 1: 2½″ x 8¾″ (6.4 × 22.2cm)

Border 2: 2½″ x 10¾″ (6.4 × 27.3cm)

Border 3: 2¾″ x 10¾″ (7 × 27.3cm)

Border 4: 2¾″ x 13″ (7 × 33cm)

Mock prairie points (page 30): Cut 2 rectangles 2¾″ x 40″ (7 × 101.6cm) from *Fb*; make 12.

FOUNDATION STRIP-PIECED BORDER

Cut each rectangle the width below x 7″ (17.8cm) long.

1¼″ (3.2cm): *Ff*, cut 3.

1½″ (3.8cm): *Fa2* cut 2; *Fb*, cut 2.

1¾″ (4.4cm): *Fe*, cut 3, *Fd*, cut 3.

2″ (5.1cm): *Fa1*, cut 2; *Fc1*, cut 2; *Fg*, cut 3.

2¼″ (5.7cm): *Fc2*, cut 2.

2½″ (6.4cm): *Fh1*, cut 2.

3″ (7.6cm): *Fh2*, cut 2.

EXTRAS

Fabric circles (page 31): *Fi*, cut 5 circles 2″ (5.1cm) diameter.

fast2fuse: Cut 5 circles 1¼″ (3.2cm) diameter.

Batting: Cut 5 circles 1⅛″ (2.9cm) diameter.

Fabric yo-yos (page 31): *Fj*, cut 11, *Fk*, cut 10, *Fl*, cut 8 circles 2⅛″ (5.4cm) diameter.

ADDITIONAL PIECES

Muslin

Cut 1 square 7″ x 7″ (17.8 × 17.8cm).

Cut 1 rectangle 7″ x 13″ (17.8 × 33cm).

Cut 1 rectangle 7″ x 18″ (17.8 × 45.7cm).

Shape-Flex: Cut 1 square 15″ × 15″ (38.1 × 38.1cm).

Backing: *Fh*, cut 1 square 15″ x 15 ″ (38.1 × 38.1cm).

Batting: Cut 1 square 15″ x 15″ (38.1 × 38.1cm).

SEWING THE BLOCKS

1. Block 1: Follow the directions for Foundation Piecing (page 27), using the pattern pieces and muslin square. Make 1 block. Trim the block to 6″ x 6″ (15.2 × 15.2cm).

2. Block 2: Follow the directions for the Disappearing Seam (page 28), using the pattern pieces. Make 5 blocks. Trim the blocks to 3¼″ x 3¼″ (8.3 × 8.3cm).

FOUNDATION STRIP-PIECED BORDER

See Making Multiple Pieced Borders (page 39).

1. Stitch the 7″ x 13″ (17.8 × 33cm) piece of muslin with this pattern: *Fa1, Fb, Fh1, Fc1, Fg, Fe, Fd, Ff, Fa2, Fc2, Fh2.*

2. **Border 5:** Cut 2 lengths 3″ x 13″ (7.6 × 33cm) for the vertical borders.

3. Follow Step 1 with the 7″ x 18″ (17.8 × 45.7cm) piece of muslin, adding *Fg, Fe, Fd, Ff.*

4. **Border 6:** Cut 2 lengths 3″ x 18″ (7.6 × 45.7cm) for the horizontal borders.

BASE DESIGN DETAILS

Refer to Basic Base Instructions (page 36), the block diagrams (page 123), and the Wedge-Pieced Block and Crazed Crumbles Block Table Covering Blueprints (page 126).

Note: Block 2A *is flipped 180°,* **Block 2B** *is flipped 90° to the right.*

1. Stitch a vertical row with **Block 2A** and **Block 2B**.

2. Stitch this to the right vertical edge of **Block 1**.

3. Stitch a horizontal row with **Block 2A, Block 2B,** and **Block 2A**.

4. Stitch this to the bottom horizontal edge of **Block 1**.

5. Follow **Option D** under Base Design Options (page 36) with the batting square.

6. Follow Step 2 of the Finished Seam Option (page 37), stitching **Border 1, Border 2, Border 3**, and **Border 4** in place. This is now referred to as the **base**.

Option: *See Free-Form Machine Quilting (page 40).*

7. Pin and hand stitch the mock prairie points in place.

8. Cut the trim to fit the seam; hand stitch in place.

Note: *The raw edge of a trim is covered by the following length.*

Seams 1 and 2: *Rb*

Seams 3, 4, 5, and 6: *Ra* and *Rc*

9. Stitch 29 fabric yo-yos (page 31). Hand stitch 1 in each open space **1**.

10. Stitch 5 fabric circles (page 31). Hand stitch 1 in each vignette intersection **1.**

11. Pin and stitch the **Border 5** rectangles to the vertical edges of the **base**; follow the Finished Seam Option (page 37).

12. Stitch *Rb* on each **Border 5,** ½″ (1.2cm) from seam.

13. Repeat Step 1, with the **Border 6** rectangles on the horizontal edges of the **base**.

14. Follow Step 12, with *Rc* on each **Border 6**.

15. Hand stitch 1 fabric yo-yo on the seam, even with the center of each mock prairie point.

16. Follow the directions for Embroidery and Embellishment Design (page 126), then Finishing (page 126).

EMBROIDERY AND EMBELLISHMENT DESIGN

Refer to the block diagrams (page 123) and Wedge-Pieced and Crazed Crumbles Blocks Table Covering Blueprints (below).

Block 1

Vignette intersection 1: fabric circle; center: stacked bead stitch with sequin and size 11° sb; outer edge, stacked bead stitch with 1 size 6° and 11° sb.

Seam 1, Seam 2, and spokes: continuous bead stitch fancy, stacked bead stitch with 1 size 6° and 11° sb between spokes.

Seam 3: spine vine stitch (beaded).

Seam 4: cross stitch long arm row (beaded).

Seam 5: serpentine stitch v-shape (beaded), stacked bead stitch with size 6° and 11° sb.

Seam 6: feather stitch fancy (beaded), stacked bead stitch with 1 size 6° and 11° sb.

Open space 2: 1 button, grouped bead stitch with size 11° sb; open space 3: 3 buttons with grouped bead stitch with size 11° sb; open space 4: alternate between 3 flower with petite petals (beaded) and 2 buttons, grouped bead stitch with size 11° sb

Block 2

Seams 1, 2, 3, 4: outer edge, bead combination stitch with 2 size 11° sb and 1 size 8° sb; corner section: stacked bead stitch with sequin and 1 size 11° sb; inner edge, stacked bead stitch with 1 size 6° and 11° sb.

*Fabric yo-yos open space **1:** middle, single bead stitch size 6° sb; outer edge, single bead stitch size 11° sb; open space **5: Block 2A** floret stitch (beaded); **Block 2B** stacked bead stitch with sequin and 1 size 11° sb.

Base

Seams 3, 4, 5, and 6: *Ra* and *Rc*, alternate between stacked bead stitch with sequin and 1 size 11° sb and stacked bead stitch with size 6° and 11° sb; **Seams 1 and 2:** *Rb*, stacked bead stitch with size 6° and 11° sb; mock prairie points, outer edge bead combination stitch 2 size 11° sb and 1 size 8° sb, inner edge, stacked bead stitch with size 6° and 11° sb; seams between **Block 2A** and **Block 2B**, stacked bead stitch with sequin and 1 size 11° sb; fabric yo-yos, see *

FINISHING

1. Follow Step 1 of the Border-Edge Assembly (page 42) with the backing and Shape-Flex squares.

2. Continue with Steps 4–6 to finish the edges.

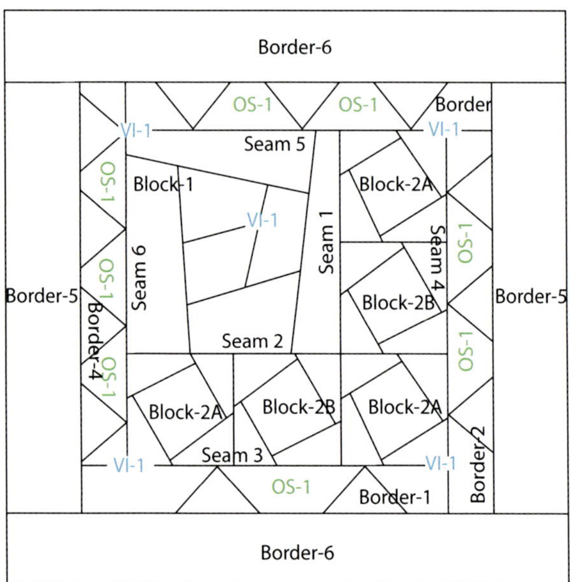

Wedge-Pieced and Crazed Crumbles Blocks Table Covering Blueprints (In diagram, OS is open space, VI is vignette intersection)

Crazy-Pieced Block Wall Hanging with Custom Hanger

The Crazy-Pieced Block (page 25) was made with the four-fabric combination, with three different fabrics used for the disappearing seam border (page 38) and binding. Additional fabric scraps were used for the mod hexies (page 29) and fabric yo-yos (page 31). Embellishments include ribbons, rickrack and rococo trims, buttons, and charms.

3 Bs: Birds, Butterflies, and Bees, 10″ x 10″ (25.4 × 25.4cm)

Creative Option Make additional fabric yo-yos, and stitch them to each corner.

SWATCHES

Fabrics

Perle cotton, cotton floss

Trimmings

1. Mod hexie **2.** Fabric yo-yo

Buttons

Embellishments

Materials

FABRICS

Fa, Fb, Fc, Fd, Fe, Ff: 6″ × 9″ (15.2 × 22.9cm)

Fg: ⅜ yard (34.3cm)

Additional scraps *Fh–Fl*: 6 pieces about 3″ × 3″ (7.6 × 7.6cm)

TRIMMINGS

Ra: ¼″ (6mm) novelty ribbon, 1 yard (1m)

Rb: ⅜″ (10mm) woven ribbon, 1 yard (1m)

RT: ½″ (12mm) rococo trim, 1 yard (1m)

EMBROIDERY MATERIALS IN A VARIETY OF COLORS

Perle cotton (pc): #8

Cotton floss (cf)

BUTTONS AND EMBELLISHMENTS

Novelty charms: birds, 3; butterflies, 3; bees, 3; bird's nest, 1

Dome snaps: 5

Hook eyes: 2

Novelty buttons: beehive, 1; pail, 1; bird house, 1; leaf, 2; bee, 4; flower, 6

Shank and 2-hole button, for spiders: 2 sets

Variety of 2- and 4-hole buttons: 23

Shank buttons: 4

Muslin: 7″ x 7″ (17.8 × 17.8cm)

Décor-Bond: 3″ × 9″ (7.6 × 22.9cm)

Batting: 11″ x 11″ (27.9 × 27.9cm)

fast2fuse, heavy: 10″ x 10″ (25.4 × 25.4cm)

Sewing and beading threads: neutral colors

Knitting needle or chopstick

Cutting Instructions

BLOCK

Follow Steps 1–3 of Pieced Blocks (page 27) with the Crazy-Pieced Block pattern (page 170). Refer to the Crazy-Pieced Block Diagram (page 130).

Cut 1 piece from each pattern to make 1 block.

Pattern piece 1: *Fa*

Pattern pieces 2 and 5: *Fb*

Pattern pieces 3 and 7: *Fd*

Pattern pieces 4 and 6: *Fc*

BORDERS

Border 1: *Fe*, cut 2 rectangles 2½″ x 8″ (5.7 × 20.3cm).

Border 2: *Ff*, cut 2 rectangles 2½″ x 8″ (5.7 × 20.3cm).

EXTRAS

Mod hexies (page 29): 3 from scraps

Décor-Bond: 3 of hexie pattern

Fabric yo-yos (page 31): 3 circles 2⅛″ (5.4cm) diameter, from scraps

Note: *12 additional yo-yos can be made for corners.*

ADDITIONAL PIECES

Muslin: Cut 1 square 7″ x 7″ (17.8 × 17.8cm).

Backing: *Fg*, cut 1 square 10″ x 10″ (25.4 × 25.4cm).

Binding vertical seams: *Fg*, cut 2 rectangles 3″ x 10″ (7.6 × 25.4cm).

Binding horizontal seams: *Fg*, cut 2 rectangles 3″ x 11″ (7.6 × 27.9cm).

SEWING THE BLOCK AND EXTRAS

1. Follow the directions for Foundation Piecing (page 27), using the pattern pieces and muslin squares. Make 1 block. Trim the block to 6″ x 6″ (15.2 × 15.2cm).

2. Stitch 3 mod hexies (page 29).

3. Stitch 3 fabric yo-yos (page 31).

Optional: *Make an additional 12 for the corners.*

BASE DESIGN DETAILS

Refer to Basic Base Instructions (page 36) and the Crazy-Pieced Block Wall Hanging Blueprints (below).

1. Follow **Option C** under Base Design Options (page 36) with the batting square.

2. Follow the directions for a Disappearing Seam Border (page 38), using the **Border 1** and **Border 2** rectangles.

3. Draw curved lines and follow the directions for Hand Quilting (page 40).

4. Cut the ribbon to fit the seam or section of the block; hand stitch in place.

Border 1: Stitch *Rb* in the open space **5**, from across **Border 2.** Stitch *Ra* on top of *Rb*.

Border 2: Stitch *RT* in the open space **6,** up to the seam of **Border 1**.

5. Hand stitch the group of fabric yo-yos in vignette intersection **6** position, covering the raw edges of *RT*.

6. Hand stitch the group of mod hexies in vignette intersection **8** position, covering the raw edges of *RT*.

7. Follow the directions for Embroidery and Embellishment Design (page 131), then Finishing (below).

FINISHING

1. Trim the base to 10″ x 10″ (25.4 × 25.4cm).

2. Follow the directions for the Bound Edge Assembly (page 41) with the 10″ x 10″ (25.4 × 25.4cm) backing:

Vertical seams: 3″ x 10″ (7.6 × 25.4cm)

Horizontal seams: 3″ x 11″ (7.6 × 27.9cm)

3. Follow the directions for the Custom Hanger (page 43), using *Rb* and the knitting needle or chopstick.

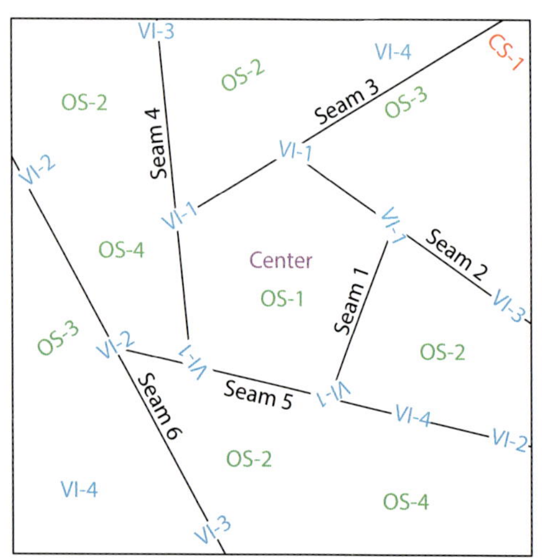

Crazy-Pieced Block Diagram (In diagram, CS is corner section, OS is open space, VI is vignette intersection)

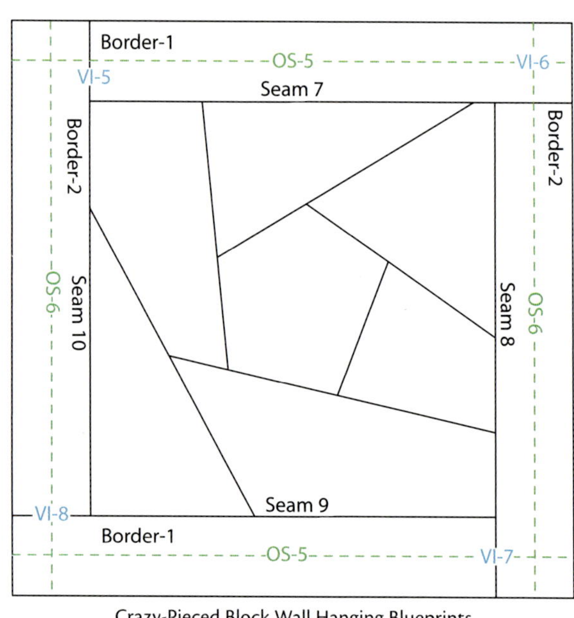

Crazy-Pieced Block Wall Hanging Blueprints (In diagram, OS is open space, VI is vignette intersection)

EMBROIDERY AND EMBELLISHMENT DESIGN

Refer to the Crazy-Pieced Block Diagram (page 130) and Crazy-Pieced Block Wall Hanging Blueprints (page 130).

Note: *Use 3 strands of cotton floss.*

Color Choices **The border row used for this project is variations of the blanket stitch, worked in one color of perle cotton. The decorative stitches and detail stitches are worked in several different color combinations for each seam.**

Block

Center: Fill in with running stitches.

Seam 1: border row, blanket stitch up and down pc, 2-wrap French knot stitch cf; decorative stitches and detail stitches, alternate between 2 lazy daisy stitches pc, 2 straight stitches pc, and fly stitch pc, 3-wrap French knot stitch cf.

Seam 2: border row, blanket stitch short-long pc, work the long stitch almost twice the length of the short stitch, long spokes; decorative stitches and detail stitches, lazy daisy stitch pc, 2-wrap French knot stitch cf; embellishment stitches, dome snap, short spokes, fly stitch pc, 2-wrap French knot stitch cf.

Seam 3: border row, blanket stitch alternate between straight and closed, straight spokes; decorative stitches and detail stitches, lazy daisy tulip stitch pc, fly stitch pc, lazy daisy stitch pc, 2-wrap French knot stitch cf, closed spokes, 3-wrap French knot stitch cf.

Seam 4: border row, blanket stitch angled pc, 3-wrap French knot stitch pc; decorative stitches and detail stitches, alternate between fly stitch offset pc, looped tendril stitch pc, and lazy daisy stitch pc, 2-wrap French knot stitch cf.

Seam 5: border row, blanket stitch crossed pc, straight stitches pc; detail stitches, alternate between 3-wrap French knot stitch cf and 2-wrap French knot stitch cf; open space between stitches, decorative stitches and detail stitches, alternate between lazy daisy 6-petal flower pc, 2-wrap French knot stitch cf, and cross stitch with straight stitches pc.

Seam 6: border row, blanket stitch pc; decorative stitches and detail stitches, alternate between 2 lazy daisy stitches pc, fly stitch pc, 3-wrap French knot stitch cf, and 1 lazy daisy stitch pc, 2-wrap French knot stitch cf.

Additional Areas

Corner section **1**: blanket stitch cobweb pc; open space **1**: novelty button; open space **2**: 2- or 4-hole button; open space **3**: button spider stitch; open space **4**: steampunk bug; vignette intersection **1**: 2- or 4-hole button; vignette intersection **2**: bird charm; vignette intersection **3**: bee charm; vignette intersection **4**: butterfly charm.

Borders

Seams 7 and 9: border row, blanket stitch pc; decorative stitch, 2 lazy daisy stitches pc every other tip; detail stitch, 3-wrap French knot stitch pc every tip.

Seams 8 and 10: border row, blanket stitch pc; decorative stitch, 2 lazy daisy stitches pc; detail stitch, 3-wrap French knot stitch pc.

Vignette intersection **5**: novelty button group, 1 house, 3 flowers, 1 bee button.

Vignette intersection **6**: fabric yo-yos, 1 bee button, 2 shank buttons, 1 2- or 4-hole button.

Vignette intersection **7**: novelty button group, 1 pail, 3 flowers, 1 bee button.

Vignette intersection **8**: mod hexies, 3 2-or 4-hole buttons, 2 shank buttons, 1 bird's nest charm, 1 bee button.

Border 1: Open space **5**: 3 2- or 4-hole buttons in the center of *Ra*.

Border 2: Open space **6**: 2 2-or 4-hole buttons, 1 leaf button in the center of the *RT*.

Crazy-Pieced and Stripped Crumbles Blocks Wall Hanging

The seven-fabric combination was used for the two Crazy-Pieced Blocks (page 25), and the five-fabric combination for the two Stripped Crumbles Blocks (page 26). Details include sashing (page 37), fabric yo-yos (page 31), and mod hexies (page 29). Rickrack, upholstery trim, buttons, and beads complement the design.

Lumber Jack Picnic, 16″ x 16″ (40.6 × 40.6cm)

Creative Option To change the pattern, rather than flipping the second vertical row, place the blocks in the original position, or stagger the blocks similar to the positioning of the blocks in *Time for Tea* (page 102).

SWATCHES

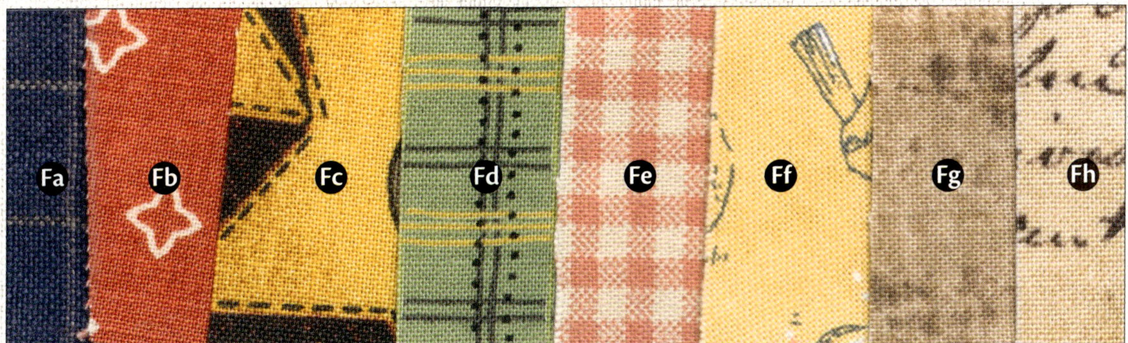

Fabrics

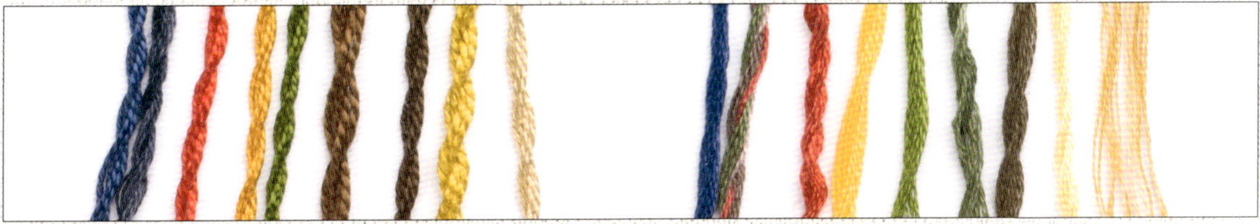

Perle cotton, cotton floss

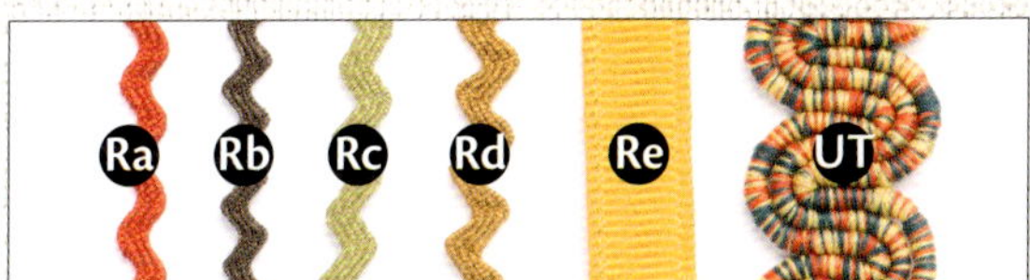

Trimmings

Seed beads

1. Mod hexie 2. Fabric yo-yo, 3. Ribbon button

Buttons

Materials

FABRICS

Fa, Fb, Fc, Fd, Fe, Ff, Fg: fat quarters

Fh: ½ yard (45.7cm)

TRIMMINGS

Ra: ⅛″ (3mm) rickrack, 1½ yards (1.4m)

Rb: ⅛″ (3mm) rickrack, ½ yard (45.7cm)

Rc: ⅛″ (3mm) rickrack, 1 yard (1m)

Rd: ⅛″ (3mm) rickrack, 2 yards (1.9m)

Re: ⅜″ (1cm) grosgrain ribbon, 1½ yards (1.4m)

UT: ¾″ (1.9cm) upholstery trim, 1 yard (1m)

EMBROIDERY MATERIALS IN A VARIETY OF COLORS

Perle cotton (pc): #8

Cotton floss (cf)

Seed beads (sb): sizes 6°, 8°, 11°, 15°

EMBELLISHMENTS

8mm beads: 100

Hooks: 6

Buttons

Novelty buttons: heart, 2; star, 1; snail, 4; bird house, 2; butterfly, 4; frog, 2; owl, 1; chicken, 1; rooster, 1; bug, 2

Variety of 2- or 4- hole buttons: 56

Shank buttons: 8

Muslin: ¼ yard (22.9cm)

Décor-Bond: about 6″ × 9″ (15.2 × 22.9cm)

Batting: ½ yard (45.7cm)

Sewing and beading threads: neutral colors

Cutting Instructions

BLOCKS

Follow Steps 1–3 of Pieced Blocks (page 27). Refer to the block diagrams.

Crazy-Pieced Block 1

Follow the Crazy-Pieced Block pattern (page 170), cutting 2 pieces from each pattern to make 2 blocks.

Pattern piece 1: *Fa*

Pattern piece 2: *Fb*

Pattern piece 3: *Fc*

Pattern piece 4: *Fd*

Pattern piece 5: *Fe*

Pattern piece 6: *Fg*

Pattern piece 7: *Ff*

Stripped Crumbles Block 2

Follow the Stripped Crumbles Block pattern (page 171); disregard the crumble pieced lines and cut 2 pieces from each pattern to make 2 blocks.

Pattern piece 1: *Fa*

Pattern piece 2: *Fb*

Pattern piece 3: *Fd*

Pattern piece 4: *Fc*

Pattern piece 5: *Fh*

SASHING AND BORDERS

Sashing: *Fe*, cut 2 rectangles 2¼″ x 13″ (5.7 × 33cm).

Border 1: *Fa, Ff*, cut 2 rectangles from each fabric 2″ x 7½″ (5.1 × 19.1cm). Follow the directions for Stripped Borders (page 38).

Border 2: *Fh*, cut 2 rectangles 2″ x 14½″ (5.1 × 36.8cm).

EXTRAS

Mod hexies (page 29): *Fe*, cut 6.

Décor-Bond: Cut 6 of mod hexie pattern.

Fabric yo-yos (page 31): *Fa, Fb, Fd*, cut 4 from each fabric to make 12.

Ribbon buttons (page 32): *Re*, cut 6 lengths.

ADDITIONAL PIECES

Muslin: Cut 4 squares 7″ x 7″ (17.8 × 17.8cm).

Backing: *Fh*, cut 1 square 16″ x 16″ (40.6 × 40.6cm).

Hanging sleeve: Cut 1 rectangle 4″ x 14″ (10.2 × 35.6cm).

Batting: Cut 1 square 16″ x 16″ (40.6 × 40.6cm).

Binding horizontal seams: *Fg*, cut 2 rectangles 3″ x 16″ (7.6 × 40.6cm).

Binding vertical seams: *Fg*, cut 2 rectangles 3″ x 17″ (7.6 × 43.2cm).

SEWING THE EXTRAS AND BLOCKS

Sewing the Extras

1. Stitch 6 mod hexies (page 29).

2. Stitch 12 fabric yo-yos (page 31).

3. Stitch 6 ribbon buttons (page 32).

Sewing the Blocks

1. Follow the directions for Foundation Piecing (page 27), using the pattern pieces and muslin rectangles and the specifics for each block (below).

2. Trim each block to 6″ x 6″ (15.2 × 15.2cm).

3. Follow the Embroidery and Embellishment Design (page 136).

CRAZY-PIECED BLOCK 1

1. Make 2 blocks.

2. Cut the trim to fit the seam; hand stitch in place.

Note: *The raw edges will be covered with embroidery or embellishment stitches.*

Open space 1: *Rc*

Open space 2: *Rb*

Open space 3: *Rd*

Open space 4: *Ra*

3. Hand stitch 3 ribbon buttons in vignette intersection 1.

STRIPPED CRUMBLES BLOCK 2

1. Stitch pattern pieces 1, 2, and 3 together.

2. Center: *Rc*, hand stitch 3 stems.

3. Stitch the remaining pattern piece.

4. Stitch 1 mod hexie onto each stem.

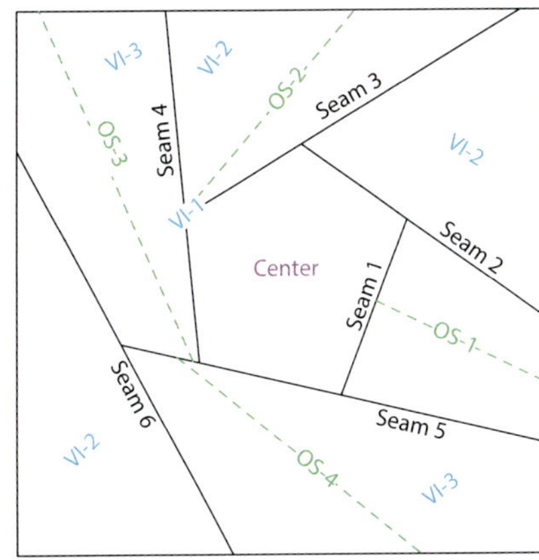

Block 1 Crazy-Pieced Block Diagram (In diagram, OS is open space, VI is vignette intersection)

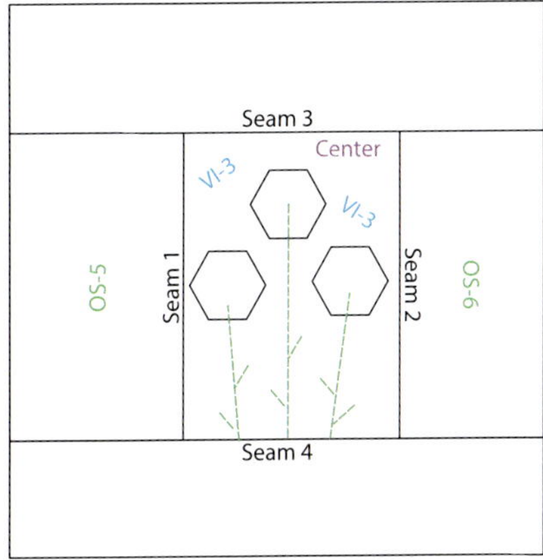

Block 2 Stripped Crumbles Block Diagram (In diagram, OS is open space, VI is vignette intersection)

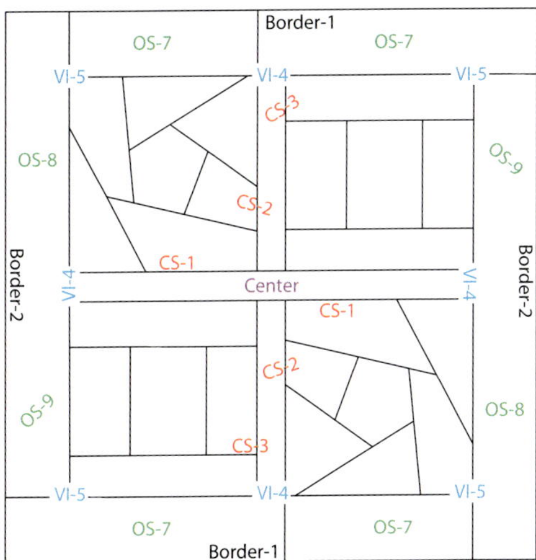

Crazy-Pieced and Stripped Crumbles Blocks Wall Hanging Blueprints (In diagram, CS is corner section, OS is open space, VI is vignette intersection)

EMBROIDERY AND EMBELLISHMENT DESIGN

Refer to the block diagrams and Crazy-Pieced Block and Stripped Crumbles Block Wall Hanging Blueprints (page 135).

Note: *Use 3 strands of cotton floss.*

Block 1

Center: cross stitch pc, stacked bead stitch with 1 size 6° and 11° sb.

Vignette intersection **1:** ribbon buttons, shank button, 2 groups of 3 stacked bead stitches with size 6° and 11° sb.

Seam 1: border row, fly stitch row pc; decorative stitch, straight stitch cf; embellishment stitch, single bead stitch with size 11° sb; open space **1**: *Rc*, 2-wrap French knot stitch cf, 2 buttons.

Seam 2: border row, herringbone long arm stitch pc, straight stitch cf; long arm, decorative stitches and detail stitches, lazy daisy tulip stitch pc, group of 3 2-wrap French knot stitches cf, straight stitch pc; short cross, detail stitches, 2-wrap French knot stitch cf; embellishment stitch, stacked bead stitch with size 6° and 11° sb.

Seam 3: border row, blanket stitch up and down; decorative stitches, every other spoke group of lazy daisy stitches pc, pistil stitch pc; detail stitch, 3-wrap French knot stitch cf; embellishment stitch, single bead stitch 1 size 11° sb; open space **2**: *Rb*, 2-wrap French knot stitch cf.

Seam 4: border row, chain stitch zigzag pc; decorative stitches, alternate between bell flower stitch pc, single bead stitch with size 11° sb, and fly stitch pc, grouped bead stitch, 2 size 11° sb; detail stitch, 2-wrap French knot stitch cf; open space **3**: *Rd*, 2-wrap French knot stitch cf, lazy daisy stitch cf, 1 button, 3-wrap French knot stitch pc.

Seam 5: border row, blanket stitch closed pc, stem stitch pc; detail stitch, straight stitch pc; embellishment stitches, alternate between stacked bead stitch with size 6° and 11° sb and 3 stacked bead stitches with size 6° and 11° sb; open space **4**: *Ra*, 2-wrap French knot stitch cf, lazy daisy stitch cf, 2 buttons.

Seam 6: border row, feather stitch double pc; decorative stitches and detail stitches, alternate between 3 lazy daisy stitches pc, 2 straight stitches pc, 3 2-wrap French knot stitch cf, and lazy daisy stitch pc, fly stitch pc; embellishment stitch, single bead stitch, alternate between 1 size 6° and 1 size 11° sb.

Vignette intersection **2**: 1 button; vignette intersection **3:** steampunk bug.

Block 2

Center: *Rc*, 2-wrap French knot stitch cf, feather stitch (for leaves) pc, mod hexies, straight stitch pc, 3-wrap French knot stitch cf, button; vignette intersection **3**: steampunk bug.

Seam 1: border row, blanket and chain stitches pc; decorative stitches and detail stitches, alternate between 3 lazy daisy stitches pc, 2 pistil stitches cf, 3 3-wrap French knot stitch cf, and fly stitch pc; open space **5**: alternate between 3 buttons and stacked bead stitch with 1 size 6° and 11° sb.

Seam 2: border row, herringbone stitch pc; decorative stitches, one edge fleet stitch pc, other edge stacked bead stitch with 1 size 6° and 11° sb, cross stitch pc; detail stitch, 3-wrap French knot stitch cf; open space **6**: 1 heart button bug, 2 buttons.

Seam 3: border row, chevron stitch pc; decorative stitches and detail stitches, one edge 2 lazy daisy stitches pc, 2 2-wrap French knot stitches cf, other edge 2-wrap French knot stitch cf; detail stitch, straight stitch pc; embellishment stitch, stacked bead stitch with 1 size 6° and 11° sb.

Seam 4: border row, snail trail stitch pc; decorative stitches, alternate between looped tendril stitch pc, single bead stitch with size 11° sb, and 2 3-wrap French knot stitch pc.

BASE DESIGN DETAILS

Refer to Basic Base Instructions (page 36) and the Crazy-Pieced Block and Stripped Crumbles Block Wall Hanging Blueprints (page 135).

1. Follow **Option C** under Base Design Options (page 36) with the batting square. Place the blocks on batting with a 1″ (2.5cm) spacing between the blocks in this order: **Block 1**, rotate **Block 2** 180°, **Block 2**, rotate **Block 1** 180°.

2. Follow Steps 2–3 of Fabric or Ribbon Sashing (page 37) for each sashing rectangle. Place 1 rectangle horizontally across and overlapping the raw edges of blocks and then add the remaining sashing rectangle vertically.

3. Hand stitch *UT* vertically and then horizontally across the sashing rectangles.

4. Follow directions for the Disappearing Seam Border (page 38), using **border 1** and **border 2** rectangles.

5. Cut the trim to fit the seam; hand stitch in place.

Note: *The raw edges are covered by buttons.*

Border 1: *Rd*

Border 2: *Ra*

7. Hand stitch 3 fabric yo-yos in each vignette intersection **4** position.

Additional Embroidery and Embellishments

Sashing: embellishment stitches: *UT*, single bead stitch with 8mm beads.

Vignette intersection **4:** embellishment stitches, single bead stitch with size 6° sb in the center, 2 groups of 3 stacked bead stitches with 1 size 6° and 11° sb, snail button.

Remaining buttons:

Vignette intersection **5:** group of 3 buttons covering the raw edges of the rickrack trims.

Center: star button; open space **7**: 3 buttons in each section; open space **8**: bird house; open space **9**: 2 butterfly buttons; corner section **1**: 2 frogs, or owl buttons; corner section **2**: chicken or rooster buttons; corner section **3**: bug button.

ASSEMBLY AND FINISHING

1. Follow the directions for Hanging Sleeve (page 41), using the backing and hanging sleeve rectangle.

2. Follow the directions for the Bound Edge Assembly (page 41):

Horizontal seams: 3″ x 16″ (7.6 × 40.6cm)

Verticall seams: 3″ x 17″ (7.6 × 43.2cm)

Stripped Crumbles Block Wall Hanging with Custom Hanger

Pick a random mix of fabrics for this enlarged Stripped Crumbles Block (page 26). Details include stripped borders (page 38), with grosgrain ribbons covering the raw edge seams. Embroidery and embellishment stitches were worked in perle cotton and seed beads, with buttons and larger bead details.

A Range of Rust, 12¾″ x 13″ (32.4 × 33cm)

Creative Option To change the look, you could substitute fabric circles (page 31) and ribbon buttons (page 32) for the large and medium size buttons and/or substitute a hanging sleeve for the custom hanger.

SWATCHES

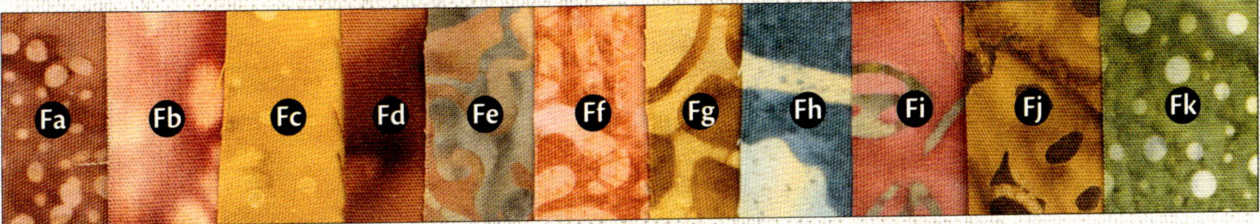

Fabrics

Seed beads

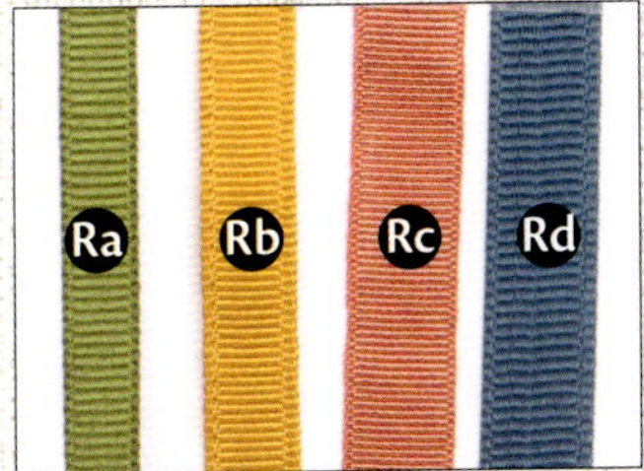

Trimmings

Perle cotton

Embellishments (not all sizes and shapes are shown)

Materials

FABRICS

Scrap fabrics: about ¾ yard total of 11 or more fabrics (68.6cm)

Backing and binding: ½ yard (45.7cm)

TRIMMINGS

Ra: ¼" (6mm) grosgrain ribbon, 1 yard (1m)

Ra: ⅜" (10mm) grosgrain ribbon, 1 yard (1m)

Ra: ⅜" (10mm) grosgrain ribbon, 1 yard (1m)

Ra: ⅜" (10mm) grosgrain ribbon, 1 yard (1m)

EMBROIDERY MATERIALS IN A VARIETY OF COLORS

Perle cotton (pc): #8

Seed beads (sb): sizes 6°, 8°, 11°, 15°

EMBELLISHMENTS

Buttons 2- or 4-Hole

Ba: X-Large, 1¼" (3.2cm), 2

Bb: Large, 1" (2.5cm), 7

Bc: Medium, ¾" (1.9cm), 5

Bd: Small, ⅝" (1.6cm), 7

Be: Smaller, ½" (1.2cm), 8

Large Beads

7mm round bead: 34

10mm flower bead: 12

13mm round bead: 10

16 × 13mm shell bead: 4

15 × 8mm oblong bead: 3

18mm round bead: 7

Muslin: ½ yard (45.7cm)

Shape-Flex: ½ yard (45.7cm)

Batting: ½ yard (45.7cm)

Sewing and beading threads: neutral colors

Knitting needle or chopstick

Cutting Instructions

BLOCK

Enlarge the Stripped Crumbels Block pattern (page 171) by **20%**.

Follow Steps 1–3 of Crumbles Block (page 28). See Stripped Crumbles Block Diagram (below) for piecing suggestions.

Cut 1 piece from each pattern piece to make 1 block.

BORDERS

See Stripped Crumbles Block Wall Hanging Blueprints (below) for piecing suggestions; cut 1 each.

Border 1: 2¾″ x 7¼″ (7 × 18.4cm)

Border 2: 3″ x 10″ (7.6 × 25.4cm)

Border 3: 2¾″ x 10¼″ (7 × 26cm)

Border 4: 2¾″ x 12¾″ (7 × 32.4cm)

ADDITIONAL PIECES

Muslin: Cut 1 square 7¼″ x 7¼″ (18.4 × 18.4cm).

Shape-Flex: Cut 1 rectangle 12¾″ × 13″ (32.4 × 33cm).

Batting: Cut 1 rectangle 12¾″ × 13″ (32.4 × 33cm).

Backing: Cut 1 rectangle 12¾″ × 13″ (32.4 × 33cm).

Binding horizontal seams: Cut 2 rectangles 3″ x 12¾″ (7.6 × 32.4cm).

Binding vertical seams: Cut 2 rectangles 3″ x 14″ (7.6 × 35.6cm).

Pattern Piece 4
OS-5
OS-4
OS-2
Seam 3
Pattern Piece 1
Pattern Piece 2
Pattern Piece 3
OS-1
OS-2
Seam 1
OS-3
OS-2
Seam 2
Seam 4
Pattern Piece 5

Stripped Crumbles Block Wall Hanging Diagram
(In diagram, OS is open space)

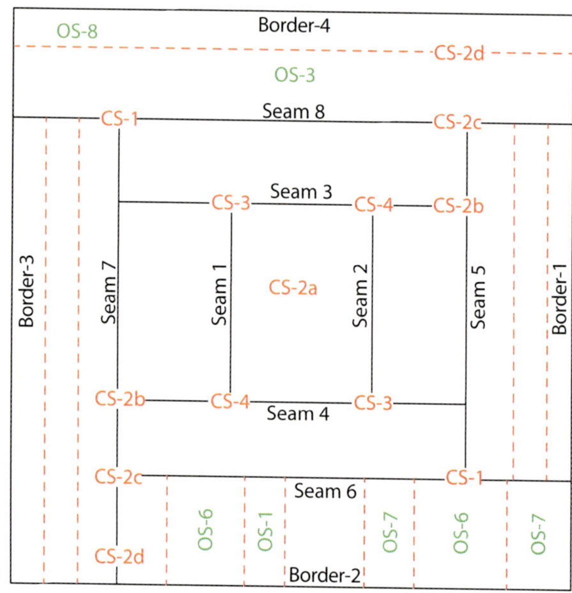

Stripped Crumbles Block Wall Hanging Blueprints
(In diagram, CS is corner section, OS is open space)

BASE DESIGN DETAILS

Refer to Basic Base Instructions (page 36) and the Stripped Crumbles Block Wall Hanging Blueprints (page 140).

1. Follow Steps 4–5 of the Crumbles Block (page 28), using the pattern pieces and muslin square. Make 1 block.

2. Cut the trim to fit the seam; machine or hand stitch in place.

Note: *The raw edge of a trim is covered by the following length.*

Seam 1: *Rb*

Seam 2: *Ra*

Seam 3: *Rd*

Seam 4: *Rc*

3. Follow **Option C** under Base Design Options (page 36); place the block on the batting rectangle 12¾″ x 13″ (32.4 × 33cm).

4. Follow the directions for Adding a Border (page 37), Raw Edge Option (page 37), using **Border 1, Border 2, Border 3,** and **Border 4**.

5. Follow Step 2 with the following trims.

Seam 5: *Rb*

Seam 6: *Rd*

Seam 7: *Ra*

Seam 8: *Rc*

6. Follow the Embroidery and Embellishment Design (at right), then Finishing (at right).

FINISHING

1. Follow the directions for the Bound Edge Assembly (page 41) with the 12¾″ x 13″ (32.4 × 33cm) backing:

Horizontal seams: 3″ x 12¾″ (7.6 × 32.4cm)

Vertical seams: 3″ x 14″ (7.6 × 35.6cm)

2. Follow the directions for the Custom Hanger (page 43), using *Rb* and the knitting needle or chopstick.

Option 1: *Embroider top-to-bottom hole charm dangle stitches (beaded) to bottom edge, using size 6°, 7mm, 6°, 8°, 11° beads.*

Option 2: *Embroider stacked bead stitch with size 6° and 11° sb along inner binding edge.*

EMBROIDERY AND EMBELLISHMENT DESIGN

In the directions for the stacked bead stitch, 1 size 8°, 15°, or 11° sb can be used.

Button Embellishments

Refer to the Stripped Crumbles Block Diagram and Stripped Crumbles Block Wall Hanging Blueprints (page 140). Stitch the buttons in place with perle cotton first.

Corner section **1**: *Ba* button, in holes grouped bead stitch size 11° sb; corner section **2a**: *Bb* button, button bezel stitch (beaded) sb and grouped bead stitch size 11° sb, around button stacked bead stitch with 1 size 6° and 11° sb, bead combination stitch with 3 size 11° sb, 1 size 8° sb; corner section **2b**: *Bb* button, button bezel stitch (beaded) sb and stacked bead stitch with 1 size 6° and 11° sb; corner section **2c**: *Bb* button, in holes stacked bead stitch with 1 size 6° and 11° sb, around button stacked bead stitch with 1 size 8° and 15° sb; corner section **2d**: *Bb* button, in holes grouped bead stitch size 11° sb, around button stacked bead stitch with 1 size 8° and 15° sb; corner section **3**: *Bc* button, in holes stacked bead stitch with 1 size 6° and 11° sb, around button stacked bead stitch with 1 size 8° and 15° sb; corner section **4**: *Bd* and *Be* buttons, in holes stacked bead stitch with 1 size 6° and 11° sb.

Base

Refer to Stripped Crumbles Block Diagram (page 140).

Pattern Piece 1: serpentine stitch V-shape (beaded) sb, lazy daisy stitch fancy (beaded) sb.

Seam 1: *Rb*; fly stitch pc, stacked bead stitch with 1 size 8° and 15° sb.

Pattern Piece 2: double bubble stitch (beaded) sb.

Seam 2: *Ra*; fly stitch pc, alternate between stacked bead stitch with 1 size 8° and 15° sb and stacked bead stitch with 1 size 6° and 11° sb.

Pattern Piece 3: beaded vine stitch sb.

Seam 3: *Rd*; blanket stitch pc, continuous bead stitch size 11° sb, grouped bead stitch with size 11° sb.

Pattern Piece 4: blanket stitch fancy (beaded) sb, stacked bead stitch with 1 size 6° and 11° sb; open space **4**: alternate between flower with petite petals (beaded) with 6° and 11° sb and 3 stacked bead stitch with 1 size 6° and 11° sb, double bubble stitch (beaded) sb, fly stitch fancy row (beaded) sb; open space **5**: 3 single bead stitch, 13mm round bead.

Seam 4: *Rc*, see Seam 3; 3 groups of stacked bead stitches with 1 size 6° and 11° sb, single bead stitch with 13mm round bead, stacked bead stitch with 1 size 6° and 11° sb.

Pattern Piece 5: Equally space 3 *Be* buttons, alternate with herringbone stitch (beaded) sb, alternate between bead combination stitch with 3 size 11° 1 size 8° sb and stacked bead stitch with 1 size 6° and 11° sb.

Borders

Refer to Stripped Crumbles Block Wall Hanging Blueprints (page 140).

Seam 5: *Rb*, chain stitch pc, stacked bead stitch with 1 7mm round, size 6° and 15° sb.

Border 1: Equally space 2 single bead stitches with 16 × 13mm shell bead; blanket stitch fancy (beaded) sb; equally space 3 *Bd* buttons, in holes stacked bead stitch with 1 size 8° and 15° sb, around button stacked bead stitch with 1 size 8° and 15° sb, and spine vine stitch (beaded) sb.

Seam 6: *Rd*, herringbone stitch pc, straight stitch pc, stacked bead stitch with 1 size 6° and 11° sb.

Border 2: cross stitch long arm row (beaded) sb, stacked bead stitch with 1 size 6° and 11° sb, spine vine stitch (beaded) sb, chain stitch (beaded) sb, alternate between stacked bead stitch with 1 size 8° and 15° sb and bead combination stitch with 3 size 11° sb, 1 size 8° sb, feather stitch fancy (beaded) sb; fly stitch fancy row (beaded) sb, serpentine stitch V-shape (beaded) sb, stacked bead stitch with 1 size 6° and 11° sb.

Seam 7: *Ra*, see Seam 5.

Border 3: Equally space 4 *Bd* buttons, in holes grouped bead stitch size 11° sb, alternate with blanket stitch angled (beaded) sb, stacked bead stitch with 1 size 6° and 11° sb; equally space 2 groups of 3 flower with petite petals (beaded) with 6° and 11° sb, alternate with feather stitch fancy (beaded) sb.

Seam 8: *Rc*, see Seam 6.

Border 4: *Rb*, chain stitch zigzag pc, stacked bead stitch with 1 size 6° and 11° sb, bead combination stitch with 5 size 11° sb, 1 size 8° sb.

Additional Areas

Open space **1**: 2 single bead stitch with 13mm round bead; open space **2**: bead combination stitch with size 11° sb, oblong bead, size 11° sb; open space **3**: 3 single bead stitches with 13mm round bead; open space **6**: single bead stitch with 16 × 13mm shell bead, 2 stacked bead stitches bead 7mm round, size 6° and 15° sb; open space **7**: *Bd*; open space **8**: 3 *Be* buttons.

Stripped Crumbles Block Table Covering

To make this table covering, choose the five-fabric combination for the four reduced-in-size Stripped Crumbles Blocks (page 26). The base has double-strip borders (page 38) with mock prairie points (page 30), fabric circles (page 31), crazy-pieced fabric yo-yos (page 31), and added trims.

Jaipur Spring, 15½" x 15½" (39.4 × 39.4cm)

Creative Option Use large prints that offer a variety of pattern opportunities for small pieces like fabric circles and mock prairie points.

SWATCHES

Fabrics

Perle cotton, cotton floss

Seed beads

Trimmings

1. Fabric circle **2.** Fabric yo-yo **3.** Rosette

Buttons (not all sizes shown)

Materials

FABRICS

Fa: ½ yard (45.7cm)

Fb, Fc, Fd, Fe, Fg: fat quarters

TRIMMINGS

LT: 2 yards (1.9m)

Ra: ⅜" (10mm) grosgrain ribbon, 1 yard (1m)

Rb: ⅛" (3mm) satin ribbon, 1 yard (1m)

⅝" (16mm) hemtape, 2 yards (1.9m)

EMBROIDERY MATERIALS IN A VARIETY OF COLORS

Perle cotton (pc): #8

Cotton floss (cf)

Seed beads (sb): sizes 6°, 11°, 15°

BUTTONS

Ba: ⅜"(10mm), 32

Bb: 1¼" (3.2cm), 1

Bc: 1½" (3.8cm), 4

fast2fuse, heavy: ½ yard (45.7cm)

Batting: ½ yard (45.7cm)

Sewing and beading threads: neutral colors

Cutting Instructions

BLOCKS

Reduce the Stripped Crumbles Block pattern (page 171) to **75%**, *disregard the crumble pieced lines.* Follow Steps 1–3 of Pieced Blocks (page 27).

Cut 4 pieces from each pattern to make 4 blocks.

Pattern piece 1: *Fb*

Pattern piece 2: *Fc*

Pattern piece 3: *Fd*

Pattern piece 4: *Fe*

Pattern piece 5: *Fa*

BORDERS

Border 1

See stripped borders (page 38); stitch sections of *Ff, Fg* together.

Border 1A: 1¾" x 8½" (4.4. x 21.6cm)

Border 1B: 1¾" x 11" (4.4. x 27.9cm)

Border 2

See stripped borders (page 38) and follow the crumbled option in Step 1; stitch sections of *Fe, Fa* together.

Border 2A: 3" x 11" (7.6 × 27.9cm)

Border 2B: 3" x 13½" (7.6 × 34.3cm)

Border 2C: 3" x 13½" (7.6 × 34.3cm)

Border 2D: 3" x 16" (7.6 × 40.6cm)

EXTRAS

Mock prairie points (page 30): *Fb*, cut 1 rectangle 2" x 16" (5.1 × 40.6cm); make 4.

Fabric circles (page 31): *Fb*, cut 4 circles 2" (5.1cm) diameter.

fast2fuse: Cut 4 circles 1¼" (3.2cm) diameter.

Batting: Cut 4 circles 1⅛" (2.9cm) diameter.

Crazy pieced yo-yos (page 31): *Fb, Fc:* 6 circles 2⅛" (5.4cm) diameter.

Rosettes: 6 *Ra* and *Rb* 3" (7.6cm) lengths each

ADDITIONAL PIECES

Batting: Cut 1 square 16" x 16" (40.6 × 40.6cm).

Backing, *Fa:* Cut 1 square 15½" x 15½" (39.4 × 39.4cm).

fast2Fuse: Cut 1 square 15½" x 15½" (39.4 × 39.4cm).

Hem tape binding vertical seams: Cut 2 lengths 16" (40.6cm).

Hem tape binding horizontal seams: Cut 2 lengths 16¼" (41.3cm).

SEWING THE BLOCKS AND EXTRAS

1. Make 4 blocks, following the directions for Foundationless Piecing (page 28).

2. Trim the blocks to 4½" x 4½" (11.4 × 11.4cm).

Note: *Refer to Stripped Crumbles Block Table Covering Blueprints (page 146).*

3. Pin Block 1 to Block 2, rotated 90° to the right.

4. Machine stitch with a 1/4" (6mm) seam allowance. Press the seams open.

5. Pin Block 3, rotated 90° to the left, to Block 4, rotated 180°. Follow Step 4.

6. Pin the first and second row together, aligning the seams. Follow Step 4.

7. Stitch 4 fabric circles (page 31).

8. Stitch 6 crazy pieced fabric yo-yos (page 31).

9. Stitch 6 rosettes (page 32) from *Ra*. Tie each length of *Rb* into an overhand knot and thread through the center of each rosette.

BASE DESIGN DETAILS

Refer to Basic Base Instructions (page 36) and Stripped Crumbles Block Table Covering Blueprints (below).

1. Follow **Option C** under Base Design Options (page 36) with the batting square.

Note: *See Adding a Border (page 37)* and *Finished Seam Option (page 37).*

2. Stitch **border 1A** to the horizontal sides.

3. Stitch **border 1B** to the vertical sides.

4. Hand or machine stitch the mock prairie points in place.

5. Stitch the remaining borders in this order: **border 2A, border 2B, border 2C, border 2D**.

6. Stitch fabric circles in place.

7. Open space: Hand stitch *LT* over vertical **border 2**; repeat for the horizontal **border 2**, stopping and ending at the vertical edges of *LT*.

8. Evenly space and stitch 3 fabric yo-yos on vertical **border 2** and 3 rosettes on the horizontal **border 2**.

9. Follow the Embroidery and Embellishment Design (page 147).

Option: *Add extra details with hand quilting (page 40) through block sections and through borders.*

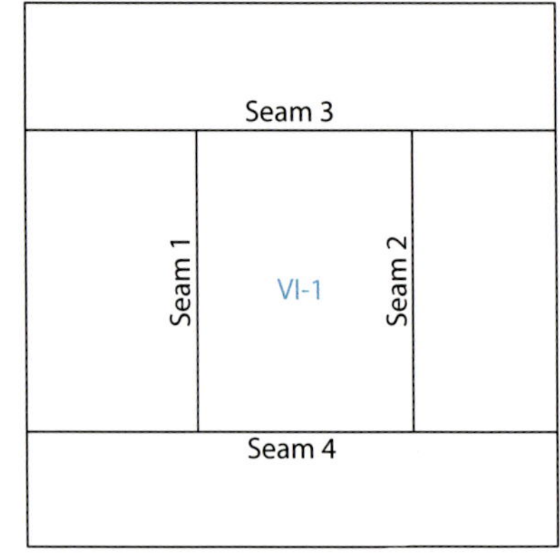

Stripped Crumbles Block Table Covering Diagram
(In diagram, VI is vignette intersection)

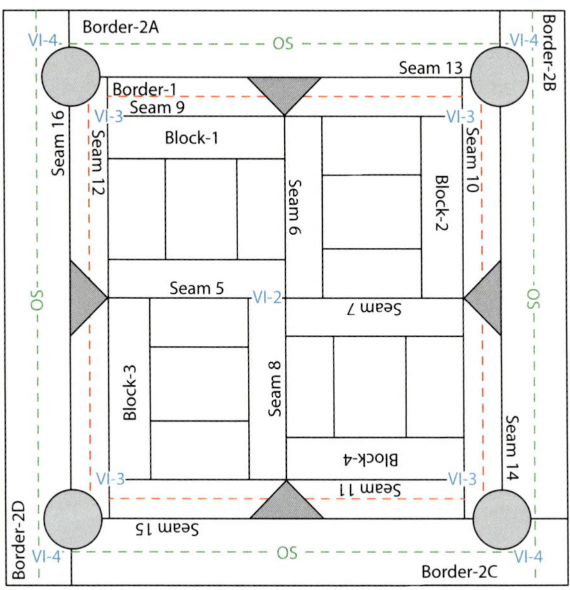

Stripped Crumbles Block Table Covering Blueprints
(In diagram, OS is open space, VI is vignette intersection)

EMBROIDERY AND EMBELLISHMENT DESIGN

Refer to the Stripped Crumbles Block Table Covering Diagram (page 146) and Stripped Crumbles Block Table Covering Blueprints (page 146).

Note: *Use 3 strands of cotton floss.*

Base

Vignette Intersection **1:** 3 spiderweb roses cf, 2 groups of 3 lazy daisy stitches pc, 3-wrap French knot stitch cf, 2 chain stitch vines pc, 2 continuous bead stitches size 11° sb, *Ba*.

Seams 1 and 2: border rows, stem/outline fern stitch pc; embellishment stitch, single bead stitch with size 8° sb.

Seam 3: border row, blanket and chain stitch pc, 2-wrap French knot stitch cf; decorative stitches and detail stitches, alternate between 6-petal lazy daisy flower pc, straight stitch cf, stacked bead stitch with 1 size 6° and 11° sb, and bead combination stitch with 3 size 11° sb, 1 size 8° sb.

Seam 4: border row, stem stitch vine pc, chain stitch branch pc; decorative stitch, lazy daisy stitch pc; detail stitch, 2-wrap French knot stitch cf; embellishment stitch, stacked bead stitch with 1 size 6° and 11° sb.

Seams 5, 6, 7, 8: border rows, chain stitch pc; embellishment stitches, grouped bead stitch with 2 size 11° sb every other stitch, facing into pattern piece 5.

Seams 9, 10, 11, 12: border rows, chain stitch pc; embellishment stitches, grouped bead stitch with 2 size 11° sb every other stitch, facing into **Border 1**.

Border 1

Seam: border row, stem/outline fern stitch pc; embellishment stitch, 2-wrap French knot stitch cf.

Mock prairie points: Start and finish with a *Ba*, stacked bead stitch with size 6° and 11° sb.

Fabric circles: in the center floret stitch (beaded), around the edge stacked bead stitch with 1 size 6° and 11° sb.

Seams 13, 14, 15, 16: border rows, chain stitch pc; embellishment stitches, * grouped bead stitch with 2 size 11° sb 2 stitches, one on either side, skip 1, repeat from *.

Border 2

Leaf trim: straight stitch across vine, center of leaves, grouped bead stitch 2, size 11° sb off each leaf, lazy daisy stitch pc, single bead stitch 1 size 11° sb next to each leaf.

Work the following pattern in between the rosettes or fabric yo-yos, next to a leaf, or in the space between leaves:

Ba

Group of 3 3-wrap French knot stitches pc

Spiderweb rose stitch cf, 2 groups of 2 lazy daisy stitches pc, 1 straight stitch cf

Group of 3 3-wrap French knot stitches pc

Bellflower stitch, group of 3 3-wrap French knot stitches

Additional Areas

Vignette intersection **2:** *Bb*; vignette intersection **3:** Ba; vignette intersection **4:** *Bc*.

FINISHING

1. Follow the directions for Ribbon-Edge Binding (page 42), using the backing square and the hem tape binding.

2. In Step 3, sandwich the fast2Fuse square between the **base** and the backing.

Wedged Crumbles Block Wall Hanging

Choose a random mix of fabrics for the nine reduced Wedged Crumbles Block (page 26) to make this wall hanging and wedge-pieced borders (page 39). Use trim to cover the raw edge seams and a variety of threads, beads, and buttons for the embroidery and embellishments.

Snowflake Serenade, 15½″ x 14½″ (39.4 × 36.8cm)

Creative Option You can change the look of any of the projects by increasing or decreasing the size of the blocks used to create the base.

SWATCHES

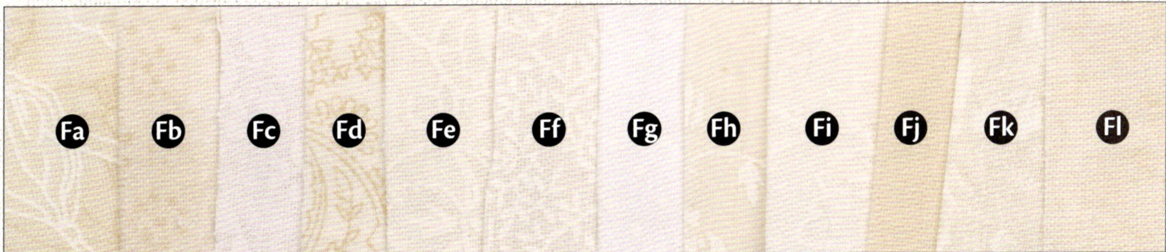

Fabrics

Seed and other beads

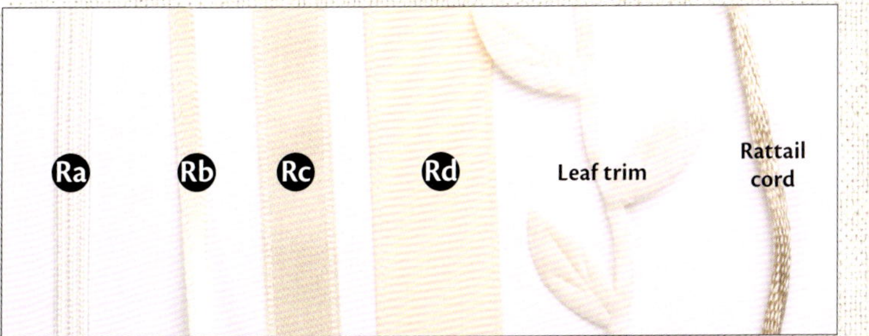

Trimmings

Perle cotton

Buttons

Glass components

Materials

FABRICS

Scrap fabrics: 10–12 fabrics, totaling about ⅝ yard (57.2cm)

Backing, hanging sleeve: ½ yard (45.7cm)

TRIMMINGS

Ra: ¼" (6mm) middy braid, 1 yard (1m)

Rb: ⅛" (3mm) satin ribbon, 1 yard (1m)

Rc: ⅜" (1cm) satin ribbon, 1 yard (1m)

Rd: ⅝" (1.6cm) grosgrain ribbon, 3 yards (2.8m)

Leaf trim: 1 yard (1m)

Rattail cord: 2 yards (1.9cm)

EMBROIDERY MATERIALS IN A VARIETY OF COLORS

Perle cotton (pc): #8, #12

Seed beads (sb): sizes 6°, 8°, 11°, 15°

6mm bugle beads

14mm bugle beads

EMBELLISHMENTS

Buttons

Ba: ½" (1.2cm) 2-hole, 8

Bb: ⅝" (1.6cm) 2-hole, 1

Bc: ½" (1.2cm) shank, 4

Bd: ¾" (1.9cm) or 1" (2.5cm) 2-hole, 2

Be: ¾" (1.9cm) 2-hole, 4

Bf: ½" (1.2cm), 4 groups of 2 4-hole and 1 shank (12 buttons total)

Bg: ½" (1.2cm) shank, 4

Bh: ½" (1.2cm) novelty 2-hole, 6

Bi: ⅝" (1.6cm) 2-hole, 10

Bj: ½" (1.2cm), 6 groups of 3 novelty buttons (18 buttons total)

Bk: ½" (1.2cm) shank, 4

Glass Components

8mm bead: 1 strand

Gba: 24 × 20mm butterfly bead, 4

Gbb: 24 × 12mm butterfly bead, 14

Gbc: 14mm flower rondelle, 12

Gbd: 16 × 12mm tulip, 8

Gbe: 14 × 10mm tulip, 18

Gbf: 15 × 12mm leaf, 16

Muslin: ⅓ yard (30.5)

Batting: ½ yard (45.7cm)

Sewing and beading threads: neutral colors

Cutting Instructions

BLOCKS

Reduce the Wedged Crumbles Block pattern (page 172) to **60%**. Follow Steps 1–3 of Crumbles Blocks (page 28).

1. Select groups of fabrics to make 3 color combinations, 1 for each pattern piece (or use a random mix).

2. Cut 9 pattern pieces from each group to make 9 blocks.

BORDERS

Border 1: Cut 1 rectangle from muslin 6" x 10" (15.2 × 25.4cm).

Border 2: Cut 1 rectangle from muslin 7" x 15" (17.8 × 38.1cm).

Follow the directions for Foundation-Pieced Borders, Multiple-Pieced Border Option B. Wedge-Pieced Border (page 39), using scrap fabrics.

ADDITIONAL PIECES

Backing: Cut 1 rectangle 15½" x 14½" (39.4 × 36.8cm).

Hanging sleeve: Cut 1 rectangle 4" x 12½" (10.2 × 31.8cm).

Batting:

Cut 2 rectangles 15½" x 14½" (39.4 × 36.8cm).

Ribbon binding:

Horizontal seams: *Rd*, cut 2 each 14½" (36.8cm).

Vertical seams: *Rd*, cut 2 each 15½" (39.4cm).

SEWING THE BLOCKS AND BORDERS

Blocks

1. Follow the directions for Foundationless Piecing (page 28). Make 9 blocks. Trim the blocks to 3½" x 3½" (8.9 × 8.9cm).

Note: *Refer to Basic Base Instructions (page 36) and the Wedged Crumbles Block Wall Hanging Blueprints (page 151).*

2. Follow the directions for the 9-Patch Block Base (page 35), now referred to as the **center**.

Borders

Cut 2 rectangles each from the foundation-pieced border strips:

Border 1: 2½" x 9½" (5.1 × 24.1cm)

Border 2: 3" x 14½" (7.6 × 36.8cm)

BASE DESIGN DETAILS

1. Follow **Option D** under Base Design Options (page 36), with the 1 batting rectangle.
2. Cut the ribbons to fit the seam or section.

Note: *The raw edges are covered by the following lengths of ribbon, or seams.*

Seams 1 and 2: *Rb*

Seams 3 and 4: *Ra*

3. Place **Border 1** flush with the **center**. Place *Rc* over the raw edges, following the directions for Fabric or Ribbon Sashing (page 37).
4. Place **border 2** flush with the **center**. Place *Rd* over the raw edges, following the directions for Fabric or Ribbon Sashing (page 37).
5. Hand stitch the leaf trim over *Rd*.
6. Follow the Embroidery and Embellishment Design (below).

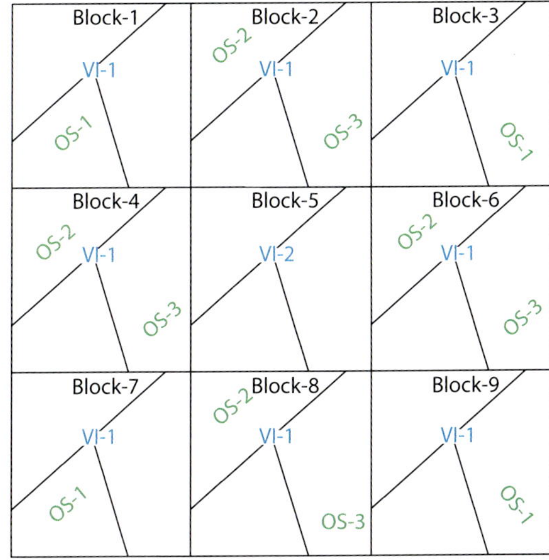

Wedged Crumbles Block Wall Hanging Center Diagram (In diagram, OS is open space, VI is vignette intersection)

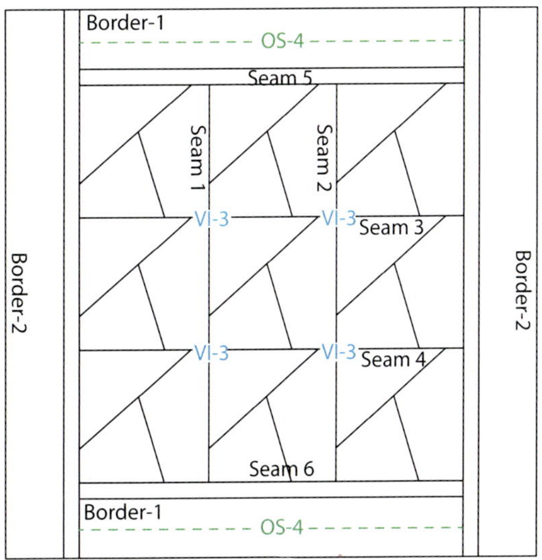

Wedged Crumbles Block Wall Hanging Blueprints (In diagram, OS is open space, VI is vignette intersection)

EMBROIDERY AND EMBELLISHMENT DESIGN

Refer to the Wedged Crumbles Block Wall Hanging Center Diagram and Wedged Crumbles Block Wall Hanging Blueprints (above).

Center

Blocks 1, 3, 7, and 9: vignette intersection **1:** *Ba* stacked bead stitch with 1 size 8° and 15° sb in holes and around button, single bead stitch 6mm bugle bead; open space **1**: single bead stitch *Gba.*

Blocks 2, 4, 6, 8: vignette intersection **1:** *Ba* stacked bead stitch with 1 size 8° and 15° sb in holes and around button; open space **2**: group of 3 stacked bead stitches with 1 size 6° and 11° sb; open space **3**: single bead stitch *Gbb.*

Block 5: vignette intersection **2:** *Bb* in holes, grouped bead stitch with size 11° sb, button bezel stitch (beaded), bead cascade stitch, size 6° and 3 size 11° sb.

Base

Seam 1 and 2: *Rb*; feather stitch pc, lazy daisy stitch fancy (beaded) sb, single bead stitch size 8°.

Seam 3 and 4: *Ra*; chain stitch zigzag pc, 3-wrap French knot stitch pc, stacked bead stitch with 1 size 6° and 11° sb.

Vignette intersection **3:** *Bc*.

Seam 5 and 6: *Rc*; chain stitch pc, stacked bead stitch with 1 size 6° and 11° sb, single bead stitch size 11° sb.

Border 1

Open space **4:** center: *Bd* in holes grouped bead stitch with size 11° sb, around button bead cascade stitch with size 6° and 3 size 11° sb. Work the following pattern from * on either side of *Bd*:

* Stacked bead stitch with *Gbd* and size 11° sb, 2 single bead stitches with *Gbf*

Be, stacked bead stitch with 1 size 8° and 15° sb in holes and around button

Bf, single bead stitch size 11° sb in holes, 3 stacked bead stitches with 1 size 6° and 11° sb between each button

Bg, 3 bead combination stitches, 1 size 11° sb, 1 14mm bugle bead, 1 size 11° sb, single bead stitch *Gbb*

Border 2

Leaf trim: straight stitch across vine, lazy daisy stitch pc in each leaf. Begin the pattern at the bottom of the vine from *; work the stitches next to a leaf or in the space between leaves:

**Bh*, in holes grouped bead stitch size 11° sb, stacked bead stitch with 14mm flower rondelle and size 11° sb

3 bead cascade stitches with 14 × 10mm tulip and 5 size 11° sb

Bi, stacked bead stitch with 1 size 8° and 15° sb in holes and around button

Bj, in holes grouped bead stitch with size 11° sb, beaded pistil stitch with 3 size 11° sb in center of group, 1 stacked bead stitch with 1 size 6° and 11° sb between each button

Bk, stacked bead stitch 14mm flower rondelle and size 11° sb

Single bead stitch with *Gbb*

3 bead combination stitches with 1 size 11° sb, 6mm bugle bead, 1 size 11° sb

Stacked bead stitch *Gbd* and size 11° sb, 2 single bead stitches with *Gbf*

Bi, stacked bead stitch with 1 size 8° and 15° sb in holes and around button

Repeat pattern from *, filling in any open spaces with 1 or 3 stacked bead stitches with 1 size 6° and 11° sb.

FINISHING

1. Layer the backing on top of the second piece of batting. Follow the directions for Free-Form Machine Quilting (page 40) or hand quilt. Trim this to 14" x 15" (35.6 x 38.1cm).

2. Follow the directions for the Hanging Sleeve (page 41), using the hanging-sleeve rectangle.

3. Follow Steps 1–5 for Ribbon-Edge Binding (page 42) with the ribbons.

4. Follow the directions for the Couched Cord Edge (page 156) with the rattail cording.

Wedged Crumbles Block Pillow

The three-fabric combination was used for the nine reduced-in-size Wedged Crumbles Block (page 26) to make this pillow. Perle cotton, beads, and buttons were used for the embroidery and embellishment stitches.

Café au Lait, 8¾″ x 8¾″ (22.2 × 22.2cm)

Creative Option To change up this pattern, use the Wedged Crumbles Block Pillow Blueprint (page 156) as a guide and choose 1 color combination for blocks 1, 3, 7, and 9, 1 for blocks 2, 4, 6, and 8, and 1 for block 5.

SWATCHES

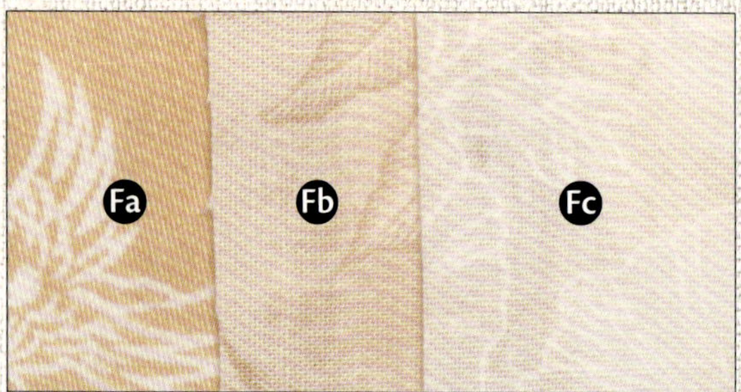

Fabrics

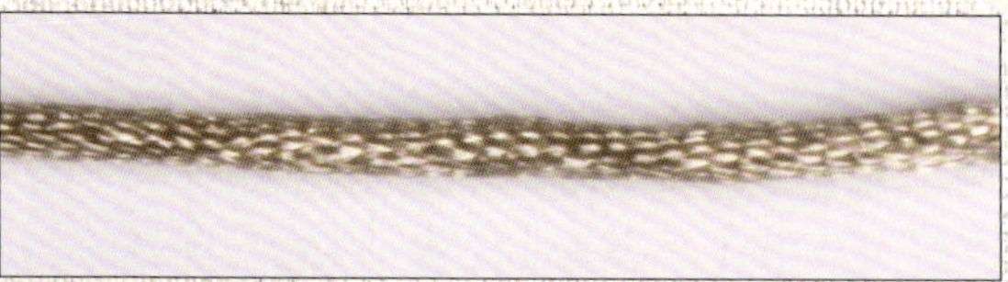
Rattail cord

Seed and 8mm beads

Perle cotton

Embellishments

Materials

FABRICS

Blocks: 3 fat quarters

Backing: 1 fat quarter

EMBROIDERY MATERIALS IN A VARIETY OF COLORS

Perle cotton (pc): #5, #8

Seed beads (sb): sizes 6°, 8°, 11, 15°

8mm beads: 2 colors, 1 strand each

EMBELLISHMENTS

9mm flower bead: 9

⅜″ (10mm) button: 4

Rattail cording: 1½ yards (1.4m)

Batting: ⅓ yard (30.5cm)

Shape-Flex: ⅓ yard (30.5cm)

Poly-fil: 1 package

Sewing and beading threads: neutral colors

Cutting Instructions

BLOCKS

Reduce the Wedged Crumbles Block pattern (page 172) to **60%**, *disregard the crumble-pieced lines.* Follow Steps 1–3 of Pieced Blocks (page 27). Cut 9 pattern pieces from each fabric to make 9 blocks.

ADDITIONAL PIECES

Backing: Cut 1 square 9½″ x 9½″ (24.1 × 24.1cm).

Shape-Flex: Cut 1 square 9½″ x 9½″ (24.1 × 24.1cm).

Batting: Cut 2 squares 9½″ x 9½″ (24.1 × 24.1cm).

BASE DESIGN DETAILS

Note: *Refer to Basic Base Instructions (page 36).*

1. Follow the directions for Foundationless Piecing (page 28), using the 3 pattern pieces. Make 9 blocks.
2. Trim the blocks to 3½″ x 3½″ (8.9 × 8.9cm).
3. Follow the directions for the 9-Patch Block Base (page 35), now referred to as the **base**.
4. Stabilize the **base** with Shape-Flex.
5. Follow the Embroidery and Embellishment Design (at right).

EMBROIDERY AND EMBELLISHMENT DESIGN

Refer to the Wedged Crumbles Block Pillow Blueprints (page 156).

Blocks

Note: *Use pc #8 in this section.*

Seam 1: border row: feather stitch pc; decorative stitch, looped tendril stitch pc; detail stitches, straight stitch, 3-wrap French knot stitch pc; embellishment stitch, stacked bead stitch with 1 size 8° and 15° sb.

Seam 2: border row: blanket stitch pc; decorative stitches, alternate between 3 lazy daisy stitches pc and 1 fly stitch pc; detail stitch, 3-wrap French knot stitch pc; embellishment stitches, stacked bead stitch with 1 size 8° and 15° sb, single bead stitch with 9mm bead.

Vignette intersection **1:** single bead stitch with 9mm flower bead; open space **1:** 3 stacked bead stitches with 1 size 6° and 11° sb.

Base

Seams 1 and 2: border row: cross stitch pc #5.

Seams 3 and 4: border row: couched stitch pc #5 and #8.

Vignette intersection **2:** button.

Follow the Finishing Directions (page 156).

FINISHING

1. Layer the backing over both of the batting pieces. Follow the directions for Free-Form Machine Quilting (page 40).

2. Staystitch the vertical edges ⅜" (1cm) from the raw edge. Repeat for the **base**.

3. Pin the **base** and the backing right sides together. Machine stitch the horizontal edges with a ⅜" (1cm) seam allowance.

4. Turn right side out. Press the seams open.

5. On one side, fold under the raw edges along the staystitched line. Press.

6. Pin and hand stitch with the ladder stitch.

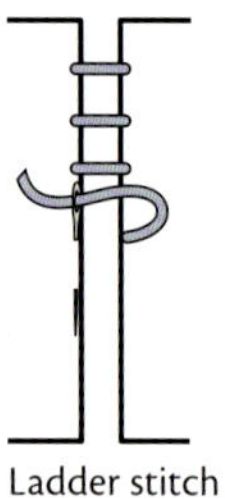

Ladder stitch

7. Repeat Step 5–6 for the remaining side, leaving a 3" (7.6cm) opening.

8. Fill with Poly-fil, using a stuffing tool. Sew the opening closed, using the ladder stitch.

9. Follow the directions for the Couched Cord Edge (at right) with the rattail cording.

COUCHED CORD EDGE

1. Knot the tail of the cord. Lay along the finished edge of the **base**, with the knot at a corner.

2. Thread a needle with perle cotton #5 or #8. Bring this through the seam, up to the knot.

3. Whipstitch the thread over the cord and through the fabric.

4. Repeat Step 3, knotting the cord at any corner of the **base**.

5. To finish, cut and knot the cord, and then knot and cut the thread.

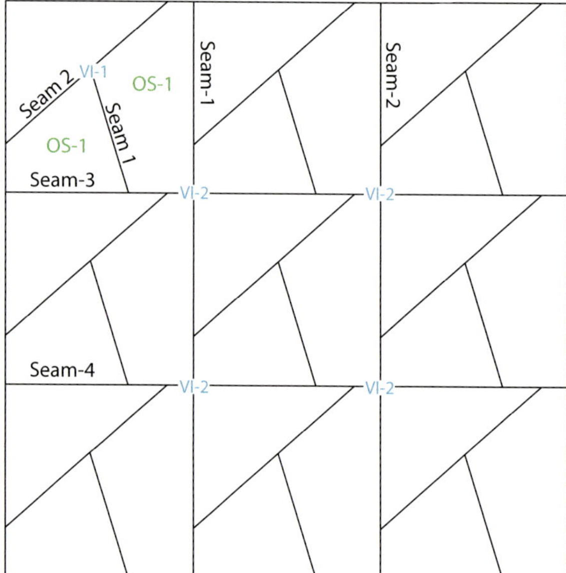

Wedged Crumbles Block Pillow Blueprints (In diagram, OS is open space, VI is vignette intersection)

Crazed Crumbles Block Table Covering

Select a random mix of fabrics for the Crazed Crumbles Block pattern pieces (page 26), crumbled strip border (page 38), prairie points (page 30), fabric circles (page 31), and fabric yo-yos (page 31). Rickrack trim, perle cotton, beads, and buttons were used for embellishments.

Wabi Sabi Tic Tac Toe, 18″ x 18″ (45.7 × 45.7cm)

Creative Option Stitch all the blocks with the same crumbled sections of fabric or use up those loose scraps from other projects. Have fun and enjoy the process!

SWATCHES

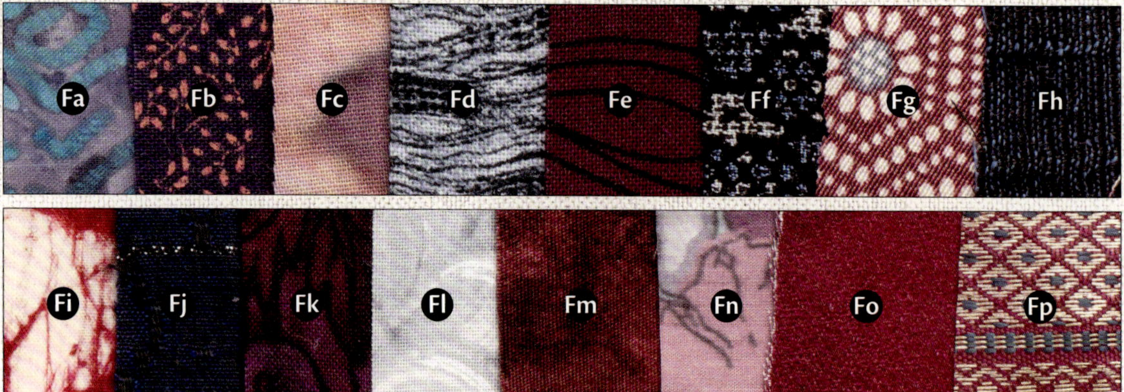

Fabrics

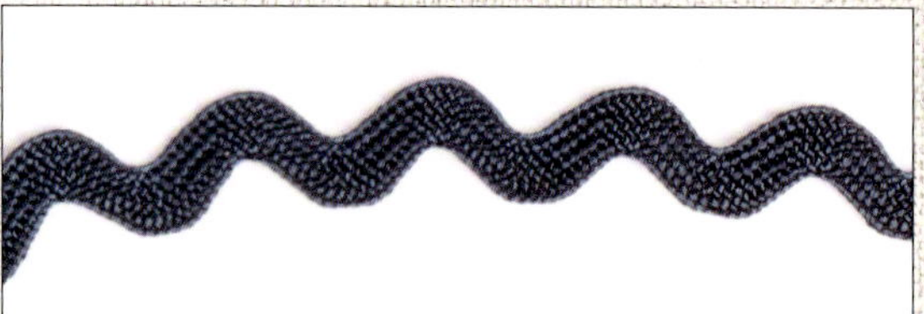

Trimming

Perle cotton, cotton floss

Seed beads

1. Fabric circle **2.** Prairie point **3.** Fabric yo-yo

Embellishments

Materials

FABRICS

Blocks and borders: 12–16 scraps totaling about 1 yard (1m)

Backing, sashing: ⅝ yard (57.2cm)

TRIMMING

Ra: rickrack, 2 yards (1.9m)

EMBROIDERY MATERIALS IN A VARIETY OF COLORS

Perle cotton (pc): #8, #12

Cotton floss (cf)

Seed beads (sb): sizes 6°, 8°, 11°, 15°

EMBELLISHMENTS

Buttons

Ba: 1⅛″ (2.9cm) button, 3

Bb: ¾″ (1.9cm) button, 4

Glass Components

Gba: 12mm flower rondelle, 8

Gbb: 12mm flower bead, 8

Gbc: 8mm flower rondelle, 26 (2 colors)

Gbd: 12mm flower bead, 18 (3 colors)

Muslin: ¼ yard (22.9cm)

fast2fuse, heavy: about 3″ × 13″ (7.6 × 33cm)

Batting: ⅝ yard (57.2cm)

Sewing and beading threads: neutral colors

Crazed Crumbles Block Table Covering Block Diagram
(In diagram, VI is vignette intersection)

Cutting Instructions

BLOCKS

Enlarge the Crazed Crumbles Block pattern (page 173) to **105%**. Follow Steps 1–2 of Pieced Blocks (page 27), then Steps 2–3 of Crumbles Blocks (page 28).

Select groups of fabrics to make 5 color combinations, 1 for each pattern piece (or use a random mix).

Cut 4 pattern pieces from each group to make 4 blocks.

STRIP-PIECED BORDERS

Border 1: Cut 2 rectangles from muslin 3″ x 12″ (7.6 × 30.5cm) vertical.

Border 2: Cut 2 rectangles from muslin 3″ x 18″ (7.6 × 45.7cm) horizontal.

Follow the directions for Foundation-Pieced Borders A (page 39). Strip-Pieced Border (page 39), using scrap fabrics.

EXTRAS

Prairie points (page 30): Use 3″ (7.6cm) wide rectangles by the length of the scrap; cut 10.

Fabric circles (page 31): Cut 10 (or 2 different fabrics: 4 and 6) circles 2″ (5.1cm) diameter.

fast2fuse: Cut 10 circles 1¼″ (3.2cm) diameter.

Batting: Cut 10 circles 1⅛″ (2.9cm) diameter.

Fabric yo-yos (page 31): Cut 76 circles 2⅛″ (5.4cm) diameter, using scraps and backing fabric.

ADDITIONAL PIECES

Muslin: Cut 4 squares 7″ x 7″ (17.8 × 17.8cm).

Backing: Cut 1 square 18″ x 18″ (45.7 × 45.7cm).

Sashing: Cut 2 rectangles 1½″ x 12″ (3.8 × 30.5cm) vertical.

Sashing: Cut 2 rectangles 1½″ x 18″ (3.8 × 45.7cm) horizontal.

Sashing: Cut 4 rectangles 1½″ x 18″ (3.8 × 45.7cm).

Batting: Cut 1 square 18″ x 18″ (45.7 × 45.7cm).

Binding vertical seams: Cut 2 rectangles 3″ x 18″ (7.6 × 45.7cm).

Binding horizontal seams: Cut 2 rectangles 3″ x 19″ (7.6 × 48.3cm).

Option: *Piece 2 fabrics together from scraps to create the binding rectangles or cut from the same fabric as the backing and sashing.*

SEWING THE BLOCKS AND EXTRAS

1. Follow the directions for Disappearing Seam (page 28). Make 4 blocks. Trim the blocks to 6¼″ x 6¼″ (15.9 × 15.9cm).

Note: *Refer to Crazed Crumbles Block Table Covering Blueprints (page 161).*

2. Pin Block 1, rotated 180°, to Block 2, rotated 90° to the left.

3. Machine stitch with a 1/4″ (6mm) seam allowance. Press the seams open.

4. Pin Block 3, rotated 90° to the right, to Block 4. Follow Step 3.

5. Pin the first and second rows together, aligning the seams. Follow Step 3.

6. Stitch 10 fabric circles (page 31).

7. Stitch 76 fabric yo-yos (page 31).

BASE DESIGN DETAILS

Note: *Refer to Basic Base Instructions (page 36) and the Crazed Crumbles Block Table Covering Blueprints (page 161).*

1. Follow **Option C** under Base Design Options (page 36) with the batting square.

2. Place **Border 1** and **Border 2** flush with the **base**. Follow the directions from Step 2 for Adding a Border (page 37) and Step 1 for Raw Edge Option (page 37).

3. Hand stitch the prairie points in place as shown.

4. Follow Steps 2–4 for the Folded Edge Fabric Sashing (page 37):

Vertical: 1½″ x 12″ (3.8 × 30.5cm)

Horizontal: 1½″ x 18″ (3.8 × 45.7cm)

This is now referred to as the **base**.

5. Stitch 1 fabric circle in each vignette intersection **1** and vignette intersection **5** position.

6. Follow the Embroidery and Embellishment Design (page 161), then Finishing (below).

Option: *Add extra details with hand quilting (page 40) through block pieces and through borders.*

FINISHING

1. Follow Step 1 for Bound Edge Assembly (page 41) with the 18″ x 18″ (45.7 × 45.7cm) backing square.

2. Fold the 4 sashing rectangles in half lengthwise and press. Pin the raw edges of each sashing to each side of the **base**.

3. Follow Steps 3–6 to bind all edges:

Vertical seams: 3″ x 18″ (7.6 × 45.7cm)

Horizontal seams: 3″ x 19″ (7.6 × 48.3cm)

4. Follow the directions for Yo-Yo Edging (page 44).

5. Stitch *Bb* in each corner section, next to the binding.

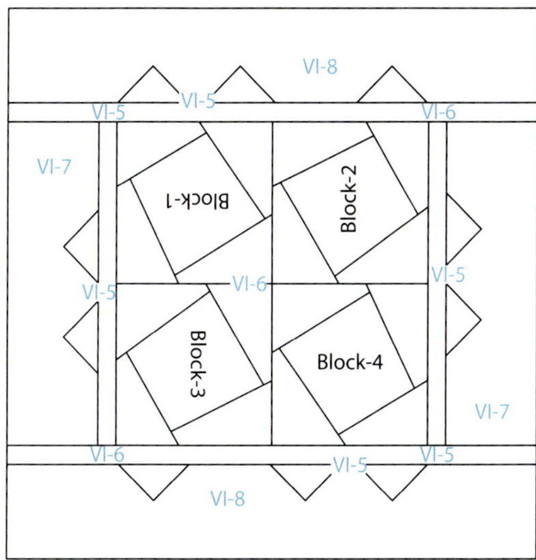

Crazed Crumbles Block Table Covering Blueprints
(In diagram, VI is vignette intersection)

EMBROIDERY AND EMBELLISHMENT DESIGN

Refer to the Crazed Crumbles Block Table Covering Block Diagram (page 159), Crazed Crumbles Block Table Covering Block Blueprints (above).

Note: *Use 3 strands of cotton floss.*

Blocks

Center: Vignette intersection **1:** straight stitch pc over fabric circle, single bead stitch *Gbd* in the center, stacked bead stitch with 1 size 6° and 11° sb around outer edge; vignette intersection **2:** bead cascade stitch with *Gbc* and 5 size 11° sb.

Seam 1: border row, blanket and chain stitch pc (tips worked into pattern piece 2); decorative stitches, 3 lazy daisy stitches pc (off every other tip); detail stitches, straight stitch pc, 3-wrap French knot stitch cf (off every tip) below border and worked into pattern piece 1; decorative stitches, fly stitch pc, 2 fleet stitches crossed pc, 3-wrap French knot stitch cf, stacked bead stitch with size 6° and 11° sb.

Seam 2: border row, feather stitch pc; decorative stitches, alternate between stacked bead stitch with 1 size 6° and 11° sb and 3-wrap French knot stitch cf, tips facing pattern piece 3; decorative and detail stitches, looped tendril stitch pc, lazy daisy stitch pc, tips facing pattern piece 1; decorative and detail stitches, 2 lazy daisy stitches pc, 3 straight stitches pc, 2 3-wrap French knot stitches cf.

Seam 3: border row, herringbone stitch pc, straight stitch pc, 3-wrap French knot stitch cf, tips facing pattern piece 4; decorative and detail stitches, lazy daisy tulip stitch pc, fly stitch pc, 3-wrap French knot stitch cf, tips facing pattern piece 1; decorative and detail stitches, fleet stitch pc, lazy daisy stitch pc, stacked bead stitch with 1 size 8° and 15° sb.

Seam 4: border row, cretan stitch pc, 3-wrap French knot stitch cf, tips facing pattern piece 5; decorative and detail stitches, 2 lazy daisy stitches pc, 3 straight stitches pc, 3-wrap French knot stitch cf, tips facing pattern piece 1; decorative and detail stitches, fly stitch with loop pc, stacked bead stitch with 1 size 6° and 11° sb.

Vignette intersection **3:** single bead stitch *Gba.*

Vignette intersection **4:** single bead stitch *Gbb.*

Base

Rickrack: straight stitch pc, stacked bead stitch with 1 size 6° and 11° sb.

Sashing: chain stitch pc, 3-wrap French knot stitch every other stitch.

Prairie points: group of 3 stacked bead stitches with 1 size 6° and 11° sb at tip and each corner, stacked bead stitch with 1 size 6° and 11° sb in center.

Vignette intersection **5:** stacked bead stitch with 1 size 6° and 11° sb around outer edge.

Vignette intersection **6:** *Ba.*

Vignette intersection **7:** single bead stitch 2 *Gbd*, 1 single bead stitch *Gb3.*

Vignette intersection **8:** single bead stitch 2 *Gbd.*

Fabric yo-yos: single bead stitch size 6° sb.

Crazed Crumbles Block Wall Hanging

Select two different five-fabric combinations to make the reduced-in-size Crazed Crumbles Blocks (page 26). Why not use a variety of luscious fabrics, including upholstery, tapestry, embroidered silk, sari borders, and a silk tie, along with grosgrain ribbons, rosettes (page 32), buttons, and beads to create this wall hanging?

Autumn Bouquet, 17¼" x 17¼" (43.8 × 43.8cm)

Creative Option This is a great project for heavier fabrics because the raw edges of the blocks are covered with ribbons.

SWATCHES

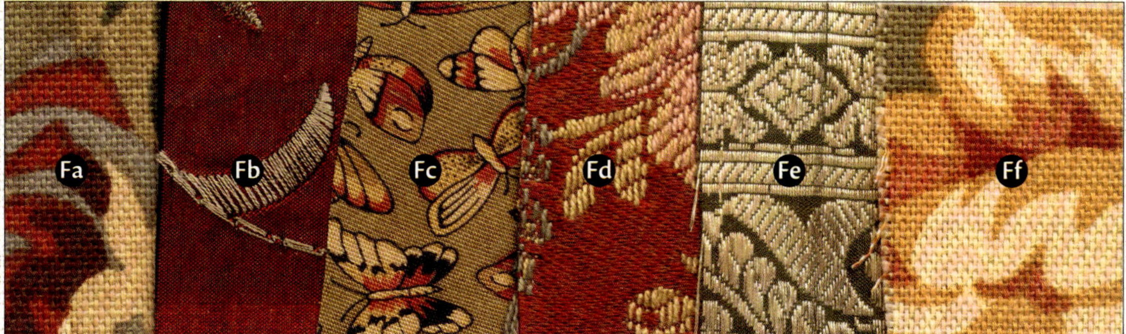

Fabrics

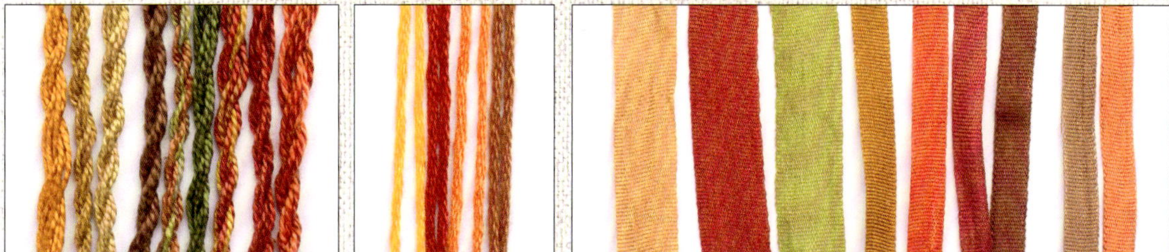

Perle cottons, cotton flosses, silk embroidery ribbons

Seed and other beads

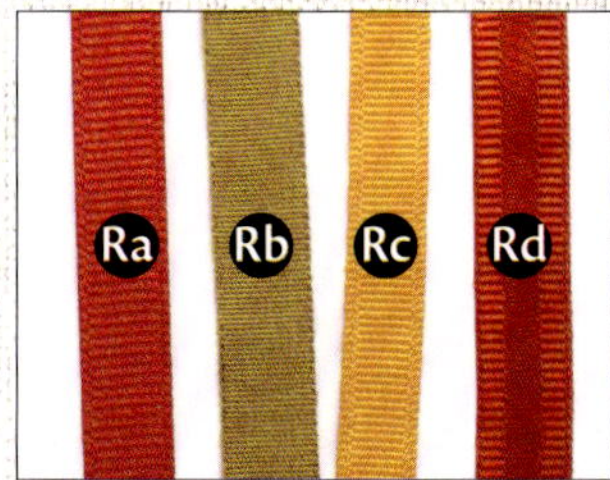

Trimmings

Rosette

Embellishments

Materials

FABRICS

Fa: ⅝ yard (57.2cm)

Note: *Choose a fabric with a variety of color choices.*

Fb, Fc, Fd, Fe: fat quarters

Note: *A silk tie can be substituted for Fc, and a wide ribbon for Fe.*

Ff: cotton solid or print (not shown), ⅝ yard (57.2cm)

TRIMMINGS

Ra: ⅜" (1cm) satin ribbon, 1½ yards (1.4m)

Rb: ⅜" (1cm) satin ribbon, 5 yards (4.6m)

Rc: ⅜" (1cm) satin ribbon, 1¾ yards (1.7m)

Rd: ⅜" (1cm) satin ribbon, 2½ yards (2.3m)

Rattail cord, 2½ yards (2.3m)

EMBROIDERY MATERIALS IN A VARIETY OF COLORS

Perle cotton (pc): #8

Cotton floss (cf)

Silk embroidery ribbon (ser): 2mm, 4mm, 7mm

Seed beads (sb): sizes 6°, 8°, 11°, 15°

Size 6° square bead: 20

8mm bead: 42

EMBELLISHMENTS

Buttons

Ba: variety of 8mm buttons or beads, 36

Bb: ½" (1.2cm) shank, 8

Bc: leaf button, 12

Bd: rose, 8

Be: flower, 4

Bf: 2- or 4-hole button, 12

Glass Components

Gba: 8 × 10mm tulip bead, 5

Gbb: 14mm flower bead, 4

Gbc: 8 × 14mm large leaf bead, 8

Gbd: 8 × 10mm flower bead, 4

Gbe: 5 × 7mm small leaf bead, 8

Gbf: 8 × 8mm medium leaf bead, 20

Gbg: 5 × 7mm pansy bead, 8

Muslin: ⅓ yard (30.5)

Batting: ⅝ yard (57.2cm)

Sewing and beading threads: neutral colors

Cutting Instructions

BLOCKS

Reduce the Crazed Crumbles Block pattern (page 173) to **85%**, *disregard the crumble-pieced lines.*

Follow Step 1 of Crumbles Blocks (page 28).

Block 1

Cut 5 pieces from each pattern piece to make 5 blocks.

Pattern piece 1: *Fb*

Pattern pieces 2, 4: *Fe*

Pattern pieces 3, 5: *Fc*

Block 2

Cut 4 pieces from each pattern piece to make 4 blocks.

Pattern piece 1: *Fd*

Pattern pieces 2, 4: *Fa* (one color combination)

Pattern pieces 3, 5: *Fa* (a different color combination)

BORDERS

Cut 2 rectangles: *Fa*, 2½" x 14" (6.4 × 35.6cm), vertical

Cut 2 rectangles: *Fa*, 2½" x 18" (6.4 × 45.7cm), horizontal

EXTRAS

Rosettes: *Rd*, cut 24 lengths 3" (7.6cm).

FF: COTTON FABRIC

Backing: Cut 1 square 17½" x 17½" (44.5 × 44.5cm).

Hanging sleeve: Cut 1 rectangle 4" x 15½" (10.2 × 39.4cm).

Cut 4 squares 4" × 4" (10.2 × 10.2cm) for binding.

Cut 4 rectangles 2½" × 15½" (6.4 × 39.4cm) for binding.

ADDITIONAL PIECES

Muslin: Cut 9 squares 5" x 5" (12.7 × 12.7cm).

Batting: Cut 1 square 17½" x 17½" (44.5 × 44.5cm).

SEWING THE BLOCKS AND EXTRAS

Refer to the Block Diagram(s) (below) to make 9 blocks.

1. Follow Steps 4–6 of Crumbles Blocks (page 28), using the muslin rectangles, slightly overlapping the pattern pieces to fit the square.

2. Cut the ribbon to fit the seam or section of the block; hand stitch in place.

Note: *The raw edge of a ribbon is covered by the following lengths.*

Block 1

Seam 1: *Rb*

Seam 2: *Rc*

Seam 3: *Rb*

Seam 4: *Rc*

Block 2

Seam 1: *Rb*

Seam 2: *Ra*

Seam 3: *Rb*

Seam 4: *Ra*

3. Trim each block to 5″ × 5″ (12.7 × 12.7cm).

4. Stitch 24 rosettes (page 32).

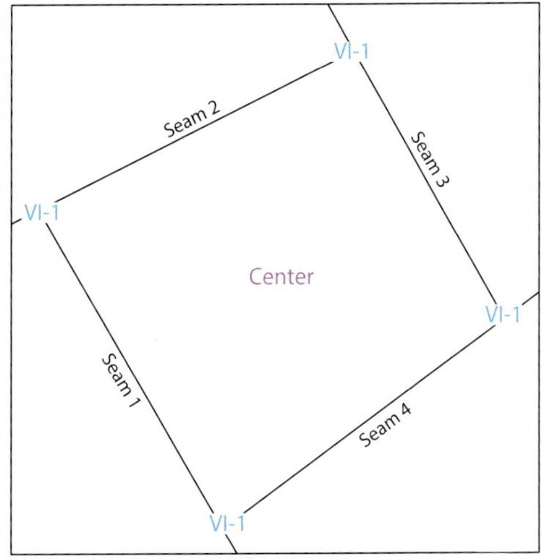

Block 1 Crazed Crumbles Block Wall Hanging Block Diagram (In diagram, VI is vignette intersection)

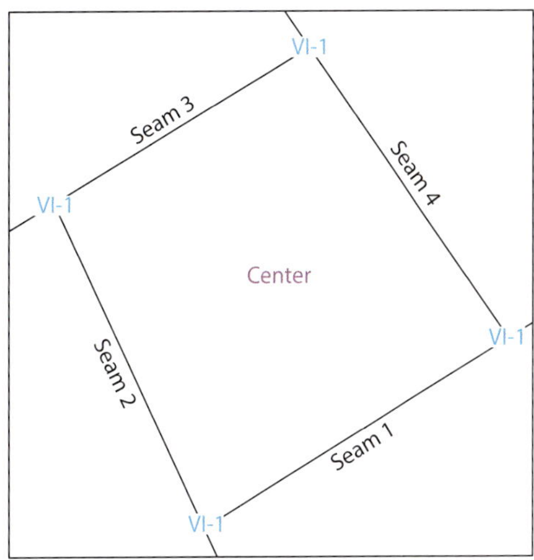

Block 2 Crazed Crumbles Block Wall Hanging Block Diagram (In diagram, VI is vignette intersection)

BASE DESIGN DETAILS

Note: *Refer to Basic Base Instructions (page 36) and the Crazed Crumbles Block Wall Hanging Blueprints (below).*

1. Follow the directions for the 9-Patch Block Base (page 35); this is now referred to as the **base**.

2. Follow **Option C** under Base Design Options (page 36) with the batting square.

3. See Adding a Border (page 37) and Finished Seam Option (page 37):

   Vertical: 2½″ x 14″ (6.4 × 35.6cm)

   Horizontal: 2½″ x 18″ (6.4 × 45.7cm)

4. Stitch *Rb* across the length of each border.

5. Vignette intersection **2** and corner section **1:** Stitch a group of 3 rosettes.

6. Follow the Embroidery and Embellishment Design (page 167), then Finishing (below).

FINISHING

1. Follow the directions for adding the hanging sleeve (page 41) to the backing.

2. Follow the directions for the Soft-Edge Assembly (page 43), using the backing, 4″ × 4″ (10.2 × 10.2cm) squares, and 2½″ × 15½″ (6.4 × 39.4cm) rectangles.

3. Follow the directions for the Couched Cord Edge (page 156) with the rattail cording.

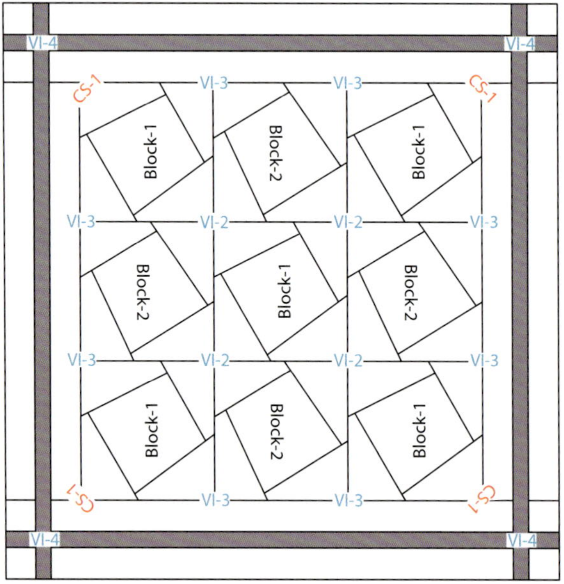

Crazed Crumbles Block Wall Hanging Blueprints
(In diagram, CS is corner section, VI is vignette intersection)

EMBROIDERY AND EMBELLISHMENT DESIGN

Refer to the block diagrams (page 165) and Crazed Crumbles Block Wall Hanging Blueprints (page 166).

Note: *Use 3 strands of cotton floss.*

Block 1

Center: 3 woven roses ser, 2 groups of 2 ribbon stitches ser, 2 groups of 3 straight stitches pc, 2 groups of 3 3-wrap French knot stitches ser; embellishment stitches, continuous bead stitch with 6 size 11° sb and *Gba*, 2 stacked bead stitches with 8mm bead and 1 size 15° sb, 2 single bead stitches with 6° square bead.

Note: *For the center block, continuous bead stitch with 12 size 11° sb, 2 rows of stem stitches pc, 2 single bead stitches with 6° square beads.*

Seams 1 and 3: *Rb*, border row, blanket stitch pc, 3-wrap French knot stitch cf; decorative and detail stitches, alternate between padded straight stitch ser, 2 lazy daisy stitches pc, grouped bead stitch with 3 size 11° sb and 3-wrap French knot stitch pc.

Seams 2 and 4: *Rc*, border row, feather stitch straight side pc, 3-wrap French knot stitch cf; decorative and detail stitches, alternate between chain stitch pc, stacked bead stitch with 1 size 6° and 11° sb and 5-wrap French knot stitch ser, 2 lazy daisy stitches pc, stacked bead stitch with 1 size 8° and 15° sb.

Block 2

Center: single bead stitch *Gbb*, 2 *Gbc*, 1 *Gbd*, 2 *Gbe*, 2 *Gbf*, 2 stacked bead stitch with 8mm flower rondelle and 1 size 11° sb.

Seams 1 and 3: *Rb*, border row, cross stitch row pc, lazy daisy stitch cf; decorative and detail stitches, alternate between stacked bead stitch with 1 size 6° and 11° sb and looped tendril stitch pc, 2 straight stitches, 3-wrap French knot stitch ser.

Seams 2 and 4: *Ra*, border row, alternate between blanket stitch and blanket stitch up down pc, 3-wrap French knot stitch cf; decorative and detail stitches, blanket stitch spokes alternate between 2 lazy daisy stitches ser, pistil stitch pc, 3-wrap French knot stitch cf, and lazy daisy stitch ser, fly stitch pc, 3-wrap French knot stitch cf; embellishment stitches, blanket stitch up down spokes stacked bead stitch with 1 size 8° and 15° sb.

Additional Areas

Center of each block: Fill in with 4 groups of 3 stacked bead stitches with 1 size 6° and 11° sb and 4 groups of 3 3-wrap French knot stitches pc.

Vignette intersection 1: *Ba*.

Vignette intersection 2: *Bb*, 3 stacked bead stitches with 8mm bead and 1 size 15° sb, 3 single bead stitches *Gbf*.

Corner section 1: *Bb*, 3 stacked bead stitches with 8mm bead and 1 size 15° sb, 2 single bead stitches *Gbf*, 2 single bead stitches with *Gbg*.

Vignette intersection 3: *Bd*.

Vignette intersection 4: *Be*.

Borders: *Rb*; border row cross stitch row pc; decorative stitches, straight stitch pc, 3-wrap French knot stitch cf, evenly space 3 *Bf* per rectangle.

Block Patterns

Blocks are 6″ x 6″ (15.2 × 15.2cm).

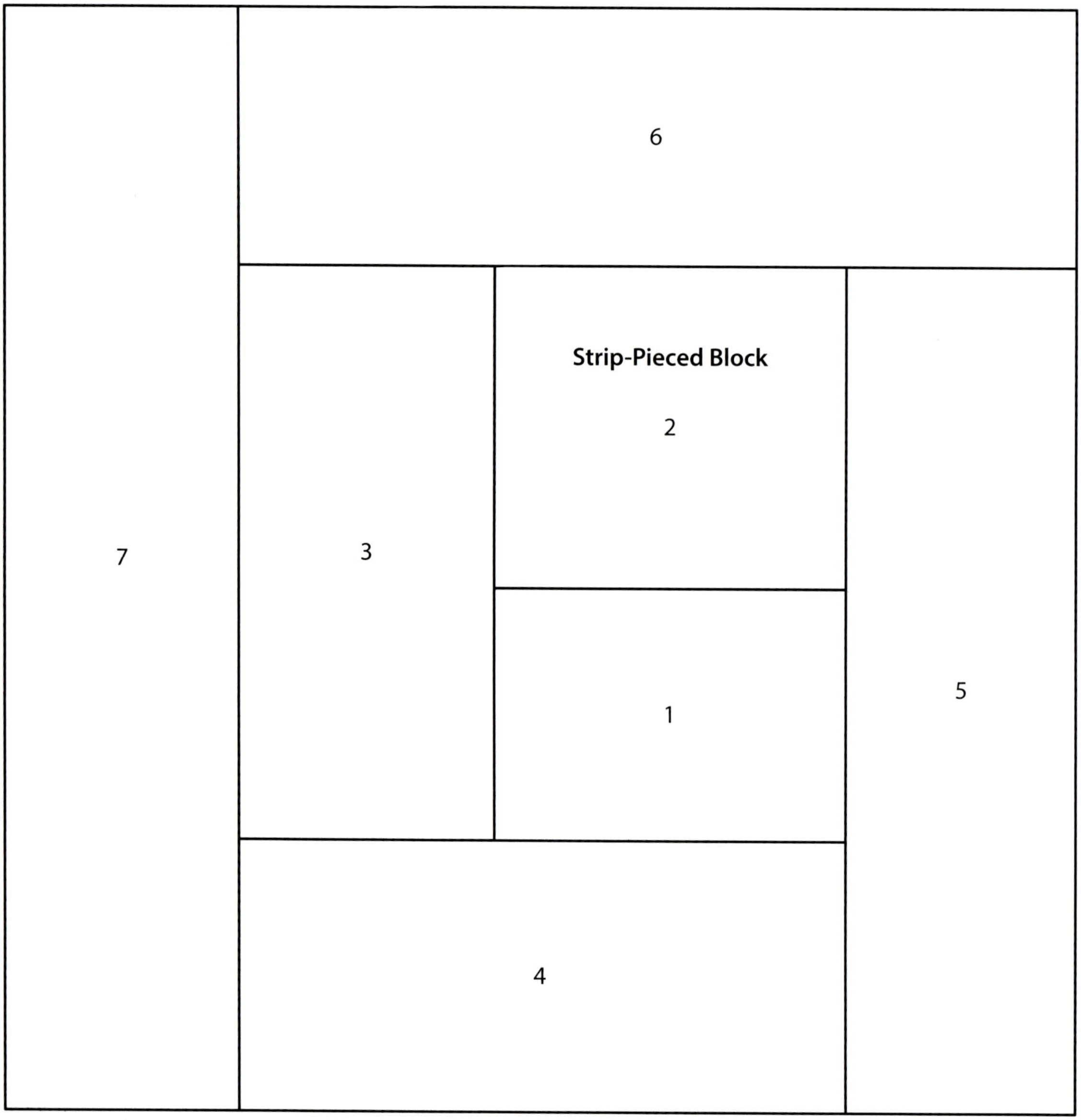

Blocks are 6″ x 6″ (15.2 × 15.2cm).

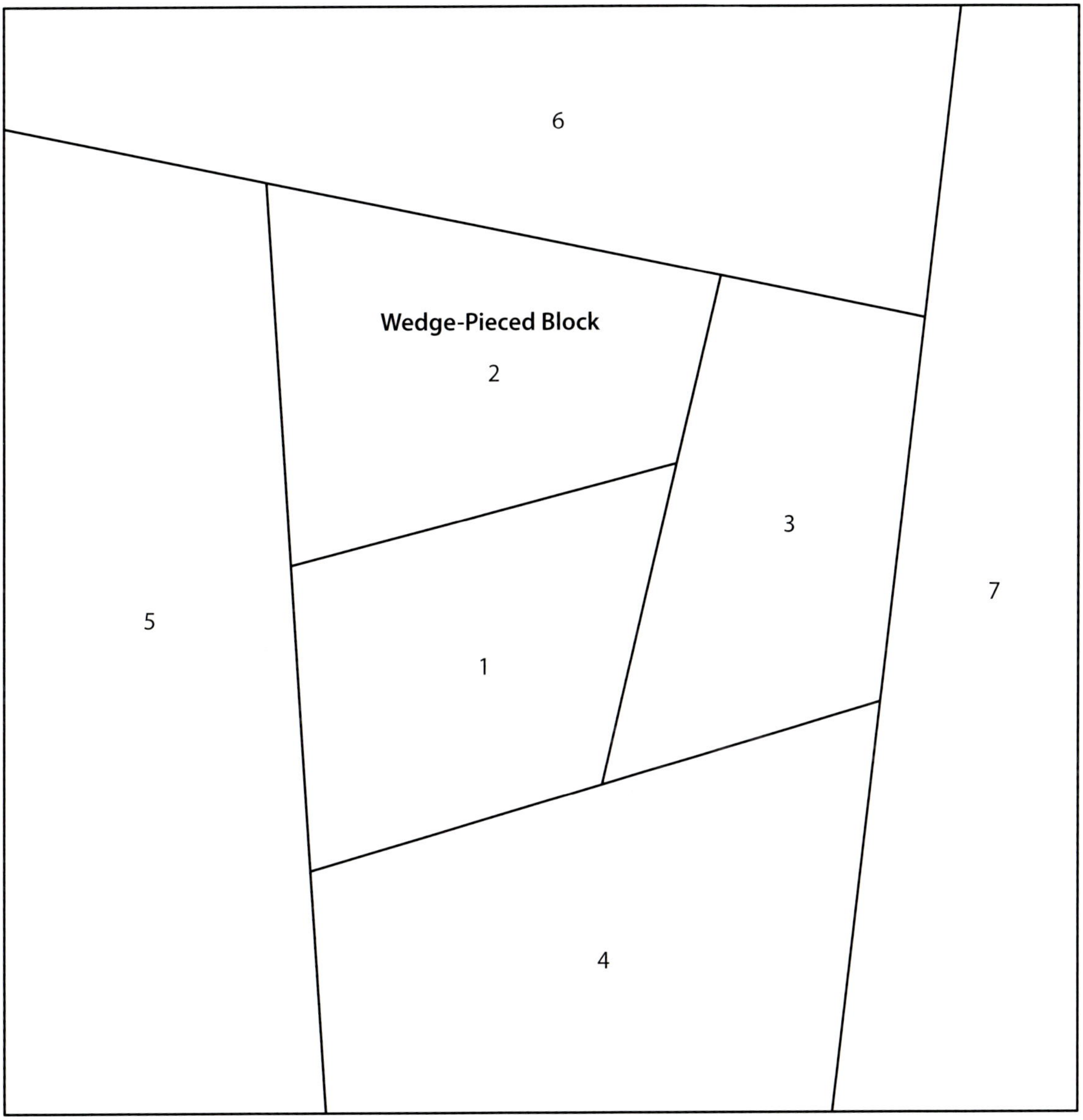

Blocks are 6″ x 6″ (15.2 × 15.2cm).

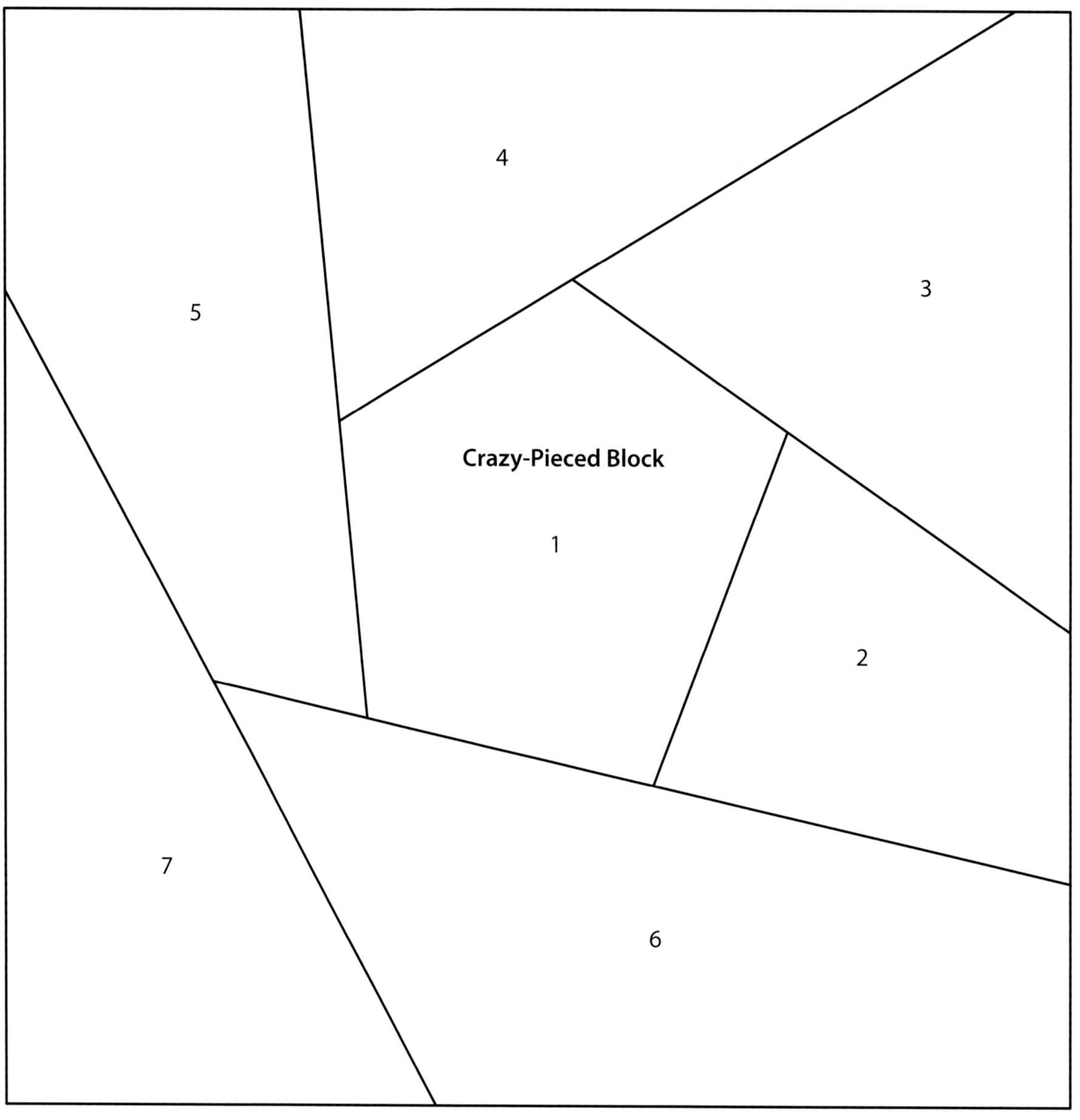

Blocks are 6" x 6" (15.2 × 15.2cm).

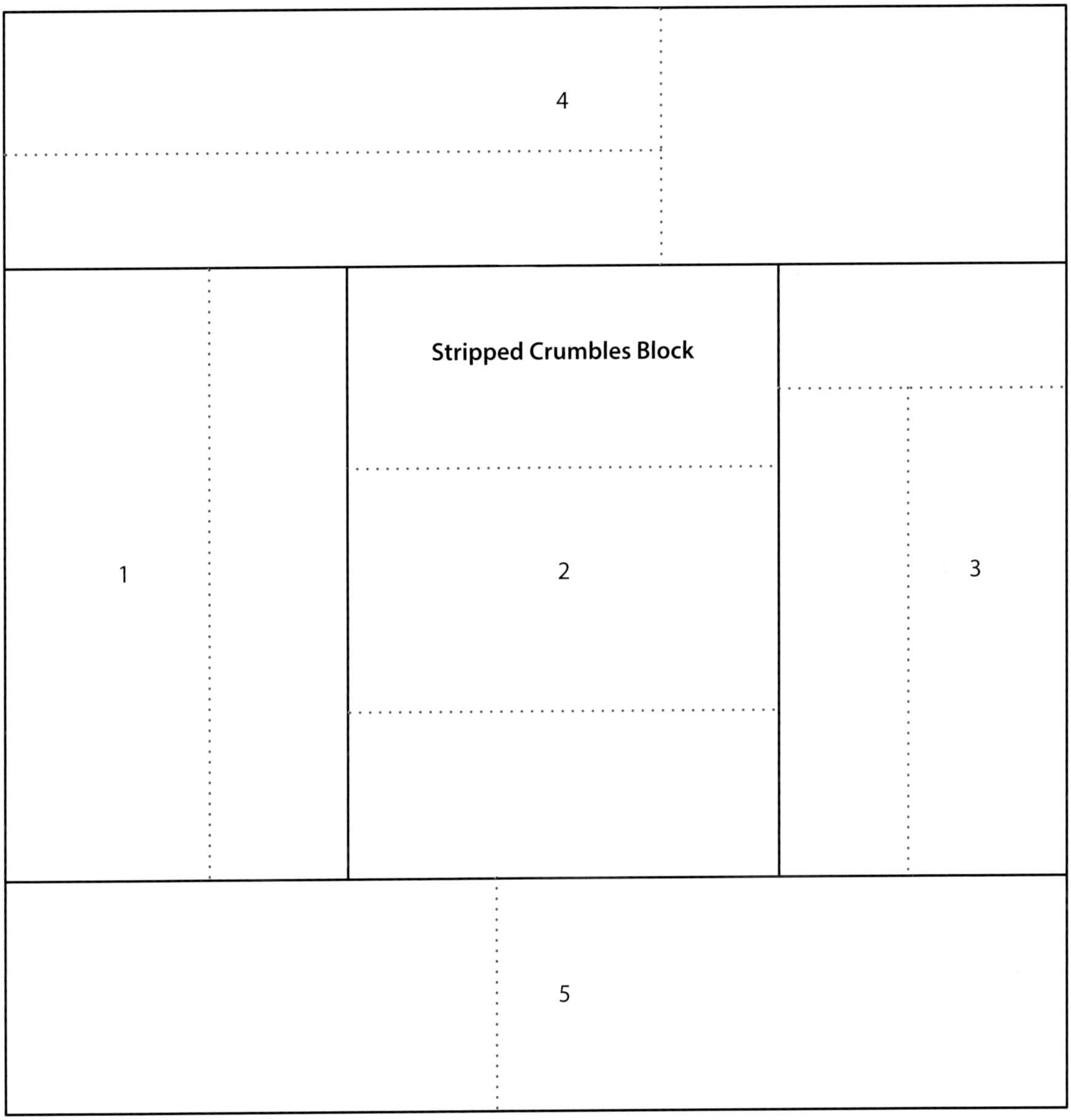

4

Stripped Crumbles Block

1

2

3

5

Blocks are 6″ x 6″ (15.2 × 15.2cm).

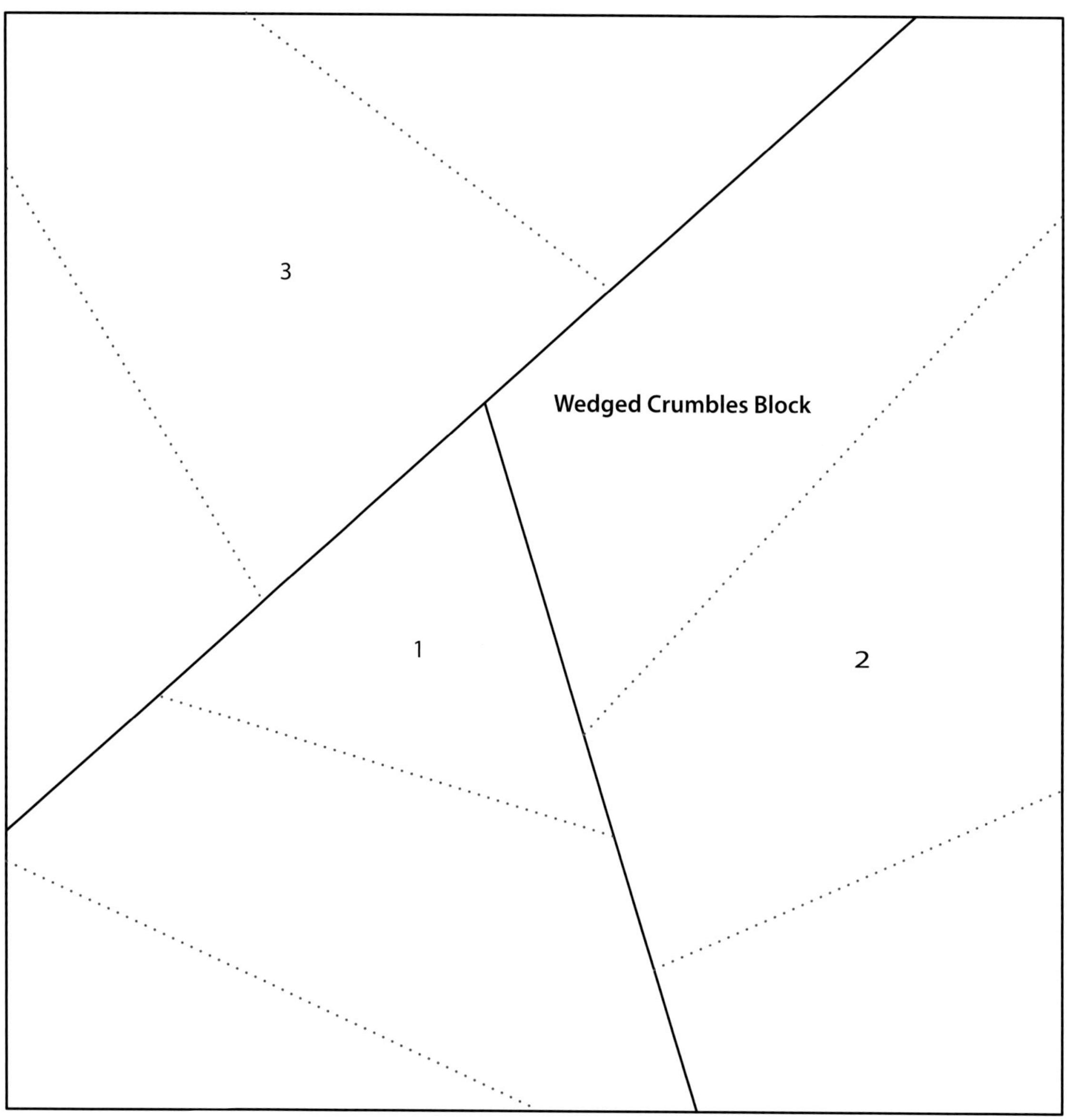

Blocks are 6″ x 6″ (15.2 × 15.2cm).

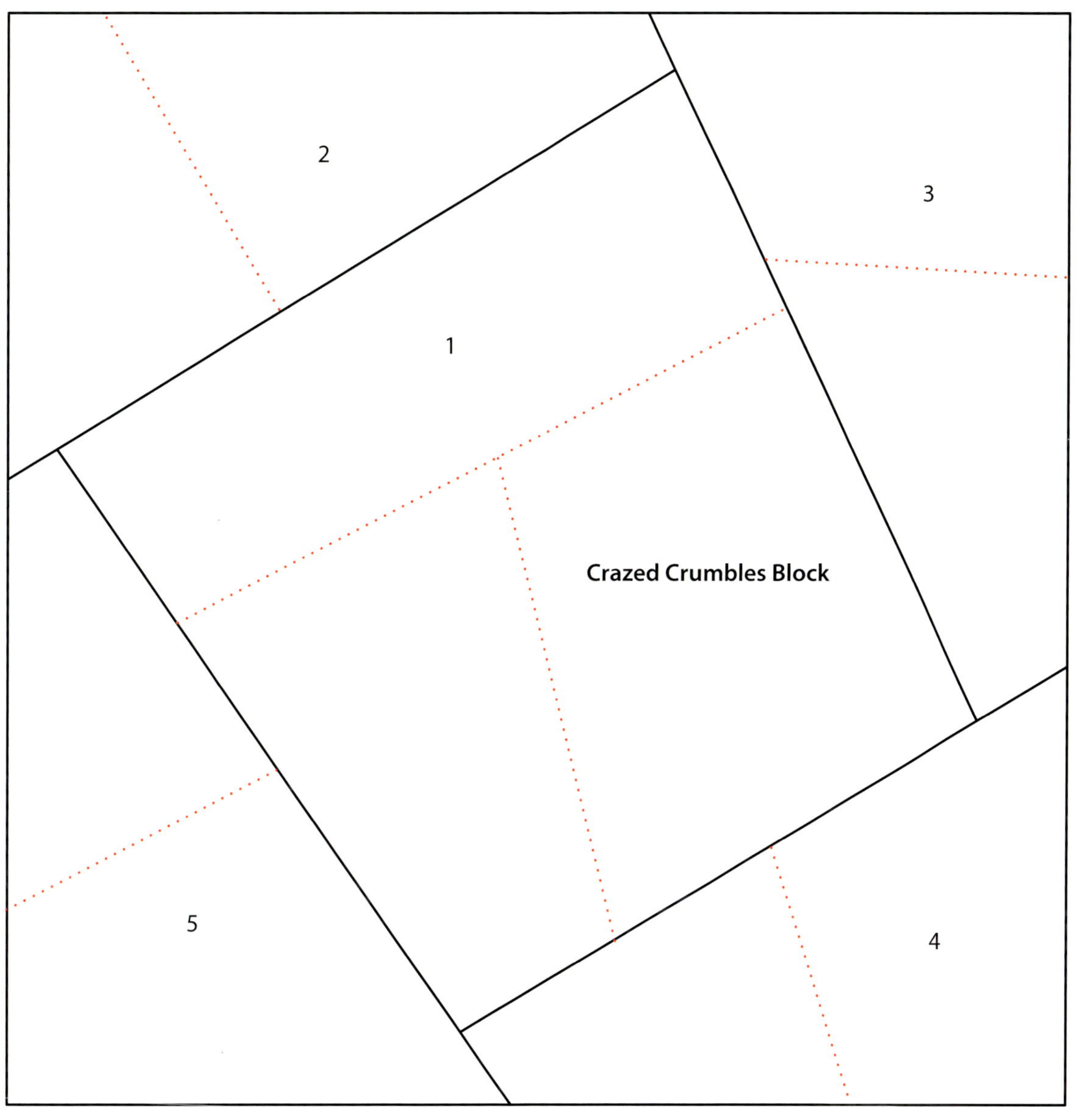

BONUS IDEA

Ghastlie Webs in the Attic

Size: 25″ x 25″ (63.5 × 63.5cm)

I made this wall hanging with the Stripped Crumbles Block pattern (page 171) and the Crumbled Strip Border (page 38), using a random mix of fabrics. I used trims to cover the raw edges of the blocks and a fun print for the sashing; see Fabric or Ribbon Sashing (page 37). I cut a vintage doily into four sections for the center of each block, with the stitches worked in perle cotton and seed beads. Additional embellishments included mod hexies and a random mix of new and vintage buttons.

About the Author

Christen came from an environment where "home-made" was the motto that her family lived by. She benefited from the talents of two creative parents, from whom she learned how to embroider, sew, knit, crochet, tat, draw, paint, metalsmith, and woodwork. In school, she continued to explore other art forms, including jewelry making, ceramics, lettering, photography, and mixed media.

Christen's first job, working at a fabric store, encouraged her passion for fiber art to blossom. She focused on designing garments, accessories, home décor, and small quilts. She has an AA in Fashion Design and began her career in the Wearable Art field in 1986. Her work has been shown in galleries and fashion shows all over the world.

Christen's design choices, color mastery, and embroidered artistry set her work aside. Each piece is deliberately designed and executed to showcase the components and the techniques she has chosen to incorporate into them.

Christen has been teaching for more than 30 years and began writing books and articles more than two decades ago. She views teaching as a joyful responsibility and appreciates the opportunity to pass on the knowledge and love of these beautiful art forms and to inspire and encourage future creative minds.

Christen identifies as an Urban Gypsy and a Mixed-Media Maven, and has been known to Embellish to the Point of Explosion! She works and teaches out of her home studio in Escondido, California. You can contact her through her website: **christenbrown.com**

Gentle Ladies Needlekeep

Christen has authored several best-selling books for C&T Publishing that include embroidery, piecing, quilting, ribbonwork, mixed media, and beadwork. The titles include:

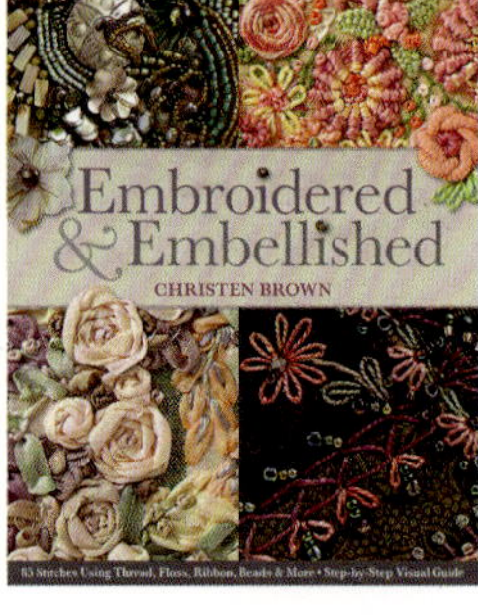

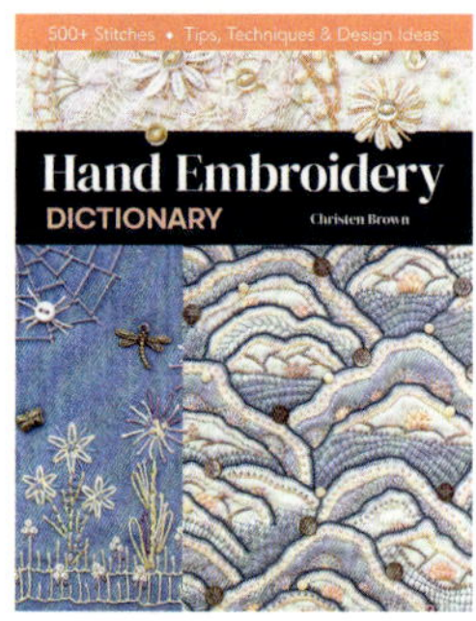

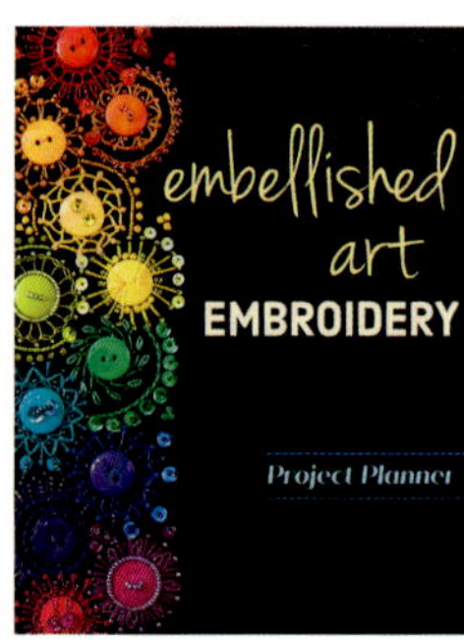

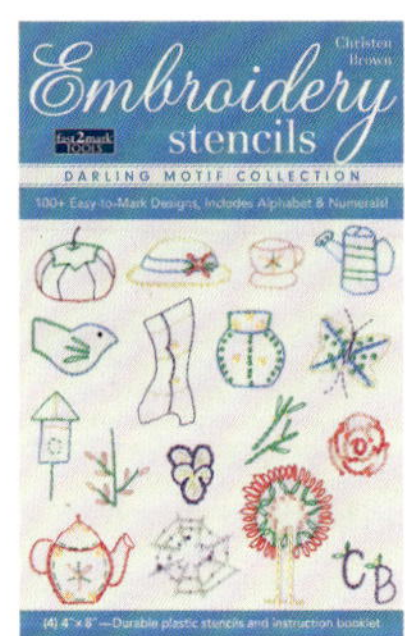

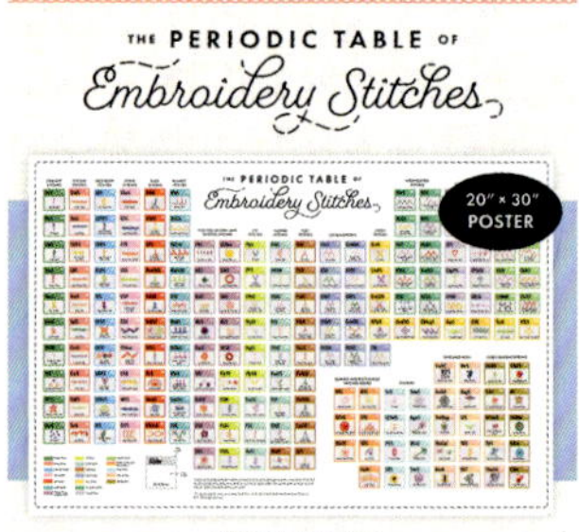